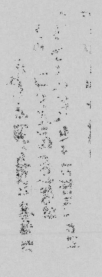

The Book of
HUMAN EMOTIONS

The Book of
HUMAN EMOTIONS

From Ambiguphobia to Umpty —
154 Words from Around the World
for How We Feel

Tiffany Watt Smith

Little, Brown and Company
New York   Boston   London

Little, Brown and Company
Hachette Book Group
1290 Avenue of the Americas, New York, NY 10104
littlebrown.com

First North American edition, June 2016

Originally published by Profile Books in partnership with Wellcome Collection in Great Britain in 2015.

Little, Brown and Company is a division of Hachette Book Group, Inc. The Little, Brown name and logo are trademarks of Hachette Book Group, Inc.

The publisher is not responsible for websites (or their content) that are not owned by the publisher.

The Hachette Speakers Bureau provides a wide range of authors for speaking events. To find out more, go to hachettespeakersbureau.com or call (866) 376-6591.

Illustrations by Tracy Shaw

ISBN: 978-0-316-26540-9
LCCN: 2015952381

10 9 8 7 6 5 4 3 2 1

RRD-C

Printed in the United States of America

To my family
with love, always

And how delightful other people's emotions were!
— much more delightful than their ideas, it seemed to him.

Oscar Wilde, The Picture of Dorian Gray

CONTENTS

CONTENTS

CONTENTS

CONTENTS

The Book of
HUMAN EMOTIONS

INTRODUCTION

Look up. Look up at the clouds. Are they gray and solemn in a windless sky? Or wisps floating carelessly on a breeze? Is the horizon drenched in a hot red sunset, angry with desire?

To the painter John Constable, the sky was full of emotion. He called it, in a letter written in 1821, the "key note" and "chief organ of sentiment in painting." It is for this reason that he dedicated much of his time to collecting and classifying the clouds. Walking out from his house in Hampstead — at that time a village near London — with a bundle of papers, and a pocket full of brushes, he would sit for hours on the heath, rapidly painting the changing shapes above him, the wind rustling his papers, raindrops pooling the colors. Once home, he arranged his sketches according to the latest meteorological classifications, noting the date, time, and weather conditions.

Constable wanted to master the language of the sky — and when you look at his paintings, it's clear that he did. But he also lived in an age obsessed with the desire to label and put into categories, a passion for taxonomy that would always sit uneasily with the melting, drifting skies. Clouds are so hard to fix. Arranging them into groups, as the art critic John Ruskin discovered forty years later, was always a matter "more of convenience than true description." The clouds fold into one another and drift away. They switch allegiances until it's hard to tell them apart.

Look at the clouds, and you might see an emotion color everything for an instant — but then the skies will rearrange themselves and it'll be gone.

* * *

Recognizing and naming our emotional weather can be just as peculiar a task. Try to describe exactly how you feel right now. Is your heart fluttering excitedly for the person who'll be waiting when you step off the train? Or your stomach tight at the thought of tomorrow's deadline? Perhaps it was curiosity that nudged you toward this book. Or reluctance, studded with giddy defiance, that is making you linger over its pages in the shop rather than returning home. Are you feeling hopeful? Surprised? (Are you bored?)

Some emotions really do wash the world in a single color, like the terror felt as the car skids, or the euphoria of falling in love. Others, like clouds, are harder to grasp. Plan a surprise for a loved one and you might feel anticipation crinkled with glee and creased at the edges with a faint terror — what if they hate it? Storm off during an argument and it might be hard to tell the precise moment at which your indignation ends and your clammy self-loathing begins. There are some emotions that are so quiet that they slip past before we've even had a chance to spot them, like that momentary sense of comfort that makes your hand reach out for a familiar brand at the supermarket. And then there are those that brood on the horizon, the ones we hurry away from, fearing they will burst upon us: the jealousy that makes our fingers itch to search a loved one's pockets, or the shame that can goad us into self-destruction.

Sometimes it feels more like we belong to our emotions, than they to us.

But perhaps it's only by paying attention to our feelings, by trying to capture them as Constable did the clouds, that we can truly understand ourselves.

What is an emotion?

Deep inside each of our temporal lobes is a tear-shaped structure called the amygdala. Neuroscientists call this the "command center" of our emotions. It assesses stimuli from the outside world, deciding whether to avoid or approach. It triggers a clatter of responses, raising the heartbeat, instructing the glands to secrete hormones, contracting the limbs or making an eyelid twitch. Recall a sad story or look at a picture of your newborn baby while lying in a brain scanner and the amygdala will be one of the areas that will appear to "light up" on the resulting computer-generated image.

With their glowing tapestries of magenta and emerald, studies of the brain can be seductive. They can even seem like the final word on how and why we feel the way we do. But to think of our emotions purely as biochemical fireworks in the brain is, in the words of the writer Siri Hustvedt, "rather like saying that Vermeer's *Girl Pouring Milk* is a canvas with paint on it or that Alice herself is words on a page. These are facts, but they don't explain my subjective experience of either of them or what the two girls mean to me."

More than that, I think, approaching emotions as first and foremost biological facts misrepresents what an emotion actually is.

The invention of emotions

No one really felt emotions before about 1830. Instead, they felt other things —"passions," "accidents of the soul," "moral sentiments" — and explained them very differently from how we understand emotions today.

Some ancient Greeks believed a defiant rage was carried on an ill wind. Desert-dwelling early Christians thought boredom could be implanted in the soul by malignant demons. In the fifteenth and sixteenth centuries, passions were not exclusive to humans, but could work their strange effects on other bodies too, so that palm trees could fall in love and yearn for one another, and cats become melancholic. But alongside this intangible realm of souls and supernatural forces, doctors also developed a complex approach to understanding the body's influence on the passions. Their insights were based on a theory of humoral medicine from the ancient Greek physician Hippocrates, which spread via the physicians of the medieval Islamic world, and flourished ultimately in the writings of the court doctors of the European Renaissance. The theory held that each person had a balance of four elemental substances in their bodies — blood, yellow bile, black bile, and phlegm. These humors were thought to shape personality and mood: those with more blood in their veins were quick tempered, but also brave, while a dominance of phlegm made one peaceful but lugubrious. Physicians believed strong passions disrupted this delicate ecosystem by moving heat around the body and rousing the humors in turn. Rage sent blood rushing from the heart to the limbs, readying a person to launch an attack. Once black bile was heated, by contrast, it sent poisonous vapors curling up to the brain and crowded it with terrifying visions. Traces of these ideas still linger: it's why we speak of people being phlegmatic or in an ill humor, or say their blood is boiling.

The origin of our modern concept of emotion can be traced to the birth of empirical science in the mid-seventeenth century. Thomas Willis, a London anatomist who dissected hanged criminals, proposed that a surge of joy or a nervous tremble was not the work of strange liquids and fumes, but of the delicate lattice of the nervous system at the center of which was a single organ: the brain. A hundred or so years later, physiologists studying reflex responses in animals went further and claimed that bodies recoiled in fright or twitched in delight because of purely mechanical processes — no immaterial soul substance was necessary at all. In a drafty Edinburgh lecture hall in the early nineteenth century, the philosopher Thomas Brown suggested this new way of understanding the body required a new vocabulary, and proposed using the word "emotion." Though already in use in

English (from the French *émotion*), the term was imprecise, describing any movements of bodies and objects, from the swaying of a tree to a hot blush spreading across the cheeks. The coinage indicated a novel approach to the life of feelings, one that used experiments and anatomical investigations to focus on observable phenomena: clenched teeth; rolling tears; shudders; wide eyes.

This provoked a flurry of interest among Victorian men of science in understanding how the body's smiles and frowns expressed — and even stimulated — internal emotions. One man in particular stands out: Charles Darwin. As early as the 1830s, Darwin was treating emotions as a topic worthy of serious scientific attention. He sent out questionnaires to missionaries and explorers across the globe asking how grief or excitement was expressed by the indigenous people they encountered. He experimented on himself, trying to isolate the muscles used when he shuddered or smiled. He even studied his infant son, William, meticulously charting his responses: "At his 8th day he frowned much...when little under five weeks old, smiled."* In 1872 Darwin published his findings in *The Expression of the Emotions in Man and Animals*, and made the audacious claim that our emotions were not fixed responses, but the result of millions of years of evolutionary processes that were still ongoing. As basic and important as breathing or digestion, as much animal as human, our emotions were there because they had helped us survive — preventing us from ingesting poisons, as in disgust, or helping us form bonds and cooperate, like love or compassion. By the 1880s, the view that emotions were inherited reflexes was so established among scientists that the philosopher

* There is some evidence that the Darwin household was not altogether supportive of his investigations. While they were still engaged, his fiancée, Emma Wedgwood, expressed her concern: "You will be forming theories about me & if I am cross or out of temper you will only consider 'What does that prove?'"

William James could argue that the bodily responses *were* the emotion, and the subjective feeling just followed. While "common sense says... we meet a bear, are frightened, and run," he wrote, it was more rational to say that we feel "afraid because we tremble." He thought the physical response came first, the subjective quality, a by-product — he called it an "epiphenomenon" — a split second later.

Not everyone approached emotions in this way. The year after Darwin published his theories on the evolution of emotional expressions, Sigmund Freud began his medical training in Vienna. By the early 1890s, however, Freud had abandoned his career as a neurologist, believing that it wasn't enough to talk about prolonged sorrow or excessive suspicion in terms only of the brain and body: "It is not easy to treat feelings scientifically," he wrote. One had also to consider the far more elusive and complex influence of the mind, or psyche. Although he never set out a comprehensive theory of what he considered emotions to be — he spoke of them, poetically, as "feeling-tones" — Freud's work added depth and complexity to the vision of emotions as biological twitches and jerks. It's through his work that many of us have come to think of emotions as things that either can be repressed, or else build up and require venting. And that some — particularly those urgent terrors and furious desires of childhood — can sink down and hide in the deepest recesses of our minds only to emerge years later in dreams, or compulsions, or even physical symptoms like an aching head or cramping stomach. It's also from Freud that we have inherited the idea that we might not even recognize some of our emotions, but that our anger or jealousy might be "subconscious," springing up like a jack-in-the-box accidentally ("Freudian slips"), or in the jokes we tell, or in habits such as persistent unpunctuality. Although many of the technical details of Freud's theories have long since been discredited, the idea that our emotions take circuitous routes through our minds as well as our bodies has been of profound therapeutic importance and left traces on today's emotional language. In this way, the Victorians are responsible for two of the most influential ideas about our feelings today: that our emotions are evolved physical responses, and that they are affected by the play of our unconscious minds.

Emotional cultures

In fact, the answer to the question "what is an emotion?" lies not only in our biology or private psychological histories. The way we feel is also enmeshed in the expectations and ideas of the cultures in which we live. Hate, anger or desire can seem to come from the most untamed, animal parts of ourselves. Yet they can also be aroused by those things that make us distinctly human: our language and the concepts we use to understand our bodies; our religious convictions and moral judgments; the fashions, even the politics and economics, of the times we live in. The seventeenth-century nobleman François de La Rochefoucauld recognized that even our most ardent urges can be conjured by the need to keep up with conventions: "Some people," he quipped, "would never fall in love if they hadn't heard love talked about." And just as talking, watching and reading can incite emotions in our bodies, they can quieten our feelings too. The Baining people of Papua New Guinea leave a bowl of water out overnight to absorb *awumbuk*, the gloom and inertia that descend when a much-loved guest departs. The ritual is reported to work every time. The influence of our ideas can be so powerful that they can sometimes shape those biological responses we think of as the most natural. How else is it possible that in the eleventh century, knights could faint in dismay or yawn for love? Or that four hundred years ago people could die of nostalgia?

The idea that emotions might be shaped by our cultures, as well as by our bodies and minds, was enthusiastically taken up in the 1960s and '70s. Western anthropologists living in remote communities became interested in the emotional vocabulary of different languages. For instance *song* — the outrage felt on receiving a less than fair share — is held in high esteem in the cooperative culture of the Pacific islanders of Ifaluk. It became clear that some cultures take very seriously certain feelings that in English-speaking cultures might seem petty. What's more, some emotions seemed to be so significant that people were fluent in their many subtle tastes and textures, like the fifteen distinct sorts of fear the Pintupi of Western Australia are able to feel. Other emotions that might seem fundamental to English speakers were missing in some languages: there is, for instance, no word that precisely captures the meaning of "worry" among the Machiguenga of Peru. This interest in emotional languages was intriguing: If different people have different ways of conceptualizing their emotions, might they *feel* them differently too?

Historians had long suspected the importance of passions to understanding the mind-sets of the past. However, a decade or so after these initial anthropological studies, they began excavating long-dead emotional cultures in earnest. Of course, they couldn't interview Roman slaves or medieval lovers about their feelings. But they could uncover the ways people of the past had understood their passions or sentiments by looking at diaries and letters, conduct manuals and medical regimens, even legal documents and political speeches. They began to ask the questions that have become so familiar to those who work in this field today. Was boredom invented by the Victorians? What made American presidents start smiling in their official portraits? Why did self-help authors in the sixteenth century encourage people to be sad, where today they'd exhort us to be happy? Why, in the eighteenth century, did artists want to broadcast the fact that they'd felt shocked? How could some emotions disappear — such as the combination of listlessness and despair the early Christians called "acedia" — and others like "ringxiety" suddenly pop into existence? To study the emotions of the past wasn't only to understand how rituals of love and grief had changed over time, or why in different historical periods some emotions could be publicly expressed, while others were hidden, or restrained through penance or prayer. The new field of study asked how these cultural values imprinted themselves on our private experiences. It asked whether our emotions were entirely our own.

Even accounts of those emotions that are sometimes thought to be "basic" or "universal," such as fear or disgust, vary across times and places. The idea that some emotions are more fundamental than others is a very old one. The *Li Chi*, a Confucian collection of precepts and rituals that can be dated back to at least the first century BCE, identifies seven inherent feelings (joy, anger, sadness, fear, love, dislike and fondness). The philosopher René Descartes thought there were six "primitive passions" (wonder, love, hatred, desire, joy and sadness). In our own time, some evolutionary psychologists argue that between six and eight "basic" emotions are expressed in the same way by all people.* The list usually includes disgust, fear, surprise, anger, happiness and sadness — though not "love," whose displays we expect to be tangled up in the rituals of different cultures. These "basic" emotional

---

* Emotionologists — those of us who study emotions from different fields — argue about this "basic emotions" theory a lot. The most well-known recent advocate of the idea that there are universal and basic emotions is the psychologist Paul Ekman. Recent researchers have disputed his claims, arguing that the facial expressions he has identified as universal in fact reflect a Western bias. Being suspicious about the universal emotions theory is not to say that we don't express and feel some emotions in very similar ways, or that we can't understand emotions from other cultures. After all, imagining the emotions of other people from past cultures is the most enjoyable part of being a historian of emotions. But saying something is very similar is not the same as saying it is identical in every way.

expressions are thought to be evolved responses to universal predicaments: a disgusted grimace ejects poisons from our mouths when we stick out our tongues; the rush of energy that comes when we are enraged may help us fight off a rival. But does it really follow that these emotions must *feel* the same way to all people in all places? Imagine a New York trader on the stock-exchange floor with sweating palms, a thumping heart and a prickling scalp. Then think of the same sensations experienced by a thirteenth-century Christian kneeling in a cold chapel in prayer, or by a Pintupi in Australia on waking in the dead of night with a stomach pain. The trader might call those feelings "an adrenaline rush" or "good fear" (or, on a bad day, "stress"). The second might view them as "wondrous fear," an awestruck terror alerting them to the presence of God. The third might feel *ngulu*, a particular sort of dread the Pintupi experience when they suspect another person is seeking revenge. The meanings we charge an emotion with change our experience of it. They determine whether we greet a feeling with delight or trepidation, whether we savor it or feel ashamed. Ignore these differences and we'll lose most of what makes our emotional experiences what they are.

It comes down to what you think an emotion is. When we talk about emotions, I think we need what the American anthropologist Clifford Geertz in the 1970s called "thick description." Geertz asked an elegant question: What is the difference between a blink and a wink? If we answer in purely physiological terms — speak of a chain of muscular contractions of the eyelids — then a blink and a wink are more or less the same. But you need to understand the cultural context to appreciate what a wink is. You need to understand playing and jokes, and teasing and sex, and learned conventions like irony and camp. Love, hate, desire, fear, anger and the rest are like this too. Without context, you only get a "thin description" of what's going on, not the whole story — and it's this whole story that is what an emotion *is*.

This book is about these stories, and how they change. It's about the different ways emotions have been perceived and performed — from the weeping jurors in Greek courts to the brave, bearded women of the Renaissance; from the vibrating heartstrings of eighteenth-century doctors to Darwin's self-experiments at London Zoo; from the shell-shocked soldiers of the First World War to our own culture of neuroscience and brain imaging. It's about the different ways our sorrowful, frowning, wincing, joyous bodies inhabit the world. And how the human world, with its moral values and political hierarchies, its assumptions about gender, sexuality, race and class, its philosophical views and scientific theories, inhabits us in return.

Emotion spotting: a field guide

Today, emotional health, and the necessity of recognizing and understanding our feelings to achieve it, is a stated goal of public policy in many countries, from Bhutan to the UK. Turn on a TV or open a newspaper, and there'll be, somewhere, tips on how to achieve lasting happiness, or why crying can be good for us. The idea that it's important to pay attention to our emotions is not new. The Stoics of ancient Greece taught that noticing the first stirrings of a passion gave you the best chance of controlling it. Catch the precise moment the hairs on the nape of your neck began to tingle, they thought, and you could remind yourself not to let blind panic set in. In the seventeenth century the scholar and great anatomist of melancholy Robert Burton also found noticing his emotions helped him — though his approach was rather different. He became curious about his feelings of despair and worry, and tried to understand them in conversation with other writers and philosophers, particularly those of the past. Eventually, his melancholy, which had once seemed so senseless, became filled with meaning — and started to loosen its grip.

Today's enthusiasm for taking our emotions seriously can largely be traced back to psychological research first popularized in the mid-1990s under the catchy heading of emotional intelligence, aka emotional quotient or EQ. Its proponents argued that being able to identify your own and other people's emotions, and to use them as a guide to making decisions, was as important in determining success as the traditional measure of IQ. Awareness of emotions has been shown to be strongly correlated with greater resilience in times of stress, with improved performance at work, with better management and negotiation skills and with more stable relationships at home. Today EQ, or some version of it, is a concept familiar to educators, business leaders and policy makers alike.

Whether you greet this excitement about emotions with a wide smile or a raised eyebrow, I hope you will agree that there are intriguing connections between our feelings and the words we use to describe them. Some emotions can fade into a smile when you know what to call them, such as umpty (the feeling that everything is "all wrong") or matutolypea (a sadness that only strikes in the morning). Some reveal themselves to be a greater part of our experience once we learn their name, such as basorexia (a sudden desire to kiss someone) or *gezelligheid* (the cozy feeling that comes from being inside with friends on a cold night). And sometimes, identifying and reading about other people's emotions can make our own seem less peculiar and isolating. In the course of writing this, many of the stories I encountered offered the consolations of shared experiences. Others resonated for different reasons, helping me to see some of my more wayward feelings from new perspectives. Most of us avoid thinking about some emotion or other. Perhaps you're ashamed of your resentfulness or scared about your apathy, or struggle with your embarrassment. But given half a chance to think about where our attitudes toward these feelings come from, we might discover they're not always the bogeymen we're sometimes led to believe. I hope some of these stories resonate with you too.

But this book is not really about helping yourself become a happier, or more successful (or even a richer!) individual. Though they are full of intriguing curiosities, understanding the cultural stories of our emotions above all helps us uncover the tacit beliefs about what "natural" (or, worse, "normal") emotional responses might be. If our emotions are so important to us today, if they are measured by governments, subject to increasing pharmaceutical intervention by doctors, taught in our schools and monitored by our employers, then we had better understand where the assumptions we have about them come from — and whether we really want to keep signing up.

How to use this book

In the vast literature on emotions, there are many lists of feelings. This one makes no attempt to be comprehensive, or drill down through the complexity of our inner life in the hope of striking a core. Instead, it is organized as a collection of miniature essays about emotions, presented, for the sake of convention, in alphabetical order. It acknowledges that the apparently minor and idiosyncratic — miffed (a bit), or *ilinx* (a feeling of excited disorientation such as one might get from kicking over the office recycling bin) — are as distinctive a part of the texture of our emotional lives as fear or surprise. The entries themselves similarly make no claims to being definitive. They attempt only to suggest glimpses into the historical pasts and current cultural politics of emotions, in the hope of shedding some light on why we feel the way we do today. They are something, hopefully, to get interested in and curious about, something with which to start discussions and ask questions.

It's not easy to squeeze emotions into categories. Over the time I've spent putting these entries together, I've frequently felt like a baffled Victorian cloud collector, wondering whether a particular shudder comes from pleasure or disgust (or both), or where guilt fades and remorse begins. Sometimes trying to be precise can bring insights (though *see also:* AMBIGUPHOBIA). But thinking about emotions will draw you into a maze of interconnecting passageways and revolving doors, and at times like these, the words we use to describe them become a matter more of convenience than true description. That is why this book is organized in the way it is. You can read the entries in alphabetical order. Or you can flick through its pages until something catches your eye, and then follow the cross-references — an experience that, perhaps, runs a little closer to how our emotions change shape, and melt together.

There are around 150 emotions discussed here. (There are, of course, many others that might have been…) But even if the project I embarked on is surely impossible to finish, I offer this collection, and the promise that there could have been more, as a gesture against those arguments that try to reduce the beautiful complexity of our inner lives into just a handful of cardinal emotions.

Because one thing I've learned, as a fellow explorer in this brave new emotional world, is that what we need isn't fewer words for our feelings.

We need more.

ABHIMAN

Composed around 1500 BCE, the Sanskrit Vedas are among the oldest religious writings in existence. Their hymns, incantations and rituals form the spiritual basis of Hinduism. They also let us glimpse everyday life in India 3,500 years ago.

First mentioned in the Vedas, the emotion *abhiman* (pronounced *ab*-ee-man) continues to be instantly recognizable across the Indian subcontinent. It is impossible to translate into a single English word. The literal meaning of "*abhi-man*" is "self-pride." But a clue to its deeper significance lies in the other Sanskrit word whose echoes can be heard in it: *balam* (strength).

Abhiman evokes the pain and anger caused when someone we love, or expect kind treatment from, hurts us. Sorrow and shock are at its root, but it quickly flourishes into a fierce, bruised PRIDE. It is often translated into English as "wounded dignity" or "spiteful retaliation," phrases with overtones of pettiness. In India, *abhiman* is a more acceptable, even expected, response. To recognize *abhiman* as an inevitable part of our emotional life is to know that breaking the unspoken contracts of love and respect between families and allies is an extremely serious betrayal.

Like many of the emotions linked to pride, *abhiman* can be stubborn. Often the one who feels it suffers most — a double blow. In

Rabindranath Tagore's short story "Shasti" ("Punishment"), the hero-ine Chandara lives in grinding poverty with her beloved husband, his brother, and his brother's miserable and complaining wife. When Chandara's brother-in-law accidentally kills his wife, and the police arrive, Chandara's husband panics. Attempting to save his brother, he accuses Chandara of the murder. It is not only a betrayal of their love, but of Chandara's position as a wife, and it wounds her deeply.

She draws herself up. Stiff with cold and implacable resentment, she confesses to the murder and is led silently to prison. Tagore writes that her actions are motivated by her *abhiman*, and translators have offered various versions in English: "What unrelenting resentment!"; "Such fierce, passionate pride"; "How terribly she was reacting to her hurt feeling"; and so on. As the date of her execution draws near, Chandara's husband repents and tries to intervene, but the wound still smarts. She refuses to meet his eye, even as she steps onto the gallows.

See also: HUMILIATION; LITOST; RESENTMENT.

ACEDIA

Imagine you're a Christian hermit, living in the deserts of western Egypt in the fourth century. The sun beats down on the roof of your mud-brick cell. Inside, you're praying, kneeling upon a carpet of stones — when you start to feel a little bit bored. It's a distracting, creeping feeling. Like the tickle of a gnat crawling up your arm. You must defeat it, or else risk succumbing to that most dangerous of all sinful passions: acedia.

Acedia (pronounced a-*seed*-ee-a) or sometimes called accidie, is an emotion that has no real equivalent today. It was a short-lived but disastrous emotional crisis, usually striking between 11 a.m. and

4 p.m. Its first signs were listlessness and irritability, but it didn't take long to turn into desolation and despair.

According to the Desert Father John Cassian, acedia felt like the mind was gripped by a "foul darkness." The body was affected too: as Amma Theodora, a female monastic of this period, explained, it left a sensation of being "weighed down," with weak knees, floppy limbs and a feverish head. The solitaries lived in loose-knit communities, undertaking their acts of extreme self-denial and prayer in caves and huts scattered across the desert wilderness. Under the spell of acedia, some monks picked fights with their brethren living nearby, or else complaining of their choice of vocation, attempted to set off back to the earthly delights of Alexandria or Constantinople, tempting their friends to join them. Some were found slumped and weeping in their cells; others tried to kill themselves, abandoning their bodies to the hazardous desert. Acedia was such a serious threat to the lifestyle — and lives — of these early monks that it was considered the most dangerous of the Eight Evil Thoughts, the forerunners to the Seven Deadly Sins.

Where did it come from? The Desert Mothers and Fathers believed it was sent by the Devil's minions known as "noonday demons," who whizzed about the communities infecting inhabitants with malaise. Today we might be inclined to say acedia was just a different name for the illness we now call "depression." Yet, the fact acedia struck only briefly, and only at the hottest hours of the day, and that all its victims were already feverish from their isolation and extreme acts of penitence, suggests acedia's origins were more peculiar. The phenomenon may have had more to do with isolated living in the punishing heat of desert, and suspecting that a malicious noonday demon was hovering nearby, than any "chemical imbalance" in the brain.

In the sixth century, acedia was dropped from the list of mortal sins.

Some of its symptoms were absorbed into the illness melancholia, a forerunner to our own states of depression and anxiety (*see*: MELANCHOLY). The rest became the moral vice sloth. Though people still spoke of feeling acedia, it came to mean something more like inertia — an equivalent, perhaps, to that listless feeling that descends on a rainy Sunday morning (*see*: APATHY). Perhaps it's no coincidence that the dangers of acedia abated when the center of religious thought relocated from the wilderness to the rather more congenial vineyards of Italy. Hangovers probably replaced heatstroke as the major threat to monastic life.

For more on the effects of the weather on emotions *see*: HUFF, in a.

See also: BOREDOM.

AMAE

Most of us on occasion feel the urge to crumple into the arms of a loved one to be coddled and comforted. It's important and reviving, this sensation of temporary surrender in perfect safety. The feeling it gives us is not easily captured in English, but Japanese people know it as *amae* (pronounced ah-*ma*-eh).

In Japan, *amae* is commonly acknowledged as part of all kinds of relationships, felt not only between family members, but with friends and in the workplace too. It does have shades of gray. Children may be accused of behaving in an *amaeru* way — wheedling and wide eyed, and hoping someone else will do something for them. Or a teenager might be warned against being *amai* (the adjective) for not bothering to study for a test — assuming somehow he'll pass anyway. "Behaving like a spoiled child," is one translation; "leaning on another person's good will," is another.

But these phrases do not do justice to the esteem in which *amae* is also held. According to the Japanese psychoanalyst Takeo Doi, *amae* is "an emotion that takes the other person's love for granted," there when we depend on another's help with no obligation to be grateful in return. You can even be encouraged to show some *amae* to yourself, when working too hard. For Doi, surrendering to *amae* is important because it represents a return to the indulgences and unconditional nurturing of infancy. It's the glue that allows stable relationships to flourish, an emblem of the deepest trust.

It's the fact that this combination of vulnerability and belonging has a name *at all* in Japan that has made many emotionologists curious. In the 1970s Western anthropologists became very excited about *amae*, arguing that it was evidence that even our most intimate emotions are shaped by the political and economic organization of the societies in which we live. They argued that *amae* had flourished in Japan's traditionally collectivist culture, and was a clue to the way its society continued to celebrate group dependency over individualism. Some went even further, arguing that *amae* "defined the Japanese national character," a claim that looks oversimplistic today.

Still, the fluency with which Japanese people speak about the pleasures of *amae* makes one wonder. Why do those of us who grew up speaking English fumble when we try to articulate a similar experience? Perhaps this lacuna in English speaks volumes about how hard it can be to accept other people's support. There is the worry of being thought "needy" or childish. The fear of becoming a link in an unbearable chain of obligations (*see:* GRATITUDE). And perhaps most of all, the embarrassment — of having to admit that we're not always the entirely self-sufficient adults we like to pretend to be.

See also: COMFORT; VULNERABILITY.

AMBIGUPHOBIA

An emotion coined by the American novelist David Foster Wallace to describe feeling uncomfortable about leaving things open to interpretation. E.g.: "His ambiguphobic recipe for yoghurted veal occupies seven pages and four schematic drawings."

See also: PARANOIA.

ANGER

The eyes blaze and glitter. The cheeks flush and the lips quiver. The muscles swell and are filled with a monstrous urge to destroy something. Even the hair stands on end. This could be a description of the transformation of Dr. Banner into the Incredible Hulk. It actually is how the Roman Stoic philosopher Seneca describes anger in one of the most influential and oldest anger-management texts in existence: *De Ira — On Anger —* written during the first century CE. Seneca considered anger "the most hideous and frenzied of all the emotions," a "brief insanity" during which we are closer to a wild animal than a civilized person. He thought, as had Aristotle before him, that it was caused by feeling demeaned or insulted — particularly by someone not fit to insult you (*see:* TECHNOSTRESS). And though he did recognize that anger could be useful for warriors on the battlefield, he thought it had no place in the market squares and palace corridors of Rome. Here, rages could only bring disruption: bitter quarrels and outbursts later to be regretted. So he advised exercising restraint at anger's first jolt, and rationally reflecting on the situation instead (*see:* APATHY).

Anger is an unruly class of emotion. It includes simmering RESENT-

MENT and fits of PIQUE; tantrums caused by EXASPERATION, and sudden flares of RAGE. It can be frighteningly contained, or else frenzied and physically violent. It can become abusive, ruining marriages and costing us jobs, yet it also stokes political action (*see:* INDIGNATION), and goads us into working harder (*see:* LIGET). Perhaps its one fixed point, the question to which those who have written about anger over the centuries return again and again, is whether it ought to be expressed. "I wish you'd get angry, so that we could have it out, so that we could get it out in the open," says Diane Keaton in Woody Allen's *Manhattan* (1979). To which Allen responds, "I don't get angry, okay. I mean, I have a tendency to internalize....I grow a tumor instead."

You might think the idea that expressing anger is good for our health (better out than in!) is a modern one. Not so. Some medieval and early modern doctors were also enthusiastic about unleashing fury. Though anger could deplete the body's vital spirits, there were times when it was thought beneficial. The eleventh-century Islamic scholar Ibn Butlan explained that since anger directed the body's heat to the extremities, it could revive those who had become flaccid and bed-bound through illness. He even thought it could cure paralysis. Four centuries later, in a plague tract written in 1490, the physician Lluís Alcanyís reported a story about a doctor who treated a patient for extreme weakness by sitting at the patient's bedside continually reminding him of slights from the past: the patient recovered. But the beneficial warming effects of anger did not end there. In his *Cure of Old Age, and Preservation of Youth*, the thirteenth-century physician and alchemist Roger Bacon argued that getting frequently infuriated could slow the aging process thought to be caused by the body becoming cooler and drier as it neared death. Anger, then, rather than the latest diet fads and expensive creams, was thought to give that zest for life and youthful glow coveted as much then as it is today.

In the early twentieth century the idea of healthily venting anger gained momentum. Sigmund Freud had argued that repressed emotions could cause physical symptoms ranging from headaches to gastric disturbances. Armed with this insight, a battalion of psychologists and psychiatrists in mid-twentieth-century Britain and America turned their attention to unleashing their patients' pent-up rage. One example of this approach was the "ventilation therapy" practiced at Synanon addiction rehabilitation centers in California in the late 1950s. During group therapy sessions, patients were encouraged to goad one another to dig deeper into their emotional pain. It usually didn't take long before someone snapped—and the healing was thought to begin. Primal Scream Therapy and even R. D. Laing's therapeutic community at Kingsley Hall in the late 1960s in Britain, similarly saw the expression of anger as a breakthrough in the therapeutic process. An outburst of rage was held to express an individual's authentic identity, breaking down the false selves that patients had erected to help them cope with living in a dishonest world. These therapists believed rage could reconnect patients to their true selves, releasing them from the addictions or madness that had become their refuge. For some, it worked.

Today's psychotherapists are less interested in provoking cathartic or "authentic" displays of rage than in trying to understand where anger comes from—and why we sometimes need it to help us cope with our lives. Anger flares up in strange and unexpected ways. A common response to the pain of being criticized or discovering we have been treated unfairly, anger can motivate us to try harder. But a burst of rage can benefit us in other ways too. It can create a release of muscular tension, temporarily subduing other, often more uncomfortable emotions, such as fear, or feelings of unworthiness. Perhaps an angry outburst might help us manage guilty feelings: by erupting at someone else, we shift the blame and temporarily give ourselves some RELIEF. In these cases, anger might seem "authentic," but psychoanalysts suggest it can be a decoy, a flash-in-the-pan outburst that we might unconsciously prefer to the more painful feeling it masks.

So as we think about expressing anger in the twenty-first century, the terms of the debate have shifted once again. The question is now not about whether we should express anger to keep healthy, but what other emotions our anger — whether a snarling fury or quietly seething rage — is keeping in check.

And for what happens when we keep it to ourselves, *see:* RESENTMENT.

ANTICIPATION

> *"You just wait and see," said Grandma.*
> *The lights went down, the bottom of the curtain glowed. I loved it and have always loved it best of all, the moment when the lights go down, the curtain glows, you know that something wonderful is going to happen. It doesn't matter if what happens next spoils everything; the anticipation itself is always pure.*
> *To travel hopefully is better than to arrive, as Uncle Perry used to say. I always preferred foreplay, too.*
> *Well. Not always.*
>
> — *Angela Carter,* Wise Children

Anticipation is a tiny theft of pleasure. A reckless spending of delights not yet owned.

Until the mid-nineteenth century, an anticipation was a sum of money spent before it was earned: an early payout on the dowry; an advance on next week's wages. Some emotions can be traced back to the weather and others to the landscape. Anticipation, however, is firmly embedded in the history of economics and exchange.

Perhaps it's this whiff of the scandalous ("neither a borrower nor a lender be!") that makes some adults firmly budget their children's expectations. Or perhaps, it's just their familiarity with the effects of DISAPPOINTMENT. Looking forward to an event is one thing. Savoring in Technicolor detail what will happen when the curtain goes up, however, is not for the fainthearted. "In a delicious agony of anticipation," writes Carter, the sisters knew the curtain would soon rise, "and then and then...what wonderful secrets would be revealed to us, then?"

"You just wait and see."

For more on emotions and money *see*: GRATITUDE.

See also: CURIOSITY; HOPEFULNESS.

ANXIETY

Anxiety is the dizziness of freedom.
> — *Søren Kierkegaard, The Concept of Anxiety*

The stomach lurches and the throat tightens. The eyes twitch and the mind zigzags across endless possibilities. Unlike fear or worry, which usually have a defined cause, anxiety buzzes hungrily around the buffet of life's problems, alighting on ordinary troubles and turning them into visions of disaster. It makes us fidgety and breathless. It's inhibiting. It's easy to recognize its pinched and constricted feeling from the word's Greek roots: anxiety comes from *angh* (to press tight, to strangle, to be weighted down with grief).

Anxiety is something we all experience from time to time. But today we tend to think of it as a rather pointless episode, something to be overcome and certainly not savored. We might think of sweaty, stuttering film characters — Jack Lemmon as Jerry in *Some Like It Hot*, Woody Allen in, well, anything — ratty and debilitated by endlessly imagining worst-case scenarios, and conclude that anxiety is not for the successful, or the happy. The pharmaceutical and alternative therapy industries bear this out, offering pills and potions, exercises and meditations, to calm the anxious mind and make it "free."

That anxiety is a curse seems inevitable in the twenty-first century. So it might be a surprise to discover it only became thought of as an affliction a hundred or so years ago — and that before then some philosophers spoke of feelings of fear and anguish as an enriching response to discovering one's own freedom.

The idea that anxiety might be an illness was first suggested in 1893, by the Wiesbaden psychiatrist Ewald Hecker, and two years later by his more famous Viennese colleague Sigmund Freud. They called it *Angstneurose*, and Freud thought it offered a more precise alternative to the vague catchall neurasthenia, with which many patients were diagnosed at the time. Among *Angstneurose*'s symptoms were oversensitivity to loud noises, night terrors, heart palpitations, asthma and excessive sweating. But one feature dominated: "anxious expectation," or fearing the worst. Its archetype was a fretful housewife: "She will think of influenza pneumonia every time her husband coughs when he has a cold, and in her mind's eye, will see his funeral go past," wrote Freud. He believed one of the major causes of the neurosis was an "accumulation of excitation," or, in today's terms, "sexual frustration," which is why he thought young married women were most at risk. In his view, the birth-control methods practiced at the time — condoms and coitus interruptus — inhibited female orgasm. Unspent, a woman's libido would erupt in strange ways: the heart palpitations and shallow breathing of a panic attack, for instance, which Freud understood as a substitute for the sweaty huffing and puffing of sex. For Freud, then, anxiety was libido gone sour, related to genuine desire "in the same kind of way vinegar is to wine."

In the 1940s, amid the psychological wreckage caused by the war, the poet W. H. Auden was moved to speak of an "Age of Anxiety." The governments of Britain and the United States attempted to stem the tide of anxious feelings, employing psychologists to measure and improve the population's "serenity" and "security" — an undertaking that resembles today's HAPPINESS agenda (*see also:* COMFORT). By the time Miltown, the first of the blockbuster tranquilizers, hit the market in 1955, followed by Valium in 1963, anxiety had become a multimillion-dollar industry, and the twentieth century's signature psychiatric condition. By the 1960s, however, the "Age of Anxiety" was on the wane. A new illness — a rare condition known as "depression" — was catching on, in part due to new diagnostic reclassifications encouraged by a rapidly expanding pharmaceutical industry (*see:* SADNESS). Today, anxiety is once more on the rise, and has recently overtaken depression as the most commonly diagnosed disorder in the United States, with an expansion in the different types of anxiety it is now possible to suffer (in the most recent edition of the psychiatric diagnostic bible the *DSM-V*, there are twelve). As in the late nineteenth century, more women than men are diagnosed. Are women naturally more anxious? Or, since the way the illness has historically been described is so clearly gendered, are women always more likely to meet the criteria for being diagnosed with it?

For the Danish philosopher Søren Kierkegaard, born some forty years before Freud, the idea of anxiety as a widespread psychological disorder would have been hard to countenance. He believed it was not possible to think about human existence without understanding our emotions, even the more burdensome ones. He spoke of us as trembling, terrified, sickening creatures — and one of the emotions that particularly intrigued him was, in Danish, *angest*, a combination of anguish about the present and dread about the future. With its asides and jokes, its subversions and pastiches, his 1844 treatise *Begrebet Angest*, translated into English as *The Concept of Anxiety* exactly a hundred years later, is so labyrinthine that just trying to read it would make anyone anxious. Kierkegaard argues that angst is the appropriate response to realizing life is not predetermined, but that we have absolute freedom to make any choice we want — and total responsibility for the outcome. "He whose eye happens to look down into the yawning abyss becomes dizzy," writes Kierkegaard. But though this vertigo might be unnerving, a capacity to feel it is a hallmark of a life lived authentically. Only the "most spiritless have lived without anxiety," he proclaimed. The challenge was not to avoid the panicky fretful feelings or become paralyzed by them, but to learn to acknowledge and understand the significance of the choice they offer.

So he would probably be alarmed to see how we treat anxiety today, as something to be freed from, rather than evidence of freedom itself.

Only a "prosaic stupidity," he cautioned, would dismiss such an important feeling as a mere illness.

See also: UNCERTAINTY; WORRY; COLLYWOBBLES, the

APATHY

The book falls from your hand. You stare up at the ceiling. The dog eats the leftover pizza from the box on the floor, while a phone — is it yours? you don't care — rings quietly in the next room unanswered. Unlike BOREDOM, which itches for something to do, apathy is a glorious indolence. For some of us, frankly, it's the only reasonable response to dejection and stress (see also: DOLCE FAR NIENTE). But just over two thousand years ago, philosophers gave it an even loftier role.

Stoicism, a school of philosophy founded in the third century BCE and that flourished for almost 400 years, taught that *apatheia* was essential to a harmonious and just society. From *a-* (without) *pathos* (passion), the word meant something rather different from the sluggish inertia many of us are (secretly) all too familiar with today. Stoics believed that in order for people to act in a just and rational manner, emotions like anger and jealousy should be restrained. Stoics understood emotions as a two-part process. First came "mental jolts": the hairs raising on the back of the neck in fear, or the electric shock of desire when eyes meet. Next came the emotion proper, a more potent state. Learning to interrupt one's feelings at the first involuntary stirrings and consciously *decide* to refuse them permission to flourish, was the goal of Stoic practice. Stoics didn't believe that all emotions were bad: Marcus Aurelius described the ideal Stoic character as "full of love and yet free from passion." It was just that some of the more disruptive ones needed restraining for the common good (see also: ANGER).

To many of us today, aiming to maintain life in a condition of benevolent equilibrium might seem vain, even unreasonable. We might even think that life without such emotions as envy or desire would just be brittle and dry. But a large part of the reason many of us are suspicious of apathy today can be traced back to the murder of a woman named Kitty Genovese.

In March 1964 the twenty-eight-year-old Genovese was killed in New York City in the grounds of an apartment building. The murder, though tragic, was nothing unusual. What was surprising were reports in the newspapers the next day that thirty-eight residents of the apartment block heard her screams, went to their windows and watched the attack happen without calling for help. At this time, many social psychologists thought that being part of a crowd whipped people into a frenzy. Theories of mob behavior and the "group mind" were based on the idea that being part of a crowd meant unleashing primitive emotions and irrational, impulsive behavior (*see:* PANIC). The murder of Kitty Genovese suggested something different. It was as if the watching residents had their instincts of alarm or compassion muffled, or else replaced with the assumption that someone else would help instead.

The Genovese murder became the defining image of a new disease creeping through the metropolis. The psychologists Bibb Latané and John Darley dubbed it "bystander apathy" or the "bystander effect." In the subsequent discussions, apathy was defined as more than laziness or listlessness. It was a loss of motivation or purpose, the vacuous indifference that can come when we are feeling OVERWHELMED. Apathy became aligned with a sense of defeat — and the paralysis and listlessness that can arrive when we think problems are other people's responsibility. Psychologists had worried about listlessness before: Victorian neurologists were concerned about "aboulia," or a loss of will or motivation; even earlier, the first Christians feared a condition that later became identified with the mortal sin of "sloth" (*see:* ACEDIA). But, in the decades since Latané and Darley's experiments, twentieth- and twenty-first-century psychology and sociology undergraduates have learned that apathy is not just a matter of deadly sin or diseased individual psychology but, even more insidiously, something that causes antisocial behavior yet arises from living in groups.

In fact, those first reports of the Genovese case weren't entirely true. The Chief of Police had mentioned to an editor at the *New York Times* that there had been an astonishing thirty-eight witnesses to the murder. Without checking the sources, the journalist wrote up the story describing thirty-eight witnesses watching the murder without helping. A recent investigation concluded that only three residents realized the attack for what it was and did nothing. Three is too many — of course. But the fact that the thirty-eight figure seemed believable at all is worth thinking about. Why were the general public, and the psychologists themselves, taken in?

Today we suffer from a twin inheritance. On the one hand, like the Stoics, we might welcome some relief from the strife of the passions, or believe that without emotion influencing us, we'd behave more fairly. On the other, since we have come to celebrate emotions as a motivator for all kinds of action, apathy's loss of feeling has become something fearful. The Genovese case captures so much of the nervousness we've come to feel about apathy, a condition that seems to make us unwilling to vote or pick up our litter or report a crime. And so we may go back and forth, wondering whether apathy may be good for us, or very bad, until, feeling overwhelmed, we slump listlessly back onto the sofa.

See also: BAFFLEMENT; CALM.

L'APPEL DU VIDE

Walking along a high cliff path, you are gripped by a terrifying urge to leap. As an express train hurtles into view, you itch to fling yourself in front of it. People talk of a fear of heights, but in truth anxieties about precipices are often less to do with falling than the horrifying compulsion to jump.... In Alfred Hitchcock's *Vertigo* (1958), what paralyzes James Stewart as he chases the suicidal Kim Novak up those rickety stairs of the bell tower is not dizziness. Hitchcock's clever camera trick, which makes the bottom of the stairwell swim into the foreground, also makes its vanishing point alluring. Stewart is terrified he might just give in.

The French have a name for this unnerving impulse: *l'appel du vide,* "the call of the void." Perhaps it is a kind of terrifying game the mind plays, a test serving to remind us how close danger is. But most of all, as Jean-Paul Sartre recognized, *l'appel du vide* creates an unnerving, shaky sensation of not being able to trust one's own instincts. And the fear that our emotions, with their impish irrational impulses, might be capable of leading us very far astray.

See also: PERVERSITY; ILINX; TERROR.

AWUMBUK

There is an emptiness after visitors depart. The walls echo. The space that felt so cramped while they were here now seems weirdly large. And though there is often relief, we can also be left with a muffled feeling — as if a fog has descended and everything seems rather pointless (*see:* APATHY).

The indigenous Baining people who live in the mountains of Papua New Guinea are so familiar with this experience that they name it *awumbuk.** They believe that departing visitors shed a kind of heaviness when they leave, so as to travel lightly. This oppressive mist hovers for three days, creating a feeling of distraction and inertia and

---

* The philosopher Peter Goldie has suggested that a word for lassitude felt at the *arrival* of family and friends could also be useful.

interfering with the family's ability to tend to their home and crops. So once their guests have left, the Baining fill a bowl with water and leave it overnight to absorb the festering air. The next day, the family rises very early and ceremonially flings the water into the trees, whereupon ordinary life resumes.

See also: MELANCHOLY; GRIEF.

BAFFLEMENT

During the Industrial Revolution, engineers invented a contrivance to force hot steam inside a machine to change course, restraining its natural flow. They called it a "baffler" — the old word for a magician. Bafflers are nowadays called "baffles" — and they are still tricksy. On an airstrip, for instance, they are used to drown out the roar of the engines, shooing sound waves first one way then the other until the noise dampens.

Feeling baffled is a bit like being one of those sound waves, wrong-footed by magic. It happens when too many options (*see:* UNCERTAINTY), particularly those poorly arranged in a disorderly heap (*see:* BEFUDDLEMENT), make it hard to follow, or know which direction we should proceed (*see:* OVERWHELMED, feeling), leaving us feeling frustrated (*see:* EXASPERATION), or angry (*see:* IMPATIENCE), even bilious (*see:* DISGUST), but most of all exhausted (*see:* APATHY) by a surfeit of information that creates a sense of blockage (*see:* BOREDOM), and precipitates a feeling of existential angst for the random purposelessness of things.

See also: BEWILDERMENT.

BASOREXIA

The sudden urge to kiss someone.

See also: VULNERABILITY.

BEFUDDLEMENT

Nebuchaotic sensation experienced around obscure words, incomplete lists,

See also: BAFFLEMENT.

BEWILDERMENT

Tidy. Plan. Organize. These are the principles of the industrious and efficient life.

Little room left, in this high-pressure success-oriented world of ours, for mess. Or the bewilderment that trails around it.

For the psychoanalyst Adam Phillips, feeling muddled lies at the heart of the therapeutic relationship. Mess brings people into analysis, he writes. Hoping to make sense of their destructive relationship patterns or hard-to-explain cravings, some of his patients desire above all that he will bring clarity to their minds, decluttering and reorganizing, sweeping away the cobwebs until it is pristine again. It's no surprise, this urge for tidiness. From a messy desk to the refusal to keep a diary, disorganization is sometimes presented as stubborn and self-defeating: a subconscious desire to frustrate ourselves, preventing us from pursuing our goals or achieving the success we crave.

But mess is not always an obstacle. Sometimes it can be useful. Most of us at one time or another will have discovered something of value while searching for a tedious invoice in a messy in-tray. When we root through the jumble of our minds, we might similarly find ideas we weren't looking for, or make connections between things we didn't realize were linked. For Phillips, in the end it's the clutter that is the most interesting thing about the psychoanalytic process. Above all, he is curious about the way we deliberately — albeit subconsciously — create these conditions of mess and bewilderment, tangling up our relationships or leaving chaos behind us at work, because we want to discover something new.

Among the great lost souls of literature, King Lear is perhaps one of the most vivid examples of creative disorientation. The forgetful old man moodily casts himself out onto the storm-blown heath. Confused about his identity, feeling rejected by his children and lost in the wild lands outside the castle gates, he becomes bewildered in both senses of the word. His confusion is at the heart of a feverish process of remaking himself, the feeling that makes it possible for him to ask the question that pulses through the play: "Who is it that can tell me who I am?"

We all, from time to time, find ourselves exasperated by clutter, deafened by babble and frightened by confusion. Mess is not easy to tolerate. But the confusions that force us to ask, "Who am I?" or "What does it mean?" are valuable. As we search through the jumble of possible answers, we may just turn up some idea, or image, or belief that suddenly helps things make sense.

"Anything that stops something happening is making something else possible," writes Phillips. It is reminiscent of the old homily:

lose something, and you might stumble on something far better while looking for it.

See also: DÉPAYSEMENT; OVERWHELMED, feeling.

BOREDOM

Pick up a book, and discard it. Yawn, slump, and slip into a thousand-yard stare. Wander from room to room in search of some distraction — nothing appeals. Boredom is the most contrary of emotions. It's a combination of feeling trapped, inert and disinterested: there is a vague sense of wanting something to change, but we really can't say what.

The boredom we know today was invented by the Victorians, although that is not to say that life had never felt repetitive and uninteresting before then. Pliny reputedly believed that many an "overtoiled" Roman citizen poisoned himself because of his "tedious life." And in the fifteenth century, feeling "irked" was an unpleasant combination of weariness and DISGUST, as is commonly felt when one is stuck sitting next to a dull person at dinner, or forced to listen to an incomprehensible lecture (see also: ACEDIA).

When the new emotional category of "boredom" — from the French bourrer (to stuff or satiate; literally, to be fed up) — first appeared in the English language in 1853, it was a consequence of a rapidly changing relationship to time. Pre-industrial societies had not distinguished between work and domestic drudgery, but the rapid expansion of factories and offices in cities from the late eighteenth century produced a new way of dividing up the day, inaugurating the concept of "leisure time." Leisure was quickly conceived among the middle classes as a space for self-improving recreation. A lucrative entertainment industry, which included circuses, popular science lectures and theatrical extravaganzas, rushed in to meet the growing demand to be diverted and edified, and a new tourism industry emerged to cater to the combined bourgeois excitements of consumerism and novelty (*see also:* WANDERLUST).

In this context, finding oneself at a loose end or trapped in dreary company, or feeling unable to be interested, attentive or useful, was a mark of inadequacy. Doctors debated boredom's unsavory health implications (alcoholism, onanism, excessive sleeping). Politicians vilified it as a social ill and blamed the poor and unemployed for allowing it to fester. Feminist campaigners and novelists pointed out the emotion's corrosive effects on middle- and upper-class women. In Charles Dickens's *Bleak House*, published in 1853, Lady Dedlock, separated from her true love and married to a kind but remote gentleman, is listless, lonely and "bored to death." She had succumbed, wrote Dickens in what the *Oxford English Dictionary* cites as the first use of the word "boredom" in English, to the "chronic malady" of modern life. Twenty or so years later, Gwendolen in George Eliot's *Daniel Deronda* warned this malady might have unforeseen effects on others too. Brought up like hothouse plants to "look as pretty as we can, and be dull without complaining," women could be turned poisonous to the touch by boredom.

Today, we ought to be boredom-free. With the constant stimulation of ever-smarter technologies, and the celebration of a new kind of flexible "creative worker" in whose world there is no discernible split between "labor time" and "leisure time," stress rather than boredom is the malady of our times. Yet the Victorians' worries about boredom are still with us, reframed in twenty-first-century terms. The controversial diagnosis of attention deficit hyperactivity disorder (ADHD) among growing numbers of schoolchildren has created a whole category of people understood to be neurologically prone to boredom, their lowered dopamine levels leaving them restless, fidgety and easily distracted. Those who score highly on the Boredom Proneness Scale are considered more likely to abuse alcohol, become obese, or make mistakes while driving.

This moral and medical panic about boredom may come at a price. Turn off your smart phone, and you may find yourself slipping — via irritable boredom — into that listlessness that gives rise to pleasant reverie and daydreams. Feel an itching dissatisfaction and disinterest, and you may be motivated to change your situation. There is no coincidence that many creative people, for instance the artist Grayson Perry and writer Meera Syal, have spoken of their own childhoods as immensely tedious. Their boredom propelled them to invent and imagine; as Perry puts it, boredom is "a very creative state." So perhaps we should take care not to rush in and alleviate the brattish whine of our children's "I'm bored" too quickly, or fill their schedules with endlessly interesting activities. Because it might just be, as the anthropologist Ralph Linton has argued, that "the human capacity for being bored, rather than social or natural needs, lies at the root of man's cultural advance."

See also: ACEDIA; APATHY; CHEESED (off).

BRABANT

You know it's not a good idea, and likely to backfire. But you just can't resist wondering what would happen if...

In *The Deeper Meaning of Liff* Douglas Adams and John Lloyd gave this glint of a feeling a name. Brabant: "very much inclined to see how far you can push someone."

See also: PERVERSITY; ILINX.

BROODINESS

Of a woman: feeling a maternal desire to have a(nother) baby.
— Oxford English Dictionary

It's only been since the 1980s that this word, once associated with poultry, has been applied to women. One sniff of a baby's head and the unsuspecting female is engulfed in a tidal wave of hormone-related baby lust... or so the cliché runs.

The invention of this new emotional state, and its definition "of a woman" — men started to talk of themselves as "getting broody" in the late 1990s, although the *Oxford English Dictionary* has yet to acknowledge this — is no coincidence. It came a little over twenty years after the Pill became widely available to single as well as married women in Britain and America. With reproduction more of a choice than an inevitability, broodiness, which combined a henlike instinct to breed with general moodiness or "brooding," was delineated as a powerful emotional motivator for the decision to reproduce.

Longing for a baby is not purely a cultural construct, nor specific to low-fertility societies. It can be deeply painful, a sense of something missing, a yearning, temporary feeling comparable to that experienced when separated from a loved one or home (*see:* HIRAETH; VIRAHA). And like the brooding storm-clouds that gather on the horizon, yearning for a child brings more emotional weather with it: HOPEFULNESS for a future of love; WORRY about being left behind as friends' families blossom; the DESIRE for promised joys; SADNESS at the thought that it might not happen.

To reduce broodiness to the ticktock of simple animal hormones is diminishing. But there is a long history of depicting the emotions of women as in thrall to their mysterious biology, for instance in the illnesses of hysteria or "irritable womb" (see: DISAPPOINTMENT). It runs back to Plato's announcement in the *Timaeus* that "the womb is an animal which longs to generate children. When it remains barren too long after puberty, it is distressed and sorely disturbed, and straying about in the body...[it] brings the sufferer into the most extreme anguish."

Plato's talk of wandering wombs sounds like an unscientific flight of ancient fancy today. Yet for an emotion that is imagined to exercise such tyranny over women, broodiness has been very little studied in our time. Psychologists have linked it to a heightened sex drive, which seems obvious at first glance, but less so when we consider that broodiness is also aligned to a depressive state. There is also confusion about whether it is an emotion overwhelmingly experienced by women, or can be just as pronounced — if not more so — in men. Sociologists studying the desire for a baby among involuntarily childless men have discovered a hidden world of complex emotions including sorrow and guilt, isolation and anger, and have claimed that four out of ten men describe themselves as feeling "depressed" about the situation in contrast to three out of ten women.

So there is a muddle about broodiness, and it needs sorting out. Because the idea that feeling broody is a biological inevitability for women suggests that those who choose not to reproduce are destined to suffer. And those who never feel so much as a twang of baby lust might suspect themselves to be somehow missing some crucial emotion of womanhood, and therefore not meant for parenthood.

And neither is true.

See also: TORSCHLUSSPANIK; PHILOPROGENITIVENESS.

CALM

He dreamt of a "psychocivilized society," its members capable of controlling their emotions through an electronic chip implanted in the brain. Rage, fear, lust, serenity: all could be turned on and off by remote stimulation of the limbic system via the device he called a "stimoceiver."

This is not an early draft of *The Matrix*.

It describes the ambition of José Delgado, who, in the 1960s and early '70s, was a widely celebrated neuroscientist at Yale.

Delgado's fame peaked in 1965 when dramatic photographs of one of his experiments on emotion modification made the front page of the *New York Times*. The unarmed scientist stands in a bull ring in Córdoba, Spain. In one hand he holds a matador's cape; in the other, a small remote-control box. Several meters away, a bull snorts and stamps on the ground. It charges toward the scientist. Only moments from being gored, Delgado flicks a switch that controls an electronic chip embedded in the bull's brain. The animal stops and turns away. It seems passive and relaxed. Its "aggression" and "destructive fury," reported Delgado, "ceased instantly."

It's when emotions get to be too much that we may fantasize about one of Delgado's remote controls. When anxiety sends shocks behind the eyes, or fear thuds in the chest, or love is so rapturous we fear we'll lose our footing. If we could just shut it off, even temporarily, to give ourselves a rest, *to think!* But even for masters of meditation or Stoic sages, these screeching emergency stops are hard to pull off. We might count to ten, or bite our lips, or tell ourselves "this too shall pass," but few of us can conjure calm at the opportune moment.

Certainly, the journalists reporting Delgado's experiment seemed swept up by the fantasy of calm-on-demand, although their descriptions are not altogether reliable. One of the areas of the bull's brain that was stimulated was the caudate nucleus, responsible for moving the legs to make the body turn. It's not entirely clear whether the bull's "destructive fury" had been quelled, or whether the charging bull had simply been forced to make a sudden right turn — and was, understandably, rather discombobulated as a result.

Today, smoothing the mind's scratchy edges is now largely achieved by pharmaceuticals, the so-called chemical restraints that render Alzheimer's patients in understaffed nursing homes, or prisoners on overcrowded wings, pliable and calm. In the 1970s, however, it looked as if neurotechnology might just beat the drugs to it. Though it required an invasive procedure, Delgado thought his electronic implants might ultimately offer a more elegant solution to disordered emotions than the method favored in asylums at the time: the lobotomy. However, while the technology was still at an early stage, Delgado's only human subjects were patients being treated for extreme illnesses such as epilepsy and schizophrenia at the Rhode Island Asylum. One woman with a history of drug abuse and jail time begged Delgado to implant one of his electrodes. He refused.

Deciding what counts as a "normal" emotional response can reflect the deepest prejudices of the societies in which we live. Five years after Delgado's bullring theatrics, and amid the waves of civil unrest sweeping America's inner cities in the 1960s, neurotechnology once again made the headlines. Two researchers at Harvard Medical School proposed that stimoceivers should be implanted in the brains of the rioters — most of whom were young black men. The proposal, which was never acted on, framed the RAGE of African-Americans protesting against chronic injustice as excessive and pathological, and requiring an invasive medical intervention. It is shocking today, and an incident many would rather forget. Yet this story, as with many similar ones in the history of emotions, reminds us just how politically charged — and changeable — the category of a "normal" emotional response can be.

See also: APATHY.

CAREFREE

It's impossible to watch Ginger Rogers and Fred Astaire dance without feeling a little jaunty. In the screwball comedy *Carefree*, Rogers plays a radio star who enjoys her independence so much that she keeps dodging setting a date for her wedding. Eventually, her fiancé dispatches her to a psychiatrist, Astaire, who hypnotizes her and feeds her whipped cream and cucumbers to bring on revealing dreams. Naturally, she ends up falling for him instead.

It's a ridiculous plot. But watching the pair of them whirling and tapping, joking and whistling because they're in love, raises a grin even on the stoniest days.

Feeling free is blissful and audacious. Other people and their requirements suddenly matter very little. Obligations float away. There's a sensation of lightness, of daring. The chance of adventure! Sometimes it's rebellious, a tongue poked out at the boring world of prescribed bedtimes and sensible eating. Sometimes it comes with a little warning, even a threat. This is why, in Britain, Chelsea FC supporters show off their nonchalance to unnerve their opposition, and chant this (to the tune of "Lord of the Dance"):

> *Carefree, wherever we may be*
> *We are the famous CFC*
> *And we don't care*
> *Whoever you may be*
> *'Cause we are the famous CFC.*

So it's always deflating when a little voice starts whining in your ear. What if you fall? Or can't get home? What if your negligence leaves a trail of hurt feelings behind?

For the novelist D. H. Lawrence, not caring was a skill worth cultivating. In his essay "Insouciance," he recalls a hot afternoon spent sitting on a balcony in Spain. He is pleasurably, idly absorbed in watching two men mow the green grass: "Slush! slush! sound the scythe-strokes." But then two women pipe up on the balcony next to him, talking of international politics. "They care!" he laments. "They are simply eaten up with caring. They are so busy caring about Fascism or Leagues of Nations [...] that they never know where they are."

For Lawrence, nonchalance was a revolutionary gesture. A protest against the alienation of the modern, technologized world, and a return to the natural rhythms of life. So he urged his readers to pay attention to the small things, the ephemera — the feeling of sun on one's face, the precise shade of blue of a man's trousers, the sound of scythes — rather than always rushing off into abstract thoughts and political arguments.

In this respect, Lawrence anticipates today's much-vaunted

mindfulness techniques, which are less a question of ignoring the petty distractions of daily life than tuning in to them more purposefully. Whether a passing truck is making the windows rattle, or you can hear your teenagers arguing upstairs, paying attention to noise both inside and out can help life's pressures temporarily recede. And then, later, once you've had a chance to breathe, go outside, swing your legs, or dance like Fred and Ginger.

Because that, my friend, might just be how the revolution begins.

See also: DOLCE FAR NIENTE.

CHEERFULNESS

Disney World: it's "the happiest place on earth." To work there, you must study at the Disney University, where experts in the "science of guestology" know just how to maintain beaming smiles and infectious enthusiasm while surrounded by overexcited children and their demanding parents. There are lessons (they would call them "games") in managing facial expressions and gestures; you learn, too, how to transform your inner monologue, to convert feelings of FRUSTRATION and RESENTMENT into enthusiasm and DELIGHT.

Disney employees, like many others who work in service industries where "surface acting" positive emotions is explicitly demanded, have been shown to be at greater risk of burnout. In our increasingly flexible, consumer-focused economy, it's worth asking whether we should take compulsory cheerfulness more seriously.

The emergence of cheerfulness as a workplace requirement can be traced back to America, a country well known for embracing an upbeat, can-do attitude. This is a relatively recent development. The diaries and letters of seventeenth-century Americans are as miserable in tone as those of their European counterparts. Humility, rather than the desire for change, seems to have been the appropriate response to life's hardships and injustices.

Historians have traced a change in attitude to the eighteenth century, and in particular, to the self-sufficiency and striving valued in an emerging capitalist economy. America's lack of class system has also been thought to contribute to its expectation of openness. Harriet Martineau, an English sociologist who visited the US in 1830, was set all afluster when a local cracked a joke to her at a train station. She noted, rather disdainfully, that "a general air of cheerfulness" could even be felt in the country's asylums and graveyards — presumably she was more used to European hauteur.

Among the first workers encouraged to be upbeat and enthusiastic were housewives. According to the Beecher Sisters' 1869 manual for housekeeping, women should bring a "patience and cheerfulness" to their homes. A positive attitude at home, they wrote, would ensure their family's success in the world beyond, as nourishing to their husbands and children as the casserole in the oven. This makes American housewives among the first encouraged to perform "emotional labor," the name sociologists give to the work undertaken when employees are explicitly directed to control their own feelings in order to influence those of others.

By the end of the First World War, a new sort of specialist, the industrial psychologist, entered the workplace. Charged with preventing workplace unrest and increasing productivity, they concluded that optimism and a can-do attitude (rather than raised wages or better working conditions) were the critical factors. By the 1930s, 30 percent of American companies had industrial relations departments to oversee the hiring process and test employees for "introversion" and other "temperament deficiencies." It was against this backdrop of compulsory cheerfulness that Dale Carnegie wrote one of the classics of self-help literature, *How to Stop Worrying and Start Living*, in 1948. He advised salesmen to always be "vivacious," greeting clients with a cheery smile and cracking a joke. And if the salesman happened to be dissatisfied that day? Well, the solution was easy: "Think and act cheerful," instructed Carnegie, "and you will be cheerful."

Can trying to act upbeat when you don't actually *feel* upbeat really work? There is some evidence that suggests it might, and that contorting your face into a grin might truly influence the emotions you feel.* But some psychologists and sociologists have questioned the long-term effects of sustaining a workplace rictus smile. In her seminal study of flight attendants, sociologist Arlie Russell Hochschild found that during their training they were repeatedly exhorted to be "nicer than natural" to passengers. The company's intention was for the flight attendants to elevate the status of the passengers, and make them feel that flying was a luxury experience. The cost, however, was to the flight attendants themselves. Hochschild's interviewees reported that over time, they had come to feel estranged from — even mistrustful of — their own feelings.

_____

* An experiment: try holding a pencil lengthways between your teeth and see if it improves your mood. Philosophers have long wondered whether our facial expressions of smiling and frowning can change how we feel. Today's psychologists call this idea "the facial feedback hypothesis." In 2008 a group of researchers at the Max Planck Institute in Berlin devised an ingenious experiment to test it. They compared the emotional responses of women having Botox injections before and after treatment. Before the injections, the women were asked to imitate a photograph of an angry face while in a brain scanner. Their scans showed significant activity in both sides of the amygdala, the brain region associated with emotional arousal. After the Botox, which immobilized their frown muscles, imitating the same expression produced significantly less activity in the left side of the amygdala. It remains unclear whether this effect is to do with self-consciousness (perceiving yourself as angry might make you feel so), or whether there is a direct causal link between frowning and the part of the brain that controls anger. But this question aside, the experiment seems to provide the first tentative fMRI evidence that the way our faces move might really change the way we feel.

Until recently the problems of "emotional labor" were thought to be faced only by low-paid, predominantly female service-industry employees. However, in the last ten years sociologists have studied doctors, university teachers and members of the police force on both sides of the Atlantic — and concluded that explicit demands for employees to manage their feelings are on the increase.* The requirement to be cheerful has been identified as a particular culprit, with grumpiness becoming less tolerated as anxieties about employee trustworthiness rise (*see*: DISGRUNTLEMENT). Since "emotional labor" is thought to contribute to increased levels of stress and symptoms associated with depression and ANXIETY among employees, we may find ourselves in the peculiar position where the pressure to be cheerful leads to dissatisfaction, exhaustion and alienation.

Have a nice day!

See also: HAPPINESS.

CHEESED (OFF)

The threads linking food and the heart are irresistible. The matzo ball soup that comforts. The toasted spices that transport you to your mother's kitchen. The oozing chocolate pudding bent on seduction.

For the RAF pilots who fought in the Second World War, there was an affinity between burnt cheese and boredom.

---

* Even American presidents are expected to be cheerful — at least, in their official portraits. While the founding fathers looked rather stern, by the 1940s small smiles had begun to sprout up. Harry Truman smiles in his official portrait (1947), but it's only when you get to Ronald Reagan's portrait (completed in 1991) that you see the full toothy smile that we've become familiar with today.

To get "cheesed off" was to become disgruntled while hanging around the aerodrome, waiting for a mission. Originally, this irritable feeling was described as being "browned off," the pilots comparing themselves to rusting engines. The expression "cheesed off" can be traced back to the nineteenth century, but quite why it became so popular among airmen remains a mystery. Some say it's because cheese turns brown under a grill. Others, because cheese on toast was obsessively eaten while waiting, and the men were, quite literally, fed up with it (*see:* BOREDOM).

Some situations and the emotions they provoke are so unpleasant that a silly nickname is the only hope of relief (*see also:* UMPTY; COLLYWOBBLES, the). It's easy to imagine Second World War airmen silenced by stiff upper lips. But the expression "cheesed off" is a gentle correction to this cliché. It lets us catch a glimpse of the wry smiles that lightened the grim wait.

For more emotional soldiers, *see:* HOMESICKNESS.

See also: BOREDOM.

CLAUSTROPHOBIA

It was hard to establish whether signs of life had ceased. Tickling with feathers, placing mirrors over mouths and needles under the toenails were all techniques favored by physicians diagnosing death in the eighteenth century. No wonder, then, that when corpses were exhumed, some were found with their nails worn away and their kneecaps broken, and that scratch marks were found on the inside of coffin lids.

Like many of the names we now give our most urgent terrors, claustrophobia was coined by doctors in the nineteenth century — amid a rash of newspaper reports of premature burials. The new illness described a dread of enclosed spaces: closets, small rooms, elevators, caves. The clothes tighten at the neck. Sweat prickles the palms. The risk of suffocation feels so real that there is an overwhelming urge to bolt, but you can't, feeding the trapped feeling further. Of the many popular accounts of the hours between waking up six feet under and suffocating to death that became popular at this time, Edgar Allan Poe's description in "The Premature Burial" still brings a shudder. But perhaps the campaigner William Tebb's 1895 book *Premature Burial and How It May Be Prevented* is grislier still: "They will have to undergo slow suffocation, in furious despair, while scratching their flesh to pieces, biting their tongues, and smashing their heads against the narrow houses that confine them, and calling to their best friends, and cursing them as murderers."

Since then the meaning of claustrophobia has bloated. It's not just confined spaces that can produce its panicky constricted feeling; some relationships and social situations can also leave us desperate for air. The office party from which you're eager to escape but must woodenly smile through. The lunch spent with an ex-friend, resentments bubbling beneath the stilted conversation. Gifts, help, even love can smother us. It's when other people's expectations tighten around us, and we're duty bound to enjoy or show GRATITUDE or reciprocate that we can feel most stifled — and may just start scratching in a bid to escape.

See also: DISAPPEAR, the desire to.

COLLYWOBBLES, THE

Bloated and gassy, gurgling and sizzling. It's the stomach as well as the heart that plays host to many of our emotions. When we speak of a loss being gut-wrenching, or fear knotting the stomach, these aren't just metaphors — there's a long medical tradition linking our bellies and our minds. Early moderns studiously avoided ingesting certain foods thought to cause melancholia. Robert Burton considered cabbage especially dangerous: "It causeth troublesome dreams, and sends up black vapors to the brain." In the early eighteenth century, the etiquette of undemanding "table talk" was developed to avoid over-taxing the vital spirits during digestion: men of learning, whose busy brains were thought to steal energy from the stomach, were famous for their indigestion-based misery. Research by some modern gastroen-terologists into anxiety and stress has shown that the brain and stom-ach are so closely linked that they would be best thought of as a single system.

The collywobbles (from colic and wobble) is a feeling of anxiety and unease in the pit of the stomach, giving an oily, lurching sensation. In contrast to the prettier "butterflies," the collywobbles are gelati-nous, and quiver most violently in the sleepless hours, as we anticipate tomorrow's deadline, or the conversation we must have with our mother, and everything around us starts to float.

For more on the relationship between emotions and stomachs, *see:* HUNGER.

See also: ANXIETY.

COMFORT

The suburbs are littered with tiny monuments to heartache. A dropped teddy bear propped up against a lamppost. A smiling plastic frog languishing in the gutter. The devastation of losing a favorite toy is well known to parents, who recognize the deep significance a one-eyed bunny or well-chewed blankie can have in a child's emotional world.

The idea that children are deeply connected to their toys is in part due to the work of the pediatrician and psychoanalyst Donald Winnicott. In the early 1950s he became interested in the fact that parents often give babies something soft to cuddle to help them sleep alone. Winnicott suggested that these objects were more than a reliable presence, or substitute for the parent. It must also have warmth, texture and movement, he explained, allowing the child to imbue it with a life of its own. As if they are an extension of its own mind, the child uses such "transitional objects" to act out its own desires and fears — perhaps the most famous example is Linus's comfort blanket in Charles Schulz's *Peanuts* cartoon strip, which occasionally rears up and chases off its owner's enemies. Winnicott spoke of these objects as a "bridge" or a "third world" that lay between the baby's mind and the real world. Once the baby has learned to understand and tolerate the distinction between himself and other people, the object's usefulness fades.

Yet, our need for transitional objects never disappears entirely. It's there at crisis points of GRIEF or TERROR — one reason ambulances and police cars are equipped with soft toys or "trauma teddies" is so that victims of car crashes (usually children but sometimes adults) might have something to cuddle for reassurance. In such moments, the comfort one receives from a stuffed toy may be hard for a living, breathing human to match.

What makes you feel safe in a reckless world? Perhaps it's ice cream, or a duvet. A favorite film. Cuddling the dog. The things or rituals we use to soothe ourselves in times of distress or worry provide a temporary retreat, helping us feel held, or filled, or safe. From the

Latin *confortare* (to strengthen), seeking comfort is no weakness. We acknowledge that something is missing and that we must retreat in order to go forward. In this sense, seeking comfort is a vulnerable act, and so very brave indeed.

Before the outbreak of the Second World War, many psychologists had thought that babies bonded with whoever fed them (a theory called "cupboard love"). In the wake of the traumatic separations of families during that conflict, questions of security and reassurance came to the fore (*see:* ANXIETY). As well as Winnicott's work, these questions gave rise to John Bowlby's influential research on attachment, and a new emphasis on physical contact, mainly due to the work of Harry Harlow, a primatologist at the University of Wisconsin. He had noticed that when infant rhesus monkeys were separated from their mothers at birth they became unresponsive and despondent, and lost weight even though they were being fed by the researchers. Crucially, he noticed that they clung to their cloth diapers when afraid, and this led Harlow to devise an experiment to test the effects of tactile sensation — what he called "contact comfort."

He fashioned two wire structures, or "mothers," and placed them in the cage with the baby monkeys. One of the structures was left with the wire frame exposed, but with a bottle attached to it for feeding. The other was covered in a soft terry cloth, but had no bottle. The infant monkeys went to the "wire mother" for feeding. But when they were frightened, for instance by a moving toy unleashed into their cage, they scrambled up the "cloth mother" for comfort and stayed there. The photographs of the experiment are heartbreaking to see today, but Harlow's work is a cornerstone of modern infant care. He showed that the bond between parents and children is based on more than food; that warmth, softness and "contact comfort" are also necessary for survival. One of its most well-known applications is the emphasis on "skin-to-skin" contact between newborns and their parents (also known as "kangaroo care"), which has been proven not only to soothe and calm infants, but to strengthen their immune systems too: even the tiniest babies in ICUs are thought to be more likely to thrive when given "skin-to-skin" contact.

Winnicott's and Harlow's ideas both testify to the enduring importance of comfort in our emotional lives. As adults, it can be hard to admit to vulnerability and need (*see:* AMAE). Sometimes we might feel brave enough to seek reassurance from other humans, and ask to be held or stroked or sung to. At other times we find solace furtively and in the dark, perhaps turning to "transitional objects" once again. According to Winnicott, in our adult lives paintings and films, prayers and rituals, but also addictions and compulsions, all perform the same function as a teddy bear, holding us temporarily — and giving us something to hold too. For a moment, they may allow the unforgiving outside world to temporarily yield to and mirror our painful inner emotional landscapes. They allow us to say, "Yes, that's *exactly* how I feel."

And there is little more consoling than that.

See also: RELIEF; CONTENTMENT.

COMPASSION

Compassion is never included in lists of "universal emotions," but according to the philosopher Martha Nussbaum, it could be. Most people are capable of sensing that another person is suffering. The urge to alleviate that pain can be felt as a gut response — even if over the years we have become jaded by betrayals or exhausted by other people's demands. We may see a homeless person asking for spare change, but feel unsure whether giving money is the right way to help. A friend who cries harder each time you attempt to comfort and console makes you wonder *Am I making it worse?* A desire to help surges up, but then hesitations come in the backwash. Could you do more to help? Are you going to offend or pressurize? Might you be taken advantage of? No wonder we sometimes avoid engaging, when it can feel so confusing.

For Tibetan Buddhists, the wish to free a person from suffering is ideally experienced in equanimity, with a quiet CONFIDENCE. For many of us, however, compassion is considerably more anxious territory.

The idea that compassion might be a risky, even dangerous, emotion is well established in the Western Christian tradition. An early account was written in the sixth century by Pope Gregory the Great. "When we want to stop an afflicted person from grieving," he wrote, we must "bend from our inflexible standing posture" and experience their wretchedness with them. He compared compassion — from the Latin *com* (with) *patior* (to suffer or endure) — and the desire to console that follows it, to the process of fusing two pieces of iron. As the ironmonger heats the metal pieces till they join, so the human mind "softens" in a process he called *condescensio passionis*, or the "condescension of emotion." True compassion, then, required a person to discover very vulnerable parts of themselves: not an easy experience to tolerate.

The risk was that you might become too malleable. Gregory recalled the biblical story of Job. Hearing of Job's calamities — the death of his sons, the failure of his crops, the loss of his land, his terrible illness — his friends travel from afar to comfort him. They tear their clothes, throw dust on their heads and sit with him on the ground for seven days and nights until he is ready to speak. Honorable intentions, according to Gregory. But the friends go too far. By the end of the seven days, their minds have been blackened in grief, their faith shaken, even though Job's has not. For Gregory, then, true compassion was a high-wire act. Only the wisest can bend themselves to another's pain without being rendered numb and helpless themselves: the "compassion fatigue" we hear about in the caring professions today.

Compassion may put pressure on our emotional equilibrium, but contemporary research has shown that it's well worth it — it's not only other people who will benefit from your compassionate acts, you'll experience improved feelings of well-being and contentment too (see: WARM GLOW). Researchers at the Center for Compassion and Altruism at Stanford University have suggested taking a leaf out of Buddhist practice and regularly practicing compassion meditation. This involves sitting in silence for a short while, focusing your attention on feeling compassion for yourself first, and then, in opening out concentric circles, for loved ones, for friends, for strangers, and even for people you dislike or who have hurt you. For those who enjoy more practical solutions, they advise developing habits to make compassionate acts easier to accomplish. Carry loose change in your pocket for the specific purpose of buying food for someone living on the streets, or a treat for someone having a bad day. Make small pockets of time to visit an elderly neighbor. Commit an hour a week to a charity.

And faced with the distraught friend who has lost a baby, or a student whose father is dying? According to Mandy Reichwald, a former nurse who for most of her working life has helped care for terminally ill patients and their families, true compassion is about supporting and sustaining people so they can find their own strength. She cautions against the instinct to rush in, to throw your arms around a person to comfort them, as this takes away someone's ability to gather themselves for the situation ahead. Listen. Be interested. Be still. Guard against your own eyes welling up. "It's not about you, it's about them." If you do feel overcome, be honest. She suggests that saying "I feel really shocked by what you've just said, I need to take a minute" or "That's so sad" can have a surprising effect. It's when we feel most overcome that we might retreat to the safety of PITY, tilting our heads and keeping those in pain at a distance. Honesty counters that. Even ringing someone up and admitting, "I just don't know what to say, but I wanted to see how things are," is better than avoiding them altogether.

It's not selfish to take care of our own interest first; in fact, this is the measure of true and mature compassion. Because if you become overwhelmed by other people's problems, you won't — or won't be able to — help. For Reichwald, it's those emergency instructions on an airplane that ring in her ears like an alarm when she's feeling a little frayed: "You must put on your own oxygen mask before helping other people with theirs."

See also: EMPATHY.

COMPERSION

Wander through the vintage clothes stands and record stores of San Francisco's Haight-Ashbury district and it's easy to feel a surge of ersatz nostalgia for the utopian lifestyles once experimented with there. The Kerista Commune, founded in Haight-Ashbury in 1971, reimagined many of the orthodoxies of American life — the conventions of family, ownership and, most notoriously of all, of exclusive sexual relationships.

The belief that all our sexual desires should be met by a single person is relatively new in Western culture. It's the product of an eleventh-century trope of courtly LOVE that celebrated an almost spiritual commitment to one, idealized beloved, and does not always reflect the complexity of our attractions. The Kerista community practiced polyamory, its members encouraged to pursue multiple sexual partners at once. Some of these relationships were brief, some longer lasting, but none exclusive. Explaining that they did not struggle with jealousy, Keristans coined the word "compersion" to describe how they felt instead. A spin on compassion, compersion described a vicarious tingly, excited sensation felt on discovering a loved one was attracted to, or sleeping with, someone else.

Many languages have words for shame felt vicariously (see: VERGÜENZA AJENA) or contagious fear (see: PANIC). But the idea of taking pleasure in a loved one's desire for another remains baffling to many today, so powerful are the expectations that have grown up around the idea of love in our culture. The Keristans weren't the first polyamorous community to exist since the eleventh century, when exclusive romantic love was fully formalized in the West (there are examples in the seventeenth and nineteenth centuries too). And they certainly aren't the last. Their gift of the word "compersion" continues to challenge unspoken assumptions about emotions, and is still in use in North America and Europe.

In Britain the same feeling is more commonly known as the frubbles.*

See also: JEALOUSY.

---

* And if you are in a polyamorous relationship and you do feel a bit twingey with jealousy, then don't worry — you're just having a touch of the wibbles.

CONFIDENCE

In the bleak years of the Great Depression of the 1930s, one figure of wit, charisma and a talent for survival against the odds captured the imagination of the American public: the con artist. Swindling and scamming his — and sometimes, her — way across the silver screen and the pages of noirish detective novels, they enthralled and terrified by turns.

"Of all the *grifters*, the confidence man is the aristocrat," explained a clearly enamored Professor David Maurer, writing on the secrets of the confidence trade in 1940. "Confidence men are not 'crooks' in the ordinary sense of the word. They are suave, slick and capable."

Confidence has always dazzled. We might feel a stab of envy around those who glide effortlessly into the party, shake hands, charm all the important people (everybody laughs at their jokes!). But as much as other people's lack of self-doubt shimmers with mystery — and perhaps mild SUSPICION: can they be trusted? — our own confident feelings are yet more elusive, lost as quickly as they are found. From the Latin *con* (with) *fidere* (faith), the word's earliest uses were associated with the feeling of trust in divine support: a sign in the sky or vision in a dream lent boldness to your endeavors, the blessed expectation that everything will turn out in your favor. The suspicion that confidence is beyond our control still haunts us. You know how to take the fast bend on your bike, exactly the angle to throw the paper ball into the bin, the perfect moment to pirouette on roller skates without a humiliating tumble. But you can't entirely say why or how. "Let go your conscious self," instructs Obi-Wan Kenobi as he trains Luke Skywalker to use the Force. "Act on instinct." But if a future Jedi Master struggles with overthinking it, you can bet the rest of us do too.

In the 1950s, American psychologists began to wonder if the mystery might be taken out of confidence. Thinking itself seemed to be the key. By the 1970s, self-help gurus were claiming that the only difference between you and that charismatic individual for whom doors swung wide open was confidence. And how to get it? You had to perform a confidence trick on yourself, using a simple bit of magical thinking: "Fake it till you make it." From assertiveness classes to Alcoholics Anonymous, the "fake it till you make it" mantra was adopted. Was it a little contemptuous, this attempt to fool other people into believing we felt more optimistic about our abilities than we did? If it was, then we were the real target of the con. Not least, because the "fake it till you make it" mantra may have also spawned a belief that confidence in itself could be a reasonable substitute for competence (*see*: VERGÜENZA AJENA).

More recently psychologists have come to think that tricking ourselves into being confident may leave us with more self-doubt: we end up feeling both like a shifty imposter and their target, unsure whether we can even trust the allure of our own performance. Studies have shown that if we continually pretend to be a person we're not, we lose faith in the abilities that we *do* have — or else feel terrified that we'll be found out (*see*: FRAUD, feeling like a). What's more, too much confidence can inhibit, stopping up the desire for self-improvement that drives more insecure people to work hard. Perhaps, then, instead of always chasing that glorious sensation of invincibility, we might also put some trust in smaller, quieter feelings, and learn to love UNCERTAINTY, hesitation and confusion too.

See also: FEELING GOOD (about yourself).

CONTEMPT

"It was not a simple yawn," Judge Daniel Rozak explained to the incredulous family of Clifton Williams, as he was led away for contempt of court. Watching from the gallery in an Illinois courthouse as his cousin was sentenced on a felony drug charge in 2009, Williams had arched his back, stretched out his arms, opened his mouth and let out an enormous yawn. This was no involuntary response to tiredness, Judge Rozak concluded, but an intentional attempt to ridicule the court's authority.

Whether smirking and sneering, peering down our noses or turning away in cold indifference, being filled with contempt is an aristocratic emotion. It inflates us with a sense of superiority, curled at the edges with derision or DISGUST. Even at its mildest, contempt condescends with amused detachment. No wonder then that contempt can be inflammatory and political too.

The idea that contempt can change things has not always been accepted by philosophers, many of whom have regarded contempt as lacking any value at all. Immanuel Kant argued that contemptuous feelings and the dismissive actions that surely followed contravened a basic moral principle — that all people, regardless of their social position or background, should be treated with respect and dignity. Contempt troubled Kant, because of its finality: he argued it refuses to imagine people can change. If ANGER stirs revolutions, and INDIGNATION exposes unfairness, contempt slams the door. This, for Kant, was a terrible error, as people "never lose all predisposition to the good."

Kant's description of contempt has been influential, but was he right? Clifton Williams's yawn suggests a different way of thinking. There might have been other reasons for Williams to yawn. Perhaps he was tired. Perhaps nervous — since we often yawn when we feel afraid, a relic from our animal ancestors who still open their mouths to bare their teeth when threatened, which is why skydivers and troops preparing to go into battle can often be found standing around yawning. Even if Williams's yawn was intentionally disdainful, it might have been simply a private letting off of steam, like rolling your eyes at the back of someone's head. But if he *did* intend to communicate his contempt to others in the courtroom, then it's in this awareness of performing for an audience that the political action of his yawn can be found.

In 1955 the British philosopher J. L. Austin argued that some of the things we say don't just describe reality, but change it too. Saying "I love you," for instance, isn't only an expression of a feeling: it also shifts the nature of our relationship, it is a commitment, and it might even be a kind of question demanding an answer ("Don't you love me too?"). Emotional gestures like raising our eyebrows or wrinkling our noses are like this. They *do*, as well as express, something (Austin called this their "performative" aspect): they have an effect, and often an intentional one. In the case of Williams's yawn, it might have made him *feel* higher status in a context where he could have felt less than important. But more than that, it goaded and irritated, and therefore changed the reality of his status from a passive onlooker to an active participant in the proceedings. In this sense, Williams's yawn provoked a conversation, rather than slamming shut a door.

Contempt can be a form of political protest for the disempowered. When disdain is expressed by those conventionally thought to have no business looking down on anyone (women, black people), cozy privileges can be disrupted, and a realignment of power envisaged. Historically, women have been regarded as either victims of contemptuous men, or else as excessively punished for their lack of deference. In sixteenth- and seventeenth-century Britain, for instance, amid fears about witchcraft and the unruliness of women, wives who insulted their husbands were sentenced for "scolding" — and in Scotland, some were even sentenced to wear a "scolds mask," a kind of bridle replete with spikes to hold down the tongue as a punishment.

In the twentieth century, contempt, and its close companions scorn and ridicule, became a core strategy of protest culture. In 1911 suffragettes roller-skated the night away to avoid the census ("we don't count, we won't be counted"). More recently hundreds of women joined an online campaign based around the comically named "mansplaining" — mocking the men who, assuming their female colleagues were less informed about a topic than they were, explained it to them in oversimplified (and sometimes, just plain wrong) terms. In the twentieth- and twenty-first-century history of women's rights, contempt, then, has played a crucial role, laughing in the face of convention in the hope of shifting consciousness — or at least, getting a conversation started.

See also: IRRITATION.

CONTENTMENT

Contentment is an unreliable emotion. It sneaks off, leaving us battling the tugging dissatisfactions and covetous itches alone. And when it leaves us, the possibility of accepting what we have — and who we are — seems entirely improbable. But then back it creeps in the silent flush of an early morning, or in the pub, or eating fries on the pier, and we briefly notice that life, truly, is perfectly enough, just as it is.

See also: FEELING GOOD (about yourself).

COURAGE

ALICE AYRES
Daughter of a bricklayer's laborer
Who by intrepid conduct
Saved 3 children
From a burning house
In Union Street Borough
At the cost of her own young life
April 24 1885

Love and bravery. These are the emotions we build monuments to. The entwined marble lovers in a fountain might raise a sad smile. Monuments to bravery, by contrast, are intended to inspire. Of course, they mostly depict important men on horses. Bravery has traditionally been seen as an aristocratic and overwhelmingly male virtue. It still is: "Man up." "Grow some balls."

Alice Ayres's inscription tells a different story. She was a nurse-maid who died rescuing her three charges when a fire broke out in the shop beneath their home. She quickly became immortalized by the Victorians as an exemplar of heroic duty and care for others. Several memorials were erected to her, among them an inscription on the artist George Watts's Memorial to Heroic Self Sacrifice built in Postman's Park in London in 1900. It is a simple wooden shelter lined with fifty-four small ceramic tablets, each one commemorating an act of bravery — from a laborer who died trying to rescue his friend from an explosion at a sugar refinery to a stewardess who went down with a sinking ship after giving her lifebelt away. The shelter is a celebration of the courage of working-class men, women and children and, in stark contrast to the marble horsemen who grandly peer over the City nearby, it appears rather humble in its design. With its floral ceramics and simple carving, it channels the aesthetic of the Arts and Crafts movement, which itself harks back to medieval decorative styles. It's not just its appearance that evokes the medieval world. With its emphasis on extraordinarily courageous acts performed by ordinary people — requiring not only physical stamina but also emotional fortitude — Watts's memorial also recalls a medieval attitude, in which courage was considered one of the principles that everyone should live by.

The word "courage" first entered the English language via the Old French *corage*, from the Latin *cor* (heart), and originally referred to the heart itself, understood at that time to be the seat of all feelings and the source of one's innermost desires and intentions (*see also:* MAN). The medieval heart was not the muscle we'd recognize today. Rather than a pump circulating blood, it was believed to act as a chamber for heating the body's vital spirits. The higher the temperature of these vital spirits, the more courageous a person was assumed to be. Of course, it was hard to tell how hot someone's heart was just from looking at them (although women were usually understood to be more moist and cool than hot, dry men). But medieval physicians believed one outward sign of inner heat, and therefore courage, was hair. In a physiognomic treatise written by the thirteenth-century physician Michael Scot, "lots of abundant hair…that is thick and curly" was evidence of "much heat of the heart, such as in a lion." This link between hairiness and bravery gave rise to lengthy discussions in medical books about men who were unable to grow beards, and hirsute ladies. This association between curly hair and being brave and strong still lingers today. At least, it might be why some parents, trying to persuade their children to eat a vegetable, resort to the lie "It'll make your hair curl."

But courage was not only a question of an inner fire. It could also be cultivated by striving to shape one's life according to four cardinal virtues: prudence, justice, temperance and fortitude. Though they were Pagan in origin, these virtues remained a cornerstone of medieval life, even as Europe turned to Christianity and new concepts such as forgiveness and humility crowded in. Fortitude described a steadfastness, an ability to take responsibility for one's actions and something today we call "acting with integrity." Thus, according to Thomas Aquinas in the *Summa Theologiæ*, courage was not just an ability to "stand immovable in the midst of dangers" without succumbing to the desire to attack, but also the patience to endure pain with equanimity, to have a "strength of hope" and a feeling of "magnificence"—treating all our endeavors with sincerity and importance. Courage took in a broad sweep.

Today's talk of courage is indebted to this flexible, inclusive medieval concept. The eighteenth-century philosopher Adam Smith may have argued that courage was a question of physical resilience, and distinctly a male virtue: "We esteem the man who supports pain and even torture with manhood and firmness" rather than give way to "useless outcries and womanish lamentations." But when we admire the bravery of individuals in our own time, it is not only because they are willing to put themselves in harm's way, but also because they risk social exclusion. The brave speak out against injustice, or stand up for their beliefs when threatened by oppression. It takes courage to show your difference in a culture that is all too ready to show CONTEMPT (*see also:* SHAME). We do speak of bravery as the ability to stand firm in the face of physical hardship: the bravery of childbirth, say, or recovering from a serious illness, even the self-sacrifice that Victorians so associated with the brave. But perhaps it's the emphasis on psychological fortitude, the ability to confront one's demons or flourish despite the scars of trauma, that most recalls the medieval way of thinking about courage. That, and the idea that bravery isn't just for men on horseback, but something to which the rest of us can aspire too.

For more on having the courage of your convictions, *see:* VULNERABILITY.

CURIOSITY

It's the itch to find out more. The temptation to glance at an open diary, or strain to decipher the hisses of an argument behind you on the bus. It's the restless DESIRE that made Leonardo da Vinci fill his notebooks: What makes birds fly? How does the heart beat? Without curiosity, it's hard to imagine creativity or invention at all.

Yet, even in the age historians have dubbed the "Age of Curiosity" — roughly between 1660 and 1820 — people worried about its dangers. Most cultures have stories that warn against the urge to know more: Pandora couldn't help peeking inside that intriguing box; Baba Yaga, the toothless crone of Slavic folklore, threatens to eat nosy children who ask too many questions; and then there's that poor cat.... Curiosity can overreach. It stumbles into forbidden knowledge, not stopping to think whether what emerges will be hurtful. Most of all, curiosity can rub people — particularly those guardians of the status quo, parents, teachers, politicians — up the wrong way.

The seventeenth century witnessed the outpouring of a powerful defense of curiosity. In large part, this was due to a philosophical revolution. John Locke, in his *Essay Concerning Human Understanding,* published in 1690, argued that knowledge was not implanted in the mind by God, but was learned through the perception of the senses and rational thinking. This idea, known later as empiricism, put a premium on the evidence of one's own eyes. It gave rise to the scientific method and, in turn, the pastimes of collecting, cataloguing and investigating became fashionable. Some writers celebrated curiosity, linking it to intellectual progress. Others emphasized its egalitarian nature — although in practice, to be a great *virtuoso* or *curioso*, the titles gentlemen scholars gave themselves, one needed considerable amounts of both money and leisure. Over the next 150 years insects were examined under microscopes. Experiments on birds and air pumps were conducted before intrigued audiences. Writers of encyclopedias — such as Denis Diderot and Jean Le Rond d'Alembert, who began work on theirs in 1746 — attempted to impose order and coherence on the known world.

However, the *virtuosi* and *curiosi* were not always admired. It was on the seventeenth-century stage that their failings came into sharpest relief. The legendary German character of Faust, who sells his soul to the Devil in exchange for the secrets of natural philosophy (the old word for science), epitomized the mistrust some felt for the curious scholars, with their narcissism and desire for prestige, their greediness and solitary working habits (*see:* LONELINESS). In contrast, the amateur experimenter Sir Nicholas Gimcrack of Thomas Shadwell's *The Virtuoso* (1676) was lampooned for his pointless and impractical endeavors. He collects bottles of air and learns to swim by stretching himself out on a trunk in his laboratory, interested only in "the speculative part of swimming; I care not for the practice... knowledge is my ultimate end." It was from these anti-heroes of the Age of Curiosity, the curious men who had become curiosities themselves, that our own mad scientists emerged — the Dr. Moreaus and Dr. Strangeloves, with their eyes gleaming and skin itching at the prospect of each new discovery.

Are we in the midst of another ambivalent "Age of Curiosity"? On the one hand, curiosity is celebrated for its questing spirit, its power to drive our intellectual evolution and bring rewards. "Curiosity," the name of the NASA rover sent to explore the surface of Mars, or the emotion that teachers are supposed to foster in their pupils above all others, might appear to be an unquestioned good in our times. Yet, rapidly changing technology has also brought a fear of other people's desire to find out about *us* into sharper relief. Curiosity about other people's private lives is certainly not new. Evolutionary psychologists have suggested that our natural curiosity about one another — and its main vehicle, gossip — is one key to our evolutionary success. It allows ideas to travel and enhances a sense of community. But though curiosity might be crucial to our survival, that doesn't make us any happier to be on the receiving end of someone else's. Five centuries ago in England, eavesdropping (skulking around under the eaves to overhear private conversations) was illegal — in fact, it remained on the statute books as a common law offence until 1967. Today, it is the surreptitious accumulation of "intimate capital," the photographs and snippets of information used for blackmail and by tabloid journalists to sell newspapers, that must be policed. That we suspect other people's curiosity has less than honorable motives is nicely captured by the Swedish word for an eavesdropper: a *tjuvlyssnare*, a "listen-thief." Lurking and snatching poorly guarded secrets, the listen-thief profits — with the titillations of forbidden knowledge or simply cold hard cash — from them too.

See also: MORBID CURIOSITY, SHAME.

CYBERCHONDRIA

Anxiety about "symptoms" of an "illness" fueled by Internet "research."

See also: PARANOIA.

DELIGHT

In the exquisite, jewel-like miniatures that appeared in the printed books of fifteenth-century Persia, water cascades in the background, music drifts through the scented air, flowers bloom in ornamental beds while lovers seduce one another. No holy scripture paints such a seductive portrait of the delights of paradise as the Qur'an, and the most commonly used word to describe paradise is *al-jannah*, or garden. In other cultures too, gardens are images of luxury and lightness. From the Zen rock gardens of ancient Japan to Hieronymus Bosch's strawberry-drenched *The Garden of Earthly Delights*, images of the garden are inseparable from the glistening of pure sensory presence, and a feeling of spiritual release.

Delight is close to rapture. The hands clap, the eyes sparkle, the lips tingle into a smile. For the eighteenth-century English philosopher John Locke, delight was one of the four essential feelings out of which the complexities of all human emotions flourished (the others were pleasure, pain and uneasiness). Delight comes from the Latin *delectare* (to allure, to charm, to entice away), and Locke described it as a kind of shimmering seduction. It was, he said, that intangible thing that caused a person to say they "love" something: as in "I love the apple tree" or "I love the sky." According to the *Oxford English Dictionary*, the change of spelling during the sixteenth century from the older "delite" to the modern "delight" was the result of an accident. But as is so often the case, the mistake captures the essence of the thing: luminosity and weightlessness seem to be at the heart of delight, that most of all, makes one feel like flying.

See also: LOVE; EUPHORIA.

DÉPAYSEMENT

On February 16, 1981, the French artist Sophie Calle was hired as a chambermaid in a hotel in Venice. Each day, under cover of cleaning the guests' rooms, she itemized and photographed the contents of their suitcases and bins. A postcard of the Basilica di San Marco. An Italian phrasebook with the page corner turned down. Train time-tables and holiday clothes. Pills and diaries. A torn-up love letter describing a trip to Harry's Bar.

The resulting artwork, *L'Hôtel*, for which Calle displayed the photographs and her descriptions side by side, evokes the disorientation felt in foreign places. It tells of deciphering a strange language, and squinting at peculiar currency. Of stumbling again and again over the same landmark in unfamiliar streets, and the feelings of license and anonymity that allow holiday romances to take flight. Even the form of Calle's piece excites the experience of being a stranger. Each fragmentary clue draws us in, inviting us to imagine the occupants' identities — but never quite giving their secrets away.

In France, the feeling of being an outsider is known as *dépaysement* (literally: decountrification). Sometimes it is frustrating, leaving us feeling unsettled and out of place (*see:* AMBIGUPHOBIA; PARANOIA). And then, just sometimes, it swirls us up into a kind of giddiness, only ever felt when far away from home. When the unlikeliest of adventures seem possible. And the world becomes new again.

The French seem to be particularly intrigued by emotions to do with disorientation. *See:* ILINX and L'APPEL DU VIDE.

See also: WANDERLUST.

DESIRE

It was a long time since I had longed for anything, and the effect on me was horrible.

— Samuel Beckett, "The End'

It begins with a tingle. A fleeting fantasy of revenge. A glint of attraction. We shake it off, but it sneaks up again. It can feel dangerous, alluring. Frustrating too — since without an obstacle, desire is merely a temporary state quickly dissolving into satiety. But the forbidden, the denied, glistening just out of reach? The history of our desires is the story of how we lose ourselves to them.

Whether it's a desire for a person, or an object, or something intangible like "fame" or "glory," people have long been made nervous about the way craving for or coveting something can take us over. Medieval churchgoers were warned against harboring desires for forbidden things — they knew it as the sin of Morose Delectation, from the Latin *mora* (delay or tarry) and *delectare* (to entice). The forbidden thoughts could be anything — from hating a rival to the desire to avenge a hurt. But becoming engrossed in and preoccupied by sexual temptation was the most common, and bewitching, kind. The early Victorians spoke of the disease of "monomania," all thoughts taken hostage by one single *idée fixe*: Captain Ahab's desire to kill Moby Dick, or Heathcliff's fixation on "his departed idol," Cathy. Monomania could derange a person's mind, even causing them to neglect their bodies and health. In the twentieth century, the philosopher Georges Bataille suggested that it is not only the person who is consumed with desire who finds himself disappearing under the weight of his obsessive need. The longed-for person or object begins to disintegrate too. The desired person or thing seems to fade away, replaced by a shimmering "aura," writes Bataille, and it is impossible to know whether it is "horror or fascination" that compels us toward it (*see*: MORBID CURIOSITY).

You'd be forgiven for thinking we have moved beyond the idea that our desires are something both we, and the thing or person we desire, are lost to. In a culture absorbed by the idea of self-actualization, the idea of following one's heartfelt intentions is presented as energizing and important (*see*: SATISFACTION). When it comes to sex, we might think of the twentieth century as the time when desire was liberated from the shame and confusions of religious sin, and assume that sexual desire has become ordinary, rather than something to be enchanted by, or lost in. Twentieth-century sexologists such as Alfred Kinsey and the duo William H. Masters and Virginia E. Johnson made it their business to redeem sexual desire from its older transgressive associations, and to make studying sex a respected science involving white coats and laboratories. In their studies and others that followed, desire became equated to a bodily appetite, comparable to hunger or thirst. Making a sexual urge as natural or inevitable as the need for food or shelter, this model served to simplify it too, imagining a chain of triggers and motives linking emotional desire to physical arousal, passionate intimacy to genital satisfaction. But desire is not like that, not really. Arousal can take place even when you don't feel desire; a craving might not always lead to a satisfying ending. More than a biological instinct, desire follows circuitous routes through the imagination: it is strange and estranging too.

Perhaps it's because desire runs so close to fear that it can feel, as Beckett knew, so horrible. The habit among theologians, doctors and even sexologists to attribute our desires to some other part of ourselves — something the Devil sent, or the product of a diseased mind, or even a biological instinct implanted over millennia of evolution — may be partly a response to how uncomfortable longing can be. Perhaps our urges frighten us because they might lead us astray, hurting those we love and disrupting the status quo. Perhaps we suspect we idealize the desired object, and fear the tumult we'll create: we cling to those we desire, and fling them aside, adore and despise them in turns. Part of what makes desire so hard to tolerate is the FRUSTRATION and DISAPPOINTMENT that so often come with it. But perhaps more hidden is its SHAME: the way longing for someone exposes us, forcing us to admit we lack something that we don't already have and can't easily obtain.

See also: MAN; VULNERABILITY.

DESPAIR

A man lies dead in the street. A fox saunters past. In an upstairs apartment, a prostitute entertains her client. This scene in George Grosz's *Suicide* (1916), painted in Germany during the First World War, expresses the kind of nihilism that few of us are willing to reflect on for very long. Not even granted a name, the man lies unnoticed. And the world barely breaks its step.

The sensation that your life no longer fits you drifts in so slowly you hardly notice it coming. The clothes that seem to belong to someone else. The job that once seemed satisfying, but is now to be endured. What might begin as alienation or a sense of purposelessness can quickly dissolve into shame of the most claustrophobic kind. You imagine your family's CONTEMPT and DISAPPOINTMENT. You see looks of PITY and DISGUST in the eyes of strangers. Once it gets going properly, despair, from the Latin *de* (without) *sperare* (to hope), crashes in your ears. You hear your own heartbeat as you stare into the empty sink. You are unable to bear yourself any longer but unable to abandon yourself either. Despair is a gnawing sensation, a torturous vacillation.

There is some relief in recognizing the futility of our attempts to change things ("She never empties the dishwasher. I despair!"). But the despair we feel in our deepest selves is different. It tucks itself in behind expertly conducted polite conversations. It stays hidden. In 1849 the Danish philosopher Søren Kierkegaard wrote in *The Sickness Unto Death* that "the greatest hazard of all, losing one's self, can occur very quietly in the world as if it were nothing at all. No other loss occurs so quietly; any other loss — an arm, a leg, five dollars, a wife, etc. — is sure to be noticed."

From its earliest writings, the Christian tradition had depicted despair as something you give in to, a sin and temptation, otherworldly and barely seen. The hermits who lived in the Sinai desert in the first centuries after Christ thought it was carried by noonday demons who infected them with malaise (*see:* ACEDIA). In later centuries despair was depicted as a beguiling creature who lured men and women to their deaths. In Edmund Spenser's *The Fairie Queene*, Despair is a shrunken man living in a hollow cave in a gray, desolate landscape. Though miserable in appearance, he can twist arguments into fantastical shapes, coaxing the Red Cross Knight with the promise of "eternall rest / And happie ease, which thou doest want and crave." Despair differed from the illness of melancholia, though both were characterized by deep sorrow and the threat of suicide (*see:* MELANCHOLY). The despairing were healthy. It was their souls' ability to withstand temptation that had failed.

In the early twentieth century Existentialists such as Sartre and Camus suggested a different account of despair. For them, it was not an irrational crisis, and certainly not a sin. Rather, they saw it as a fundamental condition of living in a universe without fate, without God and without purpose. For this reason, they saw despair — losing hope of ever finding meaning in life — as both painful and liberating; the source of both terror and great happiness.

For Camus, the Greek myth of Sisyphus expressed this optimistic aspect of despair. The mortal Sisyphus, for his impudence and overreaching, is condemned by the Gods to a hopeless labor. He must roll a huge stone up a slope, his face screwed up with the effort, his shoulder braced against it. Up and up he pushes the rock, until at the top the rock rolls back down, at which point Sisyphus must begin to push it up again. Camus is most interested in the moment when Sisyphus walks back down the hill to begin again. What does he feel during that pause? Most of us might imagine weeping in frustration, raging with indignation. And then, eventually, on realizing that the task will never end, and that it is entirely without purpose, falling backwards into a dark silence.

But for Camus, it was precisely by losing hope in ever finding a meaning that Sisyphus became free. "I see that man going back down with a heavy yet measured step toward the torment of which he will never know the end," he wrote. Sisyphus realizes his fate is simply the sum of his actions, a life created by him. Rather than giving up, he simply adjusts to the pointlessness of it all. And out of his despair at the futility of his predicament, a strange lightness comes. He becomes, writes Camus, "stronger than his rock."

See also: HOPEFULNESS; SADNESS.

DISAPPEAR, THE DESIRE TO

There's a man in New York who helps people vanish. He'll forge you a new identity. Brush over your tracks using digital misdirection. And then send you off with a prepaid phone, and a one-way train ticket — paid for, of course, in cash.

It's a tantalizing service. Who hasn't, at one time or another, felt that urge to disappear completely? When life's tangle of expectations and disappointments creeps in ever closer, when the CLAUSTROPHOBIA of debts and obligations stifles, running away is seductive. In Neil LaBute's play *The Mercy Seat*, Ben is offered "a chance...to totally erase the past," on September 11, 2001. He was holed up with his lover when they should have been at work together in the World Trade Center. Now they can start a new life, officially, blamelessly dead.

For most of us it remains a fantasy, too seismic to risk even thinking about. Yet once in a while you dare yourself to try. You deliberately miss the next train or put off charging your phone. Then steal a few moments of pure solitude, and experience, briefly, the sensation of being outside everything — and glimpse what it might feel like to be truly inside yourself.

See also: DÉPAYSEMENT; LONELINESS; WANDERLUST.

DISAPPOINTMENT

Dog owners know a lot about disappointment.

Charles Darwin had a large Labrador called Bob, who, like all dogs, loved to be taken out walking. Whenever Darwin set off into the gardens of Down House, Bob eagerly accompanied him, showing "his pleasure by trotting gravely before me with high steps, head much raised." Bob expected to be going for a long march around the grounds, but sometimes Darwin intended only to visit his experimental plants. When they got to the door of the hothouse, Bob would be overcome with a "great disappointment." The head drooped, the whole body sank, the ears fell, "the tail was by no means wagged." The family nicknamed the pitiful look Bob's "hothouse face." Darwin himself confessed it could soften his heart, hinting that the dog's defeated appearance was often enough to make him abandon his hothouse and set off on the hoped-for walk instead.

Disappointment means to be "deprived of an appointment," to be "dispossessed." It's there when the beliefs and trappings we've arranged about us like a well-appointed house are suddenly upturned. Or some anticipated rise in status, or hoped-for new identity ("I'm getting my PhD!/Becoming Head of Sales!/Almost certainly passing my driving test this time!") is snatched away. Disappointment may be overwhelmingly a feeling of loss or defeat, but there are other feelings there too that give disappointment its slightly restless, tremulous edge. For Darwin, Bob's disappointment was mostly confusion: "He did not know whether I should continue my walk." Sometimes a feeling of disbelief recurs, as when we can't help wondering if this morning's rejection letter was sent to the wrong address, or some mistake has been made.

Disappointments, then, do not only leave traces of SADNESS. BEWILDERMENT is felt too, raising the exhausting prospect that life must, once again, be reshaped.

Disappointment has a long history of making trouble. Among eighteenth-century doctors, disappointments, especially thwarted romantic affairs, were thought to spark off bouts of insanity (in the medical jargon of the time, disappointment was a "moral" — i.e., nonphysical — cause of mental disturbance). A century later the emotional effects of having ones hopes dashed in love were still being taken seriously. In 1865 Mary Harris went on trial in Washington DC for murdering Adoniram Burroughs after he married another woman. Since she was known to be usually a meek and god-fearing woman, Harris's lawyers argued she had succumbed to a temporary but violent madness. Her defense was "double insanity," partly caused by a strange physical complaint known at the time as "irritability of the uterus," and partly caused by an emotional one: "disappointed affection." Harris went free.

In the early twentieth century some psychologists began to argue that disappointment could be useful. Some went so far as to suggest it was crucial for healthy mental development. Among them, Sigmund Freud stands out as the period's great theorist of disappointment. He spoke of "narcissistic wounds" or injuries, the painful assaults on our sense of identity when the fantasies we are told, or tell ourselves, are punctured. For Freud, the loss of an idealized family image hurt the ego hardest. He coined the phrase "the family romance" to describe those stories that are told to us as we grow up, and that give a dramatic importance to our arrival in the world, leaving us with the mistaken belief that we are important above all others: a "royal child." Of course, such fantasies can't last, and according to Freud it was vital they didn't. Only by being dis-appointed of our status in this way can we start to engage with life as it really is. As the psychoanalyst Melanie Klein put it, in order to move forward and develop authentic relationships, everyone has to come to the aching realization that "no really ideal part of the self exists."

The psychoanalytic story of disappointment is ultimately optimistic. It makes sense of the misery of being deprived of our mistaken beliefs about ourselves, casting it as the inevitable pain that comes when reality breaks through the myths like new teeth. Yet, though this view may ultimately be enriching, it doesn't quite capture this emotion's pervasive sense of everything having gone wrong. When we suffer the painful loss of an idealized self-image, what's left — at least immediately — isn't necessarily "the truth" but emptiness and confusion. It's a terrible slump. Or, as Wordsworth put it in *The Prelude*, "a sense of treachery and desertion in the place / The holiest that I knew of — my own soul."

See also: HOPEFULNESS.

DISGRUNTLEMENT

If not actually disgruntled, he was far from being gruntled.
— P. G. Wodehouse, The Code of the Woosters

He had been one of MI6's top agents, a specialist in cybercrime. Until he went rogue and M handed him over to the Chinese in a prisoner swap. Now he's holed up on an abandoned island full of supercomputers, and is using the skills the British government taught him to destroy M and overthrow the organization he once loved. Raoul Silva, villain of the Bond film *Skyfall*, is an archetypal expression of a very modern bogeyman: the disgruntled former employee.

Gruntles are the little snorts that pigs make while flicking flies from their snout. In the wild, boars gruntle to warn rivals to stay away. Amid the comforts of the farm, however, pigs don't gruntle out of threat so much as from habitual dissatisfaction, and it's this that gives the idea that gruntling is rather petty and pointless. Humans gruntle in their sties too, whining about the quality of the coffee, grumbling and griping on the commute home.

So talk of employees being "disgruntled" (it's one of those rare words where the "dis" exaggerates rather than negates, like "distend") might make us wonder. Disgruntled insiders, stealing intellectual property and spreading misinformation, are now thought to be a major threat to corporate life. But calling them "disgruntled"? It might suggest they could only ever be motivated by their own paltry emotions — leaving the corporate practices that alienated them in the first place in the clear.

In the early twentieth century ANXIETY, rather than disgruntlement, was considered the primary emotional challenge for corporations. Believing anxious feelings to stem from insecurity, industrial psychologists encouraged organizations to foster a sense of belonging. At IBM in the 1930s, for instance, employees were all expected to join in with the company song: "Right here and now we thankfully / Pledge sincerest loyalty / To the corporation that's the best of all..."

But do we really want to *belong* to our workplaces anymore? As the Italian Marxist philosopher Paolo Virno has argued, what used to be signs of employee disaffection are now professional ideals. In our dynamic, mobile economy, it's flexibility that is most prized. Insecurity about one's job, fear of being reshuffled, or of missing out on promotion have been translated by corporate HR departments into the values of "flexibility, adaptability and a readiness to reconfigure oneself." Yet, as online systems become more open to tampering and information more portable, employers have also become more nervous than ever about the loyalty and trustworthiness of their employees. The rise in disgruntlement may be an outgrowth of this conflicted work culture, with its demand that employees be both emotionally invested and dispensable.

Corporations have begun to use cybersecurity consultants to help guard intellectual property against "malicious insiders." Psychological profiles of those who might pose a risk have been drawn up: they usually work in technical positions such as engineering or IT; "often feel entitled to" the data; and their decision is frequently prompted by a "perceived professional set-back or unmet expectations."

Perhaps giving employees greater ownership over their work, rather than less, is the solution to disgruntlement. But in the meantime, continued monitoring of personnel is advised, including better screening to prevent hiring what cybersecurity consultants term "a problem employee." We should expect worries about the threat of disgruntlement to rise over the coming decades — and further debate about how to detect those who pose a risk. But for the time being, one of the clearest steers comes from a US government memo. It advises security agencies to monitor "despondence and grumpiness as a means to gauge waning trustworthiness."

So if you're one of life's gruntlers, consider yourself warned.

For more on workplace emotions *see*: CHEERFULNESS; VULNERABILITY.

DISGUST

You smell sour milk and your nose wrinkles. You accidentally touch dog poo and your gorge rises as you rush to the nearest tap to scrub your hands. A frothy slick of spit floating in a glass of water makes it impossible to drink. It's this quick-as-a-flash electric current, running from noxious substance to revolted feeling, that makes disgust so fascinating. You encounter a poison and your body refuses it. It's simple. As instinctive as the way your eyelid snaps shut when a fleck of hot oil from a pan jumps toward it. Disgust might seem to be a hyperefficient and practical emotion, a simple, lifesaving $2 + 2 = 4$. But little is further from the truth.

The idea that every person — whether living in the Australian outback or an apartment in Tokyo — shares a handful of emotional expressions is compelling. When evolutionary psychologists talk of "universal basic emotions," they mean that our bodies have all evolved in the same way to help us survive universal predicaments, like needing to run away from predators (fear), or scare off rivals (anger). Without these physiological responses preparing us for fighting or fleeing, we simply couldn't survive. Disgust is a prime candidate for a universal emotion: everyone seems to make retching noises and stick out their tongue when they are disgusted; everyone wrinkles their nose. Though not everyone agrees which emotions should be thought of as "basic" or "universal," disgust is always on the list, a workhorse of an emotion, forcing poisons out of our bodies and preventing them from infecting us.

However, this claim is misleading. To start with, there are at least three types of revulsion, each with distinctive responses. "Core disgust" is repulsion felt when something poisonous — usually rotten flesh or feces — comes near the mouth. It makes us recoil from the object, feel nauseous and make emetic sounds: blegh, yuck, ugh, nghm. "Contamination disgust" is felt near people or places that threaten infection. It's there when your skin crawls on entering a home that has not been washed or cleaned in years (don't touch anything!); it makes us shudder or feel reluctant even to sit down in case we are infected. The sight of someone's mouth gaping to reveal stringy saliva and gooey remnants of food, or of a bloody wound, prompts another sort of repulsion, what psychologists inelegantly term "body-envelope violation disgust," in which the threat of contamination is combined with an almost existential horror of the open body. The fact that each has different cues and responses suggests they developed along separate evolutionary paths. It would be hard to claim that one is more "basic" than the other.

More than this, so much of what prompts disgust is open to cultural interference. The boiled duck embryos eaten fresh from the egg as street food in the Philippines sicken most Western tourists. Even our responses to things we are apparently "hardwired" to find disgusting, feces or weeping wounds, depend on context. Modern-day surgeons talk of the "laudable pus" that erupts from a lanced boil (the term is a remnant from medieval humoral medicine). It may have a foul smell and texture — never mind its name; just saying "laudable pus" is enough to make me balk — but it's a welcome sight in the surgery because of the relief it brings the patient. "Dirt is matter out of place," was anthropologist Mary Douglas's summation of this problem of perspective. What we find filthy and contaminating, and therefore disgusting, is primarily a matter of what we happen to think being "in place" is.

The sense that something is "out of place" might be more important to provoking feelings of disgust than the objectively dangerous. We're all familiar with those odd little glitches, where the stomach heaves in response to some object we know can't hurt us. The hair in the mouth, or the skin on a mug of hot milk, or the soup clinging to a man's beard (just the thought of it!) that might make us bilious. So much that we find disgusting is connected to the accidentally wrongly placed; it might be no surprise to find that it's this problem of categories breaking down that lies at the heart of how the word in English came to develop.

Early moderns didn't talk of disgust. They spoke instead of the abomination felt at the spectacle of a "freak," or when crossing paths with a "witch" — an abhorrence felt toward those perceived out of the natural order of things. Historians have uncovered a tendency at this time to speak of things or people who were morally disgusting as abominable or abhorrent, while for those that were rotten or stomach-churning a much older English word, *wlatsome*, tended to be used (it meant loathsome or detestable, and was likely to have been pronounced *wlat*-some). Instead of "yuck!" or "ugh!" early moderns said "fie!" and "fum!" This may be why the giant in Jack and the Beanstalk booms "Fee, fi, fo,fum!": not out of anger, as has sometimes been suggested, but because the blood of his enemies, the English, smells rotten to him.

It wasn't until the eighteenth century that disgust as we know it entered the scene, sweeping up all kinds of aversions and repulsions behind it. Philosophers including Immanuel Kant and Edmund Burke popularized the word, from the Italian *gusto* (taste). Their disgust was primarily an aesthetic response to all that was misshapen, messy and ugly, the antithesis of Enlightenment sensibility. In a matter of only a few decades, feeling "abhorrence" began to sound old-fashioned, and "disgust" took over as the emotion that would single you out as a person of high class and learning. From this, disgust became a bloated concept, swallowing everything that did not quite fit — from the sight of something coming out of the wrong hole at the wrong time, to a badly turned vase, to inappropriate behavior.

Appropriately for an emotion concerned so much with liminality, disgust still carries this capaciousness. For instance we still speak of feeling disgusted by moral transgressions too. Though Disgusted of Tunbridge Wells probably doesn't feel the urge to vomit on hearing of the council's latest travesty *vis-à-vis* his favorite parking spot, there are moments when our senses of moral indignation and physical revulsion do overlap. In the late 1980s psychologists Paul Rozin and Carol Nemeroff conducted a peculiar experiment. They asked a group of research subjects if they would be willing to wear a pullover — most said they would. Then they added that the pullover had once belonged to Adolf Hitler. With this extra bit of news, the majority of the participants grimaced and moved away from the garment, refusing to wear it and appearing revolted and making the associated responses of "ugh" and "ew." Rozen and Nemeroff suggested that somewhere in their imaginations, the participants had feared being contaminated by some essence of "Hitlerishness" that made them recoil from the thought of the material touching their skin. In cases like these, it's clear that disgust operates far beyond the simple poison = disgust equation. It bursts its own seams, infecting our moral judgments and aesthetic tastes too.

Look close enough, then, and disgust will not be quietly reduced down to a single emotional atom, a "basic emotion" alert and ready to leap to our protection. What we speak of as "disgust" describes so many different kinds of responses — the vomitous feeling of opening the fridge and seeing rotten meat, the skin-crawling sensation that makes you not want to pick up someone's snotty hankie, the feeling of nauseated horror on seeing a person's skin flapping open, even a feeling of moral queasiness. As with so many of our emotions, it's not easy to tell where disgust begins and ends. It might shade into the squirming glee of scatological humor. Or be part of what makes certain fetishes so exciting (see: MORBID CURIOSITY). And since being too full can make us feel revolted — not only with the idea of any more food, or TV, or whatever we've indulged too much in, but also with ourselves — disgust is often linked to BOREDOM. Perhaps it's no surprise, then, that some have felt the urge to pin down this most slippery emotion. After all, disgust arises more powerfully when boundaries dissolve, meaning breaks down and things slide "out of place."

See also: AMBIGUPHOBIA.

DISMAY

In Gilbert and George's *Here* (1987), the two artists depict themselves against a photomontage of Ridley Road Market in Hackney, London. Debris litters the ground. A car is parked awkwardly as if skidded to a halt. This was at that time an area of aching poverty, abandoned and uncared for following wave after wave of race riots and clashes with police.

The artists stand upright with blank, almost startled expressions on their faces. It's not an appeal or gesture of indignation ("Do Something!"). Instead, it's a kind of helpless shrug: "What can we do?"

Dismay is a feeling of horror and paralysis. Like WONDER or BEWILDERMENT, it flattens us; like SHOCK, it might make us cover our eyes. The word originally derives from the Latin *exmagare* (to have one's abilities or courage snatched away), but came into English via the Old French *desmaier*. It's from this root that dismay picked up its strange association with fainting: while the English word descended from *desmaier* came to describe a feeling, in other European languages *desmaier* morphed into words for falling unconscious — in Spanish *desmayo* is a swoon, in Portuguese *desmaio* is a fainting fit.

In Dickens's novels, ludicrous men and oversensitive women faint in dismay. In the twelfth and thirteenth centuries, however, when the medieval romance poems were written, heroes routinely keeled over under the influence of their powerful passions. Lancelot faints on seeing a comb laced with Guinevere's hair. Boeve falls unconscious on discovering Josiane is dead. Their faints do not emasculate, but instead reveal the depth of their passions, and were easily explained by the medical beliefs of their day.

Medieval medicine held that in times of extreme emotion the heart became crushed and constricted, damming up the vital spirits that were thought to animate the body. Chaucer's *Troilus and Criseyde*, written in the 1380s, describes what happened next. It's the first night the lovers have spent together, and Troilus, his jealousy getting the better of him, accuses Criseyde of infidelity. She is distraught at the accusation. He, in turn, feels dismay at the distress he's caused. He falls to his knees, hangs down his head and is speechless: "What myghte he seyn? He felte he nas but deed" ("What could he say? He felt that he was dead"). The feeling is so profound that "sorwe so his herte shette" ("sorrow gripped his heart"). From there, his spirits become jammed, all his emotions "fled was out of towne," and even tears will not come. Finally, consciousness departs: "and doun he fel al sodeynly a-swowne."

Today, fainting from powerful emotions is still occasionally reported in medical journals (love and horror can make a person faint, though the more archaic-sounding "dismay" is less often cited as a cause). Those who suffer from Stendhal or "Florence" syndrome, for instance, can become dizzy and faint at weddings or in hospital, but are particularly known for being overcome in the presence of very beautiful or impressive amounts of art. The syndrome is named after the nineteenth-century French author Stendhal, who, on visiting Florence, was rendered so helpless by the intricate beauty of every street corner that he "walked with the fear of falling." Sometimes the only response to any kind of overwhelming emotion is to fall down and stay there.

See also: REMORSE; LOVE.

DOLCE FAR NIENTE

The pleasure of doing nothing.

See also: CAREFREE.

DREAD

One of the most terrifying things about the Great Pestilence that swept Europe in 1348–49 must have been sensing it approach. It snaked across the land, wrote the Welsh poet Jeuan Gethin in 1349, like a "rootless phantom." Pilgrims and travelers spread news of desolate streets and wretched survivors. Cities locked their gates and their inhabitants performed desperate acts of penitence. Jews were blamed for poisoning wells. Serving girls imprisoned for deliberately infecting clothes. Nothing made a difference. Some chroniclers reported that across Europe as many as nine in every ten people perished. Such reports were almost certainly exaggerated, but many believed they were witnessing the world's end, God's retribution for earthly sin.

If you hadn't already been touched by the disease, there was nothing to do but wait.

It is often said that the phrase "black death" comes from the dark blotches that discolored the skin of the infected. More likely it is a translation of the Latin *atra mors* — *mors* (death), *atra* (dark, squalid or ill fated): the dreaded end.

Unlike fear or panic, which is usually triggered by an immediate threat, dread is the cold unease felt in the approaching shadow of a menace about which we can do little. In its earliest uses, dread described a feeling of being rendered speechless and prostrate in the presence of God's awesome power (*see*: WONDER). This religious meaning continued into the early twentieth century, which is why Rastafarians dubbed themselves Dreads, and their matted hair, dreadlocks. But what to some is appropriate reverence, for others is a kind of defeatism. In his account of the outbreaks of the plague in fourteenth-century Florence, Giovanni Boccaccio lamented the "bestial behavior" and APATHY the epidemic caused. Peasants abandoned their animals and crops. Some men wandered through the empty houses, stealing food and drink, or spent their days and nights in taverns gambling away their belongings. In this atmosphere of foreboding, society's rules were made futile.

In the age of the Internet, mild dread may be a low-level hum for us all. Today's air travel allows epidemics to spread so rapidly that an approaching disease feels less like the drifting of a "rootless phantom" than a game of hopscotch played across the globe. It's harder than ever to remain ignorant each time a new pandemic — AIDS, bird flu, Ebola — appears. And since dread can feed off rumor and misinformation, the Internet provides the ideal petri dish (*see also:* CYBER-CHONDRIA). Some might panic and start stockpiling drugs, while governments conduct health checks at our borders. But for most of us there is little option but to sink backwards into a cold, gluey helplessness — and hope it doesn't come too near.

See also: PANIC.

ECSTASY

In the depths of the church of Santa Maria della Vittoria in Rome stands Bernini's sculpture *The Ecstasy of Saint Teresa*. It depicts a vision seen by a sixteenth-century nun. An angel in the form of a beautiful human man visits her, and thrusts his golden spear into her breast. "The pain was so great that I screamed aloud," wrote Teresa in her autobiography. "But simultaneously felt such infinite sweetness that I wished the pain to last eternally. It was the sweetest caressing of the soul by God." It's hard to look at Bernini's sculpture without succumbing to impure thoughts. When visitors put their coins in the illumination box, Bernini's famously orgasmic Teresa comes to life. She gasps and arches her back, her toes curl and she melts into the marble base, as if falling into a pillow of frilly mushrooms, or the rumpled sheets of a bed.

Ecstasy paralyzes us with a quivering pleasure. It blooms in the throat, reducing sentences to strangulated cries. From the Greek *ekstasis* (standing outside oneself), ecstasy involves a strange paradox: those moments when we become most connected to our body through dancing, singing, or sex are also ones when we go beyond it, experiencing a rush of boundlessness. Ecstasy feels as if the world has billowed open. As if we have, momentarily, been set free.

Such experiences have been at the heart of spiritual life for millennia. The nuns of medieval Europe scourged their flesh and fasted, in order to be rewarded with visions of falling stars and exploding cities. Long before them, the Shamans of Siberia and central Asia spun and danced till their bodies fell convulsing to the ground, and animals or ancestors appeared to lead them into spirit worlds. As the thirteenth-century Persian poet Rumi described, "When you've the air of dervishood inside / You'll float above the world and there abide." Today it's the image of sweating, hugging clubbers swept up in the fluttery whoosh of an MDMA rush that the word most readily brings to mind. That, or the giddy abandon of sex.

In European medical circles, the disenchantment of ecstasy began around the middle of the nineteenth century. Neurologists, busy organizing our mental lives along physiological lines, recategorized ecstatic states from rare and sought-after emotions to the by-products of nervous diseases. The most notorious modern ecstatics were female inmates of the Salpêtrière asylum in Paris. Diagnosed with hysteria, a pre-twentieth-century category of mental illness, these women suffered from symptoms including visions and voices, seizures and contracted limbs. Europe's elite physicians traveled to Paris in order to study them, and they helped make the career of Jean-Martin Charcot when he exhibited them as star turns in his theatrical Tuesday Lectures. These women with their flamboyant poses — their *attitudes passionnelles* — are known to us today through an album of faded asylum photographs. One is entitled "Extase 1878." Apparently at the onset of a hysterical attack (though since early photography required the patient to pose for long periods, the patient would have restaged her attitude under Charcot's direction), she kneels on the bed in her ward, among rumpled sheets, her eyes rolled upward, a beatific smile across her face. Later, Charcot would compare her to Bernini's sculpture of Saint Teresa, a secular caricature, born of madness, of a once prized spiritual experience.

Today's neurologists speak of kalopsia, a feeling that everything is intensely beautiful and radiant, and say it is caused by lesions in the right parietal cortex of the brain. Or of "autoscopic phenomena" with their doppelgänger or "out of body" effects during which one's own body is seen in outside space, as if in a mirror — thought today to be caused by damage either to the parieto-occipital cortex or temporoparietal junction. Or even of the aura of migraines, with their shooting stars and visual disturbances. Much that used to be part of the rapturous ecstasy of lovers and mystics is now reduced to defunct brain wiring. In *The Idiot*, written in 1869 on the cusp of this transition, Fyodor Dostoyevsky, who himself suffered from epilepsy, described the harmony and joy, the vivid sounds and colors, and the intense feeling of being alive that marked the onset of one of his character Prince Myshkin's fits. "What does it matter if it is a disease?" asks Myshkin. For if, "in the last conscious moments before the fit, he had time to say to himself, consciously and clearly, 'Yes, I could give my whole life for this moment,' then this moment by itself was, of course, worth the whole of life."

See also: EUPHORIA; ILINX; LOVE.

EMBARRASSMENT

The addled, constricted feeling we get when we fart loudly in a bookshop, or have "Happy Birthday" sung to us in a restaurant, or say something innocuous that others mishear as Very Rude Indeed, was largely an invention of the stiflingly polite drawing rooms of Regency England. Adopted in the 1750s, from the Old French *embarrasser* (to impede or hinder), embarrassment described feeling constrained, even crippled, following some breach of etiquette that made the conversation splutter. (The connection between embarrassment and constraint or blockage also explains the phrase "an embarrassment of riches." It comes from the French *embarras de richesses*, which refers to feeling hindered by too much choice.) This new category was free of the moral dimension of the older catchall SHAME. While shame came to be associated with the elongated miseries of self-flagellation in private, embarrassment captured social humiliations, emphasizing instead minor or fleeting transgressions before an audience.

If you're easily embarrassed, you probably envy those who allow their gaffes to roll right off them. Being lavishly praised in public or accidentally criticizing an in-law can leave one flustered and wanting to evaporate — and then, the horror! — even more discombobulated for being embarrassed. But maybe we're being too hard on ourselves. According to the sociologist Erving Goffman, embarrassment serves an important purpose. Getting flustered shows that we realize we've transgressed a social rule; it is a gesture that promises we will "prove worthy another time." Recent research from the University of California has shown that people who are more easily embarrassed are also more altruistic, and that onlookers can tell as much. In the film *Four Weddings and a Funeral*, Charles (Hugh Grant) bangs his head against a marquee pole after a joke horrifically backfires. Carrie (Andie MacDowall) smiles, not just because she's witnessing an amusing display of English repression, but because the depth of Charles's self-punitive embarrassment shows how much he cares about the offense he's caused. Because of this connection between embarrassment and maintaining social equilibrium, the philosopher Rom Harré has argued that embarrassment has taken over from shame as the major "instrument of conformity."

While stammering and staring at the ground are signs of embarrassment, blushing is its famous tell. In fact, the link between embarrassment and blushing is relatively new. Before the 1800s, one's face might grow red for a variety of reasons, including modesty and ECSTASY, PRIDE and SHAME, LOVE and ANGER. When Charlotte de Corday was executed in Paris in 1793 for assassinating revolutionary leader Jean-Paul Marat, her severed head was said to have blushed furiously, an unmistakable "sign of INDIG-NATION" at her punishment, according to the Parisian surgeon Jean-Joseph Sue. Within fifty years Victorian physiologists had rewritten the story of Corday's blush, claiming that the murderess blushed not in fury but out of involuntary shame at her wrongdoing. As Thomas Henry Burgess put it in *The Physiology or Mechanism of Blushing* in 1839, there is a distinction between the "genuine" blush of shame, and the mere facial reddenings of anger, excitement or illness. The true blush, according to Burgess, was a moral instinct implanted by God, to restrain illicit behavior. The red blotches were a powerful deterrent, staining the cheeks, the tips of noses, even the earlobes, and lighting up our guilt for all to see.

Intrigued by the possibility of an inherently moral human body, Victorian physicians set about busily recording unusual specimens of blushes. They investigated red-faced sleepwalkers and swapped tantalizing tales of female asylum patients whose thighs flushed during intimate examinations. They wondered whether people could blush when alone, and hotly debated whether people of different races could blush at all — and if not, whether this meant they were inherently deceptive. One particular "servant Negress" became something of a celebrity for a scar on her cheek that glowed red when she was "abruptly spoken to or charged with any trivial offence," though the color in the rest of her face remained unchanged. Their idea of a moral reflex, however, was reconsidered in *The Expression of the Emotions in Man and Animals* (1872) by Charles Darwin, who first cemented the link between blushing and a social experience of embarrassment — as opposed to a moral category of shame or guilt. He argued that blood rushes to the surface of the skin whenever another's "attention is vividly directed" to it, as when someone compliments our appearance. He also ventured that, since breaking taboos leaves us feeling conspicuous, blushing may have evolved as a reflex, a deterrent to rule breaking helping fledgling societies survive — an idea taken up enthusiastically by Goffman.

Darwin's theory has been very influential, but today the link between blushing, embarrassment and conformity is beginning to unravel. Echoing pre-Victorian ideas about blushing, today's physiologists argue we don't blush only when embarrassed, but also when we experience any sudden emotional change, including fear, anger and stress. In these moments, our bodies release adrenaline, which in turn dilates the capillaries in our cheeks, flooding them with blood and splattering blotches across our skin. In this picture, the idea of a "moral blush" specifically evolved to deter us from breaking the rules seems even less likely.

In fact, embarrassment doesn't always work in the way evolutionary psychologists like Darwin and Goffman suggest. While it is broadly true that a fear of embarrassing ourselves keeps us within the margins of social respectability, embarrassment can be disruptive in its own right. It can be crippling, as in the case of shyness, trapping us in its excruciating feedback loops ("I wish I didn't embarrass so easily, it's so embarrassing!"). It can be exasperating, as when teenagers, that most diligent tribe of conformists, squirm and sweat when their parents ask a stranger for directions. Sometimes embarrassment can inhibit generosity and cooperation, as when we resist the urge to offer our seat on a crowded bus for fear of drawing attention to ourselves, or assume someone is pregnant when in fact.... Embarrassment might cement our social rules, but the moments of confusion it sometimes creates can accidentally make us break them too.

See also: VERGÜENZA AJENA.

EMPATHY

In the 1890s the novelist Vernon Lee (born Violet Paget) and her friend, and probably lover, Kit Anstruther-Thomson traveled to Rome, where they performed an intriguing psychological experiment. Standing before a cast of the Venus de Milo, Anstruther-Thomson reported minuscule shifts in her internal balance that seemed, according to Lee who was scribbling it all down, to echo the sculpture's design. In high-vaulted churches, Anstruther-Thomson reported feeling her lungs fill with air. In front of Grecian urns, she felt a bulging sensation at the belly. Today their experiment seems, well, a little off-piste, but in the 1890s it was rooted in a cutting-edge psychological concept. On the Continent, *Einfühlung* (literally: in-feeling, or vicarious sensation) was being vaunted as the next big thing, a purely physiological explanation for the pleasure of looking at inanimate objects, landscapes, even weather: our bodies were primed to imitate them, and it was from this complicity that enjoyment came. Lee's experiments are particularly important to historians of psychology and emotions because she was one of the first to popularize the translation of the German *Einfühlung* into a newly coined Greek word: empathy.

Today empathy means something different. It's a feeling of emotional resonance between people rather than between people and objects, and is much celebrated (according to the psychologist Simon Baron-Cohen, as a "universal solvent": "any problem immersed in empathy becomes soluble"). The ability to intuit the distress of another, or to feel a faint echo of their excitement, and therefore respond in ways that bring the other person closer, rather than alienate them, is an overt requirement of certain professions — nursing, sales and teaching, to name a few. In emotional-literacy classes in British schools, children are taught empathy, so that alongside language and numbers a capacity for vicarious feeling is becoming an expected indicator of a child's development (and conversely, when illnesses such as autism are described, a lack of empathy is cited as the primary symptom).

As was the case in the 1890s with the concept of *Einfühlung*, the idea that fellow feeling might have a physiological basis has become most exciting of all. Are we "hardwired" to feel other people's pain or happiness? In the 1990s neuroscientists at the University of Parma discovered cells in the brains of monkeys that fire not just when the animal performs a given action — eating a banana, say — but when it witnesses another do so too. The researchers dubbed these cells "mirror neurons," and despite the fact they are yet to be found in humans, in the last twenty years the idea that we are primed to feel what others are feeling has become one of the most controversial and overhyped claims in neuroscience. Advocates of mirror-neuron theory such as the neuroscientist Vilayanur Ramachandran claim that "mirror-neurons will do for psychology what DNA did for biology," providing a unifying explanation for all human behavior. Philosophers, artists and humanities scholars have enthusiastically taken up his suggestion, and mirror-neurons have been feted as evidence of our deep interconnectedness.

But perhaps it is this frothy excitement about the *idea* of mirror neurons that is most intriguing of all. The urge to find physiological evidence of a shared response is not a new one. The origins of the word "empathy" might lie in the early twentieth century, but the desire to find a natural instinct to explain kindness goes back even further.

The sentimental philosophers of the eighteenth century — David Hume, Lord Shaftesbury, Jean-Jacques Rousseau and Adam Smith (more famous for his economic theories) among them — also believed they too had identified a bodily instinct for fellow feeling. What today is called "empathy," they called "sympathy," and saw evidence for it in the primitive physical reflexes: "When we see a stroke aimed, and just ready to fall upon the leg or arm of another person, we naturally shrink and draw back our own leg or our own arm," wrote Adam Smith in *The Theory of Moral Sentiments* (1759). "And when it does fall, we feel it in some measure, and are hurt by it as well as the sufferer...this is the source of our fellow feeling." Today's psychologists and philosophers (and politicians) speak of empathy as the panacea for an increasingly atomized society. For the moral philosophers of the eighteenth century, the promise of inbuilt sympathy countered what seemed to be a rising tide of selfishness in their society too. Theirs was a response to the pessimistic view of writers such as Thomas Hobbes, who had argued that the human urge for power was entirely natural and should be restrained: "Nature," he wrote, makes men "apt to invade, and destroy one another" (*see also:* RIVALRY).

The eighteenth-century interest in sympathy gave rise to an astonishing cult of benevolence — or what we'd call today philanthropy. "Benevolists," stirred by what was called "social affection," began to grapple with the ills of their age with utopian fever: slavery, child labor, animal cruelty. "Men of Feeling" set up schools and hospitals. "What can be more nobly human than to have a tender sentimental feeling of our own and others' misfortunes?" wrote one anonymous author in an article defending the voguish practice of "moral weeping" of 1755. The idea of crying for an extended period over someone else's distress seems rather self-indulgent today (*see:* COMPASSION), but the anonymous author thought it a spur to action: "Weeping for the affliction of others...we benevolently hasten to assist them." It was a brief flourishing of kindness. Very brief, in fact. By the end of the century tenderhearted "moral weeping" was being satirized for its self-indulgence, and the word "sentimentality" began to accrue the associations with inauthenticity and mawkishness it has today.

When we look back at the eighteenth century's turn to sympathy, its practical effects are surprising. Has the twenty-first century's interest in empathy, both as a physiological fact and a voguish moral attitude, engendered a similar wave of philanthropy? When our politicians speak of a "politics of empathy," it's hard not to feel cynical: a stilted expression of sympathy costs little, and is a poor stand-in for proper pensions or decent health care. But if we are shriveled by narcissism and in the grip of a compassion deficit, then we might just have to hope that empathy is the "universal solvent" some promise it to be.

See also: DISMAY; PITY.

ENVY

Most cultures have their traditions of the Evil Eye, a gaze motivated by envy, which poisons, curses or brings misfortune. In many Arabic countries, tradition dictates that you do not praise a beautiful or talented child: and if you do, say *Masha'Allah* — "God has willed it" — to protect the child from the bad luck brought by the *ayn al-h.asūd.* In northern India, drivers put colorful stickers on their trucks with the slogan *buri nazar wale tera muh kala* (may your face turn black, the evil-eyed one) to ward it off. In Scotland, the *Droch Shùil* is thought to dry up the milk of nursing mothers and cows. Envy is feared not only because it gives rise to a greedy desire to steal the admired object — the beautiful eyes, the healthy flock, the sumptuous home — but because it is destructive. When the envious can't have the coveted item for themselves, they don't want anyone else to have it either.

JEALOUSY, which is above all a fear of losing a loved one to another, is often credited with some romantic appeal. The same cannot be said of envy. Envy is a desire to have the material possessions and advantages of others. It's the sickness that comes on hearing another's happy sigh, the ache of contemplating their success. Left to fester, it turns to HATRED and maliciousness, laying waste to both envier and envied. The Old Irish epic the *Táin bó Cúailnge* tells of a war over a stolen bull, which began when Queen Medb and her husband Ailill decided to compare their possessions. Their wealth was equal, until Medb saw Ailill's prize white-horned bull, and "it was as if she hadn't a single penny."

With its roots in the Latin *invidus* (envious), from *in* (upon) *videre* (to see), envy has long been associated with gazing and looking. But the etymology also reminds us that those things we envy seduce us with their seemingly faultless image. Most of us, at one time or another, fall into the trap of comparing our own imperfect insides with the idealized outsides of other people's lives. This is when envy strikes, multiplying with unfamiliarity and distance. As adults, we mostly feel it as a secret vice. It's there behind the rictus grin that celebrates other people's successes. It is the opposite of GRATITUDE, which gives rise to CONTENTMENT (*see also:* MUDITA). According to the author Nancy Friday, it is "the one emotion in all human life about which nothing good can be said."

Was she right?

The essay "Envy and Gratitude" (1957) by the psychoanalyst Melanie Klein is now considered a classic in its field. Like many before her, Klein defined envy as a kind of anger, provoked by another person possessing and enjoying something desirable, and that gives rise to the impulse to "take it away or to spoil it."

The key difference was that Klein did not think envy a sin or a failure of character, but an inevitable part of all our lives. From her years observing tiny infants, she saw the envious impulse at work from only a few months old. From the security of the womb, the infant enters a world of unpleasant sensations, one of which is need. However attentive the parents are, Klein argued, a baby will always experience the frustration of food not being instantly available. So our earliest emotional life is always shaped by two sensations: of losing, and then regaining, the satisfaction of the pleasurable object, what Klein called the "good breast," or bottle. According to Klein, when the "good breast" is out of reach, the baby perceives the parent or carer as hoarding the enjoyable object, and is filled with rage and a desire to destroy the parent who has kept the food for herself. Thus the "good breast" becomes the "bad breast." It is, of course, a theory, and hard to prove with any certainty. But if Klein was right, and envy is an inevitable part of our development, then we might wonder whether we're right to try to rid ourselves of it.

Could there be something of value in the ugly impulse to want what others have — so much so that you're willing to destroy it rather than let them have it for themselves? It is worth noting that envy, which has one eye on inequalities and disparities, is one of the few emotions to be explicitly concerned with *unfairness* (for another, *see*: INDIGNATION). There are some cultures where becoming destructive and enraged as a consequence of the unfair distribution of food or wealth is considered a reasonable response (*see*: SONG). By contrast, in Britain and America, it is often made to seem petty. Cultural critics have long been exasperated by the accusation, flung at politicians on the left, that they are merely "playing the politics of envy." As left-wing theorist Fredric Jameson has argued, such phrases serve to undermine genuine political grievances, discrediting arguments for wealth redistribution by suggesting they are motivated merely by the character weakness of spite, and the "private dissatisfaction" of class hatred (*see also*: RESENTMENT).

But since the mid-1990s, neuroscientists have argued that our emotions underpin even our most apparently rational ideas, helping us weigh up our choices and motivating the decisions we make. Perhaps envy really does have a serious role to play in political debate. Sometimes the belief that others have it much better than we do is a mere trick of the light. But many have an awful lot less than they deserve. A covetous look, a twinge of envy, might just be an emotional antenna alerting you to some disparity or inequality not too far away. Whether you decide to respond with destructive fury or something a little more creative is, of course, up to you.

See also: INDIGNATION.

EUPHORIA

In January 2011, wobbly mobile-phone footage of an unforeseen uprising in Tunisia began to appear on the world's TV screens. Over the coming weeks and months, protestors poured onto the streets of Cairo, Yemen, Libya and Syria. Emboldened and defiant, they chanted *Ash-sha'ab yurid isqat al-nizam* —"the people want to bring down the regime" — against a backdrop of tear gas and burning cars. Months later, once the news cameras had left and thoughts turned to an uncertain future, those involved reflected on its feverish mood. As the Tunisian activist and blogger Lina Ben Mhenni put it, "After a few weeks of revolutionary euphoria, Tunisia is once again a police state."

It's intoxicating, infectious. It swells the heart and whirls us round and round. It's there in the breathless early weeks of a love affair, in the exhilarating highs of a strange city at night. Everything feels alight and connected, the world glows, even smells and colors seem more intense. But sometimes there is an undertow of danger. Of artifice. "What goes up must come down," we say, in a warning sort of voice — fearing our EXCITEMENT may dance too close to the biochemical manias of bipolar disease, or the false bravado of "economic euphoria," the boom that can only lead to a bust.

It wasn't always like this. When the word "euphoria," or "euphory," first entered the English language in the seventeenth century, it described a fairly ordinary feeling of physical and emotional CONTENT-MENT. From the Greek *eu* (well) *pherein* (to bear), the word literally meant "well-bearing," the predecessor of today's ubiquitous "well-being." In the seventeenth and eighteenth centuries, when formerly extremely ill patients started to show interest in their food and felt ready to get out of bed, doctors described this as euphory returning—the first reliable sign of recovery.*

It was only in the nineteenth century, with that era's obsessive categorization and pathologization of our mental lives, that euphoria picked up its undercurrent of transgression and excess. In 1896 the French physician Théodore Ribot dedicated a whole chapter of *The Psychology of the Emotions* to a phenomenon called "The Euphoria of the Dying." He and many of his fellow physicians had noted that some patients experienced states of ecstatic bliss at the end of their lives, laughing delightedly, leaping out of bed and optimistically making plans for the future, seemingly oblivious to the imminence of their demise. These patients perplexed, even outraged, doctors, who dismissed the sudden outburst of euphoria—or what they called "silly cheerfulness"—as a sign of degeneracy. Since the doctors believed it only served an evolutionary advantage to feel well when actually physically well, they concluded that the elation of dying patients consisted merely of the disordered outpourings of already corrupted minds, whose tendency to dwell on "morbid pleasures" had caused the illness in the first place.

The idea that we might experience euphoria, rather than DREAD or GRIEF, on our deathbeds has become less widespread today. In 1926 two physicians named Cottrell and Wilson found that over two-thirds of patients in the advanced stages of multiple sclerosis experienced a

---

* In case you are fondly imagining that in the old days everyone used to walk around glowing with euphory, sometimes drugs were also required. The writer of a 1701 tract on opium suggested imbibing small doses of the drug in the morning "to cause Euphory or brisk Effects," noting that the poppy encouraged "a blithe, gay and good Humor" and, enticingly, "promptitude to venery," or in other words, it ramped up one's sex drive—nowadays, it's thought to decrease it.

"prevailing mood of serenity and cheerfulness." Today, only 13 percent of patients suffering the same disease report feeling anything close to euphoric, while incidents of depression are on the rise. Why? Perhaps earlier (or our own) methods of assessing mood are to blame, or maybe the elated feelings of MS patients of the past, or the depression of those in the present, can be attributed to medication. It also seems likely that social factors, such as the waning of religious beliefs and the fact that dying is increasingly screened off in clinical settings, play their role. Either way, the link between euphoria and illness remains challenging. Early in 2013, when ex-Dr. Feelgood guitarist Wilko Johnson announced that he had been diagnosed with terminal cancer (he has now recovered), the press pounced on his descriptions of feeling "vividly alive" with a "strange euphoria" and "marvelous feeling of freedom." His interviews, though intensely uplifting, disconcertingly undermined our own calcified notions of HAPPINESS and where we should find it.

See also: ECSTASY.

EXASPERATION

See: FRUSTRATION.

EXCITEMENT

You might smell vomit. Or see enormous men, their ears smeared in Vaseline, shivering as they lace up their boots. Visit the dressing room at a rugby match, and you'll witness a strange emotion. Its traces will be there in the fear that hardens the players' faces as they walk out onto the pitch, or in the tears that fill their eyes as their national anthem swells in the stands.

The rugby player's prematch nerves seem a million miles away from the family whizzing down a snowy bank on a trash-barrel lid, pink cheeked and giggling. Or the way the heart flutters in the flurry of preparations for a party. But in fact it's impossible to talk about any of these things without talking about adrenaline. It's the kick-starter hormone secreted from the adrenal glands, which lie by the kidneys (ad-renal) and which, in an emergency, will prepare us for fight or flight. And without adrenaline, there would be no excitement at all.

When the word "excitement" first appeared in English in eighteenth-century medical books, it didn't mean quite what it does today. It was a condition of the "vital spirits," which when agitated — "excited" — would whiz around the body, sending messages to the brain and moving the limbs. Like many of the feelings we take for granted today, excitement first became understood as an emotion in the mid-nineteenth century. Charles Darwin spoke of excitement primarily as the pleasure of "high spirits," which registered in bright eyes, rapid circulation and whirlwind ideas. His favorite definition of the emotion was given to him by a child: "good spirits," the child informed the scientist, was "laughing, talking and kissing." One of Darwin's contemporaries, the psychologist Alexander Bain added to this that excitement was an "emotion of action," there with the thrill of hunting and fighting. It gave one a feeling of momentum — like those excitable "vital spirits" — and of invincibility and speed. Excitement, Bain concluded, could be full of either JOY or FEAR.

The story of excitement took a new direction in the 1890s. Dr. George Oliver was a physician from Harrogate who, according to later accounts, was in the habit of performing experiments on his family over the cold winter months. In one, he injected his young son with a purified extract of sheep and calf adrenal glands — and was surprised to notice that the boy's radial artery suddenly contracted. Subsequent experiments confirmed the extract was so potent that it could send blood pressure rocketing. Within ten years, the word "hormone" had been coined and the substance Oliver had used had been isolated and was being marketed as a new wonder drug: Adrenalin. It became a medical sensation, used for controlling hemorrhages in surgeries and suppressing allergic reactions, resuscitating stroke victims and treating the split lips of boxers. However, adrenaline didn't only catch the attention of surgeons and ringside cuts men. The era's psychologists, who studied emotions and their physiological effects, became interested in the way it caused a kind of urgent feeling, sparkling eyes and flushed cheeks — the responses that Victorian psychologists had associated with excitement. In adrenaline, they had found the secret of excitement — and the theory that our emotions might be chemical responses to life's crises was secured.

Today's medical textbooks often speak of epinephrine rather than adrenaline, and of a neurotransmitter called noradrenaline in the brain. But "adrenaline" remains a popular part of our emotional language, a byword for a burst of energy or buzzing nerves. The feeling of being hepped up, pumped and alert that Bain called "excitement," has become inseparable from the language of drugs: We speak of "adrenaline shots" and "adrenaline rushes." We talk of "adrenaline junkies." This emotion, more than any other, is a kind of chemistry, and one that we have come to admire. Following the discovery of adrenaline, the idea that a surge of excitement was good for the health became widespread — understood to be both stimulating and cathartic. Some today might prefer computer games to produce these surges of testosterone, noradrenaline and cortisol: all the excitement, none of the risk (except, perhaps, obesity). In Aldous Huxley's *Brave New*

World, written in the early 1930s, a monthly injection of an adrenaline-like substance was all that was required to maintain optimum health.

> *"Men and women must have their adrenals stimulated from time to time" [the Controller explains to the Savage ...] "It's one of the conditions of perfect health. That's why we've made the V.P.S. treatments compulsory."*
>
> *"V.P.S.?"*
>
> *"Violent Passion Surrogate. Regularly once a month. We flood the whole system with adrenin. It's the complete physiological equivalent of fear and rage. All the tonic effects of murdering Desdemona and being murdered by Othello, without any of the inconveniences."*
>
> *"But I like the inconveniences."*
>
> *"We don't," said the Controller. "We prefer to do things comfortably."*

See also: LIGET.

FAGO

"The implicit poetry in Ifaluk emotional understandings is nowhere more evident than in the concept of *fago*," wrote the anthropologist Catherine Lutz in the late 1980s. While living among the people of Ifaluk, a tiny coral atoll in the Caroline Islands of the Pacific, Lutz became fascinated by an emotion that she instinctively recognized but for which there was no English equivalent.

Fago is a unique emotional concept that blurs COMPASSION, SADNESS and LOVE together. It is the pity felt for someone in need, which compels us to care for them, but it is also haunted by a strong sense that one day we will lose them. *Fago* comes in those moments when our love for others, and their need for us, feels so unexpectedly overwhelming — and life so very fragile and temporary — that we well up.

Lutz suggested that the fact the Ifaluk, who are famed for their nonaggression, have a distinct emotion to describe a combination of sorrow, and the compassion that might go some way to relieving it, points to the importance of mutual concern in their culture. It also alerts us to the inevitability of grief in all human life.

"*Fago*," wrote Lutz, "is uttered in recognition of the suffering that is everywhere, and in the spirit of a vigorous optimism that human effort, most especially in the form of caring for others, can control its ravages."

See also: GRIEF.

FEAR

Fear has come to be seen as the most primal, the most fundamental of human emotions. We imagine our ancestors huddled in caves while the thunder rolls above them, or frozen rigid to the spot, hearts hammering against ribs, as a fearsome beast slinks past. It was Charles Darwin, in 1872, who first insisted on fear's primordial roots: "We may confidently believe," he wrote, that "fear was expressed from an extremely remote period in almost the same manner as it is now by man."

Most of the other animals who live on this planet share these involuntary responses to threat. Such reactions evolved to preserve the life of our species. The eyes widen and hearing sharpens, the heart beats rapidly and breathing becomes shallow or held in. We try to hide ourselves, or flee. Or else, riding a surge of adrenaline, we turn and fight (see: EXCITEMENT). The response is instinctive. Under threat, our bodies grab the controls, and put us on automatic pilot.

Fear is that simple. And yet...

Aren't there vast differences between worrying your partner will leave you, feeling spooked when the lights go dead and fainting in horror, as Erasmus reputedly did, at the sight of a plate of lentils? Can we really say the excited terror on the brink of an important enterprise and the blind panic felt when a car jokingly accelerates toward you are the same? Both are broadly "fear," but the first contains germs of

HOPEFULNESS and anticipation, and the second might leave us feeling ANGER and brittle with EMBARRASSMENT. In English we talk of different sorts of fear: of DREAD, WORRY, ANXIETY and TERROR. This is nothing. The Pintupi of Western Australia use at least fifteen different words to describe a whole panorama of fearful feelings, identified only by the very specific situations in which they occur (see: NGINYIWARRARRINGU).

Perhaps one of the most peculiar things of all about our friend fear — this most vital of emotions, the primal lifesaver — is our deep suspicion of it. "The only thing we have to fear is fear itself," proclaimed Franklin D. Roosevelt in 1933. The line was already a cliché: three and a half centuries earlier Michel de Montaigne had quipped, "The thing I fear most is fear." Fear might be one of our greatest allies, saving us from mortal danger, yet we depict it as a furtive enemy, stealing in like a thief, derailing rational thought, inflaming latent anxieties, hobbling purposeful action. Fear can kill. According to the seventh-century medical manual *The Book of Aurelius*, a terrifying encounter with water — heavy rain or a swollen river — could bring on lethal "hydrophobia" (literally, "fear of water," nowadays known as rabies). Ten centuries later, killer fear was still on the loose. According to the 1665 Bill of Mortality, a list of the weekly causes of death among Londoners, three unlucky souls perished after being "frighted" to death. Stampedes and desperate crushes can still kill us (see: PANIC). Or can make us feel as if we might die (see: PEUR DES ESPACES). And sometimes, with its urgent requirement that we defend ourselves against enemies at all costs, even rootless fears can leave devastation and death behind (see: PARANOIA).

In the West we live in what have been called "fear-averse" societies. Our public spaces may be festooned with security cameras, and warnings to be vigilant might boom out over our public transport systems. But these repeated exhortations to reduce risk may increase our nervousness. Continually reminded of our vulnerabilities, we may become more susceptible to political rhetoric that offers us protection in the face of global menace (*see:* TERROR). The situation is exacerbated by what sociologist Frank Furedi calls "fear entrepreneurs" — businesses or advocacy groups who stoke up threats with screaming headlines and pernicious ads ("Will eating chips cause dementia?" "Are you losing your hair?" "Are you UNFULFILLED by your JOB?"). "It did what all ads are supposed to do: create an anxiety relievable by purchase," wrote David Foster Wallace in his novel *Infinite Jest*. It's not just that fear can be stoked by so many sources, it's that new reasons to be frightened appear each day. We used to be scared of thunder and wild beasts: now seeing an ad in a newspaper or getting on a train seems to bring some new danger into focus. And it may be that we'll need more than a shopping trip to deal with it.

See also: COURAGE.

FEELING GOOD
(ABOUT YOURSELF)

There were no affirmations in the mirror. Or pep talks, willing yourself to be the best you could possibly be. In the 1890s, when the phrase "self-esteem" was first introduced into the psychological literature, feeling good about yourself was really a question of reconciling yourself to your own inadequacy.

The philosopher and psychologist William James is thought to have been the first person to use the term "self-esteem" and wonder how it might be harnessed. He thought that by giving up our fantasies of great success, and focusing our energies on the things we know are within our grasp (mastering lasagne, or remembering to meet our friends in the pub), we would feel that elusive "lightness about the heart" that comes when we surrender to exactly who we already are. "How pleasant is the day when we give up striving to be young — or slender! Thank God! we say, those illusions are gone," he proclaimed. A happy side effect might be that we would also feel emboldened to do more in the future, since self-esteem dictates what we "back ourselves to do," as he put it, but this was a sort of bonus. James summed up his insight in an elegant equation:

$$\text{self-esteem} = \frac{\text{success}}{\text{pretension}}$$

The beliefs about our future achievements (pretensions) should more or less match up with what, based on a cold assessment, we are *actually capable of* doing (success). If the expectations we have of ourselves outweigh our abilities, then we condemn ourselves to a lifetime of inadequacy and dissatisfaction. However, this did not mean that no one should strive for anything ever again: work harder to achieve a greater competency (or success), and you can set your sights on bigger and better goals. For James, then, self-esteem was a careful calibration, a question of checks and balances aimed at ensuring that one's aspirations and achievements inched along in line with one another.

James's theory of self-esteem was forgotten about for much of the first part of the twentieth century, since psychologists at that time found the topic of security more pressing (*see:* COMFORT). But as a result of the interest in positive psychology that emerged in the 1960s, "self-esteem" was revisited by a new generation of researchers. They tentatively suggested there might be a link between feeling good about yourself and behaving in more socially responsible ways. And though there was little hard evidence, the idea caught the eye of politicians. In the late 1980s, a government task force was set up, and by the 1990s schools in California were being urged to offer self-esteem-building activities to their students. These exercises were based on the idea that self-esteem could be artificially inflated using a generalized positive reinforcement. But in the excitement that self-esteem might be the secret to solving all social ills, James's elegant equation was forgotten. Rather than lowering the children's pretensions to match their skills, or raising their skills to match their pretensions, self-esteem was made a goal in itself, which then had to be succeeded at. (And those who didn't succeed — the loners, the "rude," the easily frustrated or timid — were diagnosed with a further "problem" to contend with: they "lacked self-esteem.")

In the last ten years, the self-esteem movement has come under attack, in particular by Jean Twenge, a psychologist at the University of San Diego, whose research has shown that attempting to build self-esteem creates not more, but significantly lower levels of CONTENT-MENT. An inflated belief in one's own abilities can result in narcissism and, in turn, the LONELINESS that comes from believing — or feeling you ought to believe — you are "above average" and stand apart from the crowd. Moreover, we might be more likely to feel dissatisfied and confused if we do not manage to meet our inflated expectations. Yet, we are also less likely to meet those expectations when we are poorly equipped to seek help in developing our skills: asking for the mentorship of others requires a certain humility.

Most of all, trying to secure self-esteem might make you feel bad because it is an almost impossibly difficult goal to achieve. Since being rolled out in schools on both sides of the Atlantic in the 1990s, self-esteem has been framed as a kind of permanent attribute, like knowing how to play the piano or being able to speak French. However, for James, feeling good about yourself, though it was something one could work at, was ultimately an "emotion" (specifically: he called it an emotion of the "social self"). He thought self-esteem could never be a permanent state of affairs, but that it waxed and waned. Some days we might feel optimistic and capable ("yes, I NAILED that lasagne!"). And on others, when every attempt we've made in our work or private life has crumbled, utterly hopeless. Seeing self-esteem as a fluctuating emotion rather than an accomplishment in its own right, then, might relieve us of the burden of yet another impossible task to measure up to. Give up on achieving self-esteem, and you might just find you feel much better (about yourself) as a result. •

See also: CONFIDENCE.

FORMAL FEELING, A

Sometimes life's most painful experiences can leave us eerily cold and a little mechanical. The poet Emily Dickinson described it as "a formal feeling"; the heart seems stiff and detached, our feelings wary and ceremonious. "This is the Hour of Lead," wrote Dickinson. But, she reassures us, it too will pass. First there is a "Chill," she wrote; "then Stupor — then the letting go —"

See also: GRIEF; SADNESS.

FRAUD, FEELING LIKE A

In 1919 the novelist Franz Kafka wrote a forty-five-page grievance-filled letter to his father — and never sent it. By then he was in his late thirties, but his memories of school still smarted. In the letter he complained bitterly about spending his childhood lurking about shiftily, feeling "like a bank clerk who had committed a fraud." Each new academic accolade granted to the outstanding young student left Kafka feeling increasingly anxious, compelled to work even harder just to "avoid discovery."

Are you faking your way through life? Have you fooled your boss into thinking you're more talented than you really are? Do you worry about being found out?

Then you're not alone.

In the 1970s two psychologists, Pauline Clance and Suzanne Imes, investigating this torturous experience called it the Imposter Phenomenon. They found it was particularly common among successful professional women, many of whom believed their achievements had been the result of accident or oversight. Some of Clance and Imes's subjects even believed that they'd inadvertently manipulated or flirted their way into promotion, convinced they hadn't earned their success (see: SUSPICION). Today, many successful men also admit to feeling like an imposter, and it's particularly common among first-generation professionals or those embarking on a career change.

Feeling like a fraud is undoubtedly an unpleasant experience, with its creeping sense that your hard-won gains are fragile and your achievements might, at any moment, be snatched away. But as high-profile high achievers become more vocal about their own feelings of imposterism (in recent years the former British Foreign Secretary Jack Straw and the novelist Maya Angelou have both admitted to experiencing it), it may be that feeling like a fraud is being recast as an inevitable growing pain — less something to buckle under than a feeling we must learn to bear. The suspicion that she's a phony still flickers at the periphery of Maria Klawe's vision. A renowned mathematician and computer scientist, and President of Harvey Mudd College in California, she argues that "if you're constantly pushing yourself, and putting yourself in new environments, you'll feel it over and over again." The trick, she suggests, is to learn to anticipate it, and tolerate it when it washes over you. It might even be welcomed: a sign that you've shifted out of your comfort zone, and are launching yourself bravely into new worlds.

See also: CONTENTMENT.

FRUSTRATION

See: EXASPERATION.

GEZELLIGHEID

It's no surprise that so many of northern Europe's languages have a particular word for feeling cozy (from the Gaelic *còsag*, a small hole you can creep into). It's when the rain is mizzling and the damp rises from the canals that we yearn for the feeling the Dutch call *gezelligheid*. Derived from the word for "friend," *gezelligheid* describes both physical circumstances — being snug in a warm and homely place surrounded by good friends (it's impossible to be *gezelligheid* alone) — and an emotional state of feeling "held" and comforted. The Danish *hygge* (coziness), the German *Gemütlichkeit*, which describes feelings of congeniality and companionship, and the Finnish *kodikas* (roughly: homely) have similar connotations. Riffle through the languages of the sunny Mediterranean, however, and the equivalent combination of physical enclosure and emotional comfort is much harder to find.

See also: INHABITIVENESS; COMFORT.

GLADSOMENESS

An unexpected bit of good news can change the emotional weather. A friend with a new baby; a neighbor discharged from the hospital. When good things happen to people we're fond of, a little glance of sunshine is sent in our direction too, making everything just that little bit brighter (except when it doesn't; *see:* ENVY).

It was not always this way. From the Old Norse *gladr* (bright or smooth), the earliest use of glad described the appearance of a glittering, shining thing. This meaning still lingers in the expressions "glad rags," or "glad eye" — the twinkle that attracts a lover. In the fourteenth century gladsum, or gladsomenesse, began to be used to describe a brightening of the soul too, a sparky, bouncing feeling, which today we might be more likely to call JOY.

It was probably as a result of the new fashion for being happy in the eighteenth century that the meaning of gladness became more muted. Children with a new toy could be glad, as could inanimate objects such as bells and Christmas tidings. It became linked to those moments when mild worries cease, or niggling tasks are completed —"I'm glad I caught you," "I'm glad it got fixed" (*see also:* RELIEF).

It might seem to have become a rather limp emotion — except that at this time it also became linked to pleasure felt on someone else's behalf, a particular kind of EMPATHY. This makes it a very valuable addition to the emotional lexicon. Where happiness has come to mean something we earnestly orchestrate for ourselves, gladness is the emotion of happy accidents and unexpected uplifts of the soul. And points to our willingness to be affected by the moods of other people, and celebrate on their behalf.

See also: WARM GLOW.

GLEE

Glee has never been entirely innocent. When the Norsemen arrived in England, bringing their language with them, *glý*, or *glíw*, or *glew* meant "sport" and "mockery." A *glew* was also the word for a song, loud and drunken, and *Chamber-glew* was shorthand for lewd behavior. To be motivated by *golde* and *glie* was frowned upon: it meant living in search of cash and wanton pleasure. In the seventeenth century "glee" shed some of this raucousness when it was co-opted by choir masters to describe a very precise kind of unaccompanied contrapuntal singing, a rather more staid version of the style now favored by American high school glee clubs. But today glee retains its dastardly edge. After a series of security leaks in 2013, the head of MI6 imagined Al-Qaeda terrorists "rubbing their hands with glee." This glee is a malevolent thrill, a celebration of one's own good fortune at another's expense (*see:* SCHADENFREUDE).

Body language experts disagree about the exact origins of gleeful hand rubbing, though all link it — like gleaming eyes and lip smacking — to anticipating something good coming our way. Various evolutionary tales have been ventured. Standing around in a cold cave, ready to tuck into roasted elk, for instance, our ancestors would rub their hands together to make the blood circulate faster and their fingers more nimble to pick at the flesh. Or: hand rubbing is a way of dissipating the anxious tension that is part of expectancy. Or: it's a milder version of a baby's delighted clap. Or: it comes from an ancient requirement that we cleanse our hands before receiving a gift.

But why then should it have become associated with supervillains in Hollywood films? (No one really rubs their hands in glee, do they? It's only ever a camp gesture, done in quotation marks. Members of Al-Qaeda are even less likely to — the gesture is rarely seen in Arabic countries.)

The answer can be found in John Bulwer's 1644 guide to hand gestures, *Chirologia or The Naturall Language of the Hand*, which describes two types of hand rubbing. One is rubbing the palms together as if clapping, a gesture Bulwer associates with greediness. The other, Gestus XI: "Innocentiam ostendo" ("The performance of innocence"), is an imitation of hand washing, which Bulwer links to the cleansing of imagined bloodstains — the sort of gesture Lady Macbeth might be found doing. It's for this reason that hand rubbing became so gleefully villainous: actors resorted to rubbing their hands to tip off the audience that their character, who seemed oh so innocent, was in fact very guilty indeed.

See also: ANTICIPATION; EXCITEMENT.

GRATITUDE

It might seem "hokey," as the University of California psychologist Sonja Lyubomirsky puts it, "trivial at best and corny at worst." But her experiments have repeatedly shown that keeping a gratitude journal — writing down a handful of things we feel fortunate for at the end of most days — can create measurable differences in self-reported happiness. Perhaps your neighbor put out your trash, or you noticed a beautiful spider's web covered with hoarfrost on your morning commute. Perhaps the plane landed safely or your mother made a recovery. For Lyubomirsky, gratitude is defined as "counting one's blessings." And her work has helped the gratitude journal become a cornerstone in the positive psychology movement, which aims, in the words of one of its founders, psychologist Martin Seligman, to make "the lives of relatively untroubled people happier."

One of the things that seems most to appeal about gratitude is the way it short-circuits those feelings of inadequacy and desire, which drive consumerism. Not only is consciously "counting one's blessings" free to do, it also makes us happy with what we've already got, seeming to protect us from the voraciousness of the free market. This, however, hasn't always been the case.

* * *

How does EUPHORIA create a stock-market bubble, or PANIC lead to economic depression? Emotions are an important element of the modern study of economics, but we aren't the first to think about the link between finance and feeling. The eighteenth-century philosopher and economist Adam Smith, one of the architects of modern capitalism, is usually remembered for his phrase the "invisible hand" of the free market. But he also wrote a lot about what he called "the affections of the heart," and saw the two as inexorably linked. For Smith, gratitude was central to a prosperous society: he believed it was not simply a pleasant feeling of being thankful for good things, but also created a desire to reward the people who help us. To feel grateful is to want "to recompense, to remunerate, to return good for good received," he wrote. He also thought these effects radiated outwards through a process of sympathetic resonance (*see:* EMPATHY). So even if you'd only witnessed generosity, your own gratitude buds would be tickled and you'd find yourself compelled to repay the kindness by doing a good deed for someone else.*

In the nineteenth and twentieth centuries, philosophers and psychologists who wrote about emotions seem to have been far less interested in being appreciative. There is no full discussion of it in Darwin's *The Expression of the Emotions in Man and Animals*, and it rarely appears on the many lists of emotions drawn up by psychologists over the next hundred years. Those who did write about gratitude seem to have regarded it as more burdensome. For instance in 1929 the Harvard-based psychologist William McDougall pointed out that it could provoke complex and contradictory feelings, not just awe and

---

* Smith's theory would certainly make sense to the indigenous Utku of Canada, who don't distinguish between feeling kindness and gratitude, but use one word for both: *hatuq*. In positive psychology literature, a version of this phenomenon is called "paying it forward."

admiration, but also ENVY, RESENTMENT and EMBARRASSMENT. (Some of these discomforts are identified in other languages. In Japanese we find *arigata-meiwaku*, which roughly translates as a favor someone insists on performing for you, even though you don't want them to, and when it backfires, convention dictates you must be grateful anyway. See also OIME and GRENG JAI.) While Smith had imagined gratitude as a horizontal network of exchanges, McDougall regarded it much like pity. He thought it fixed hierarchies of power, with benefactors bestowing riches on needy recipients, and the latter made painfully aware of their inability to help themselves. For this reason, McDougall thought gratitude produced "negative self-feeling," or what nowadays would be called "low self-esteem" (*see:* FEELING GOOD [about yourself]). It seems that for McDougall, writing on the eve of the Great Depression, balancing the desire for autonomy and the value of self-sufficiency with any acknowledgment of need was a troubled and complex business.

After years in the psychological wilderness, gratitude is back in vogue. But not as it was before. The sense of obligation that Smith saw as so crucial to gratitude, and which seemed so burdensome for early-twentieth-century psychologists, has been dropped. Instead, Lyubomirsky and her colleagues define gratitude as "a sense of wonder, thankfulness and appreciation" (WONDER in particular is intriguing here, as it suggests a lack of agency by any other human). Gratitude's primary value is placed in maximizing good feelings for the grateful individual. Counting one's blessings, according to Lyubomirsky, reliably increases positive mood because it helps us extract enjoyment from any situation. By stopping us taking things for granted, it also counters the effects of what psychologists call "hedonic adaptation," the all-too-familiar experience of growing used to the good things in our lives, so that they end up making us less happy. Practicing gratitude makes life's inevitable disappointments easier to bear by helping us search for the upside, and lessens the pain of envy and greed by encouraging us to value what we already have (rather than becoming preoccupied by what we think we need). All of these are impressive positive results of keeping a gratitude journal. But it's curious that there's only one brief mention in Lyubomirsky's study about the reciprocity that Adam Smith was so interested in: "The expression of gratitude is also said to stimulate moral behavior such as helping, and to help build social bonds." Feeling grateful might be quietly transformative. But it seems perhaps we have learned to value it less for its ability to ignite compassion than for how good it makes us feel about ourselves.

See also: COMPASSION; WARM GLOW.

GRENG JAI

In Thailand, *greng jai* (sometimes transliterated *kreng jai*) is the feeling of being reluctant to accept another's offer of help because of the bother it would cause them.

See also: GRATITUDE; *OIME.*

GRIEF

Her legs were amputated by a blow to the back of the knees. Scars to her back show attempts made to break the torso in two. The stone sculpture, which dates from between 26,000 and 22,000 years ago, depicts a heavily pregnant woman and was certainly destroyed intentionally. Why did she meet such a violent end?

One theory, advanced by the archaeologists who found her: the sculpture was smashed following the death in childbirth of the woman depicted. Violent ANGER as part of the agony of grief is something we all recognize. There's no reason to suppose our ancient ancestors didn't recognize it too.

Of all the emotions, the confusion and pain of grief is so personal, so unfathomable, that to speak of "it" is wrongheaded. "It's useless for me to describe," confessed Lemony Snicket in *The Bad Beginning*, which starts with the death of the children's father, "how terrible Violet, Klaus, and even Sunny felt in the time that followed....If you have ever lost someone very important to you, then you already know how it feels, and if you haven't, you cannot possibly imagine it." It's not just that other people's grief can be hard to appreciate. If we are lucky, profound grief is something we'll experience only a few times in our lives, so it is nearly always disorienting, an emotion for which we get very little rehearsal.

We may feel a debilitating SHOCK: "For a week, almost without speaking, they went about like sleepwalkers through a universe of grief," wrote Gabriel García Márquez. We may, as did the poet Emily Dickinson, experience a peculiar stiffness as if all emotion has been suspended (*see*: FORMAL FEELING, A). There may be RELIEF that a terminally ill loved one is no longer suffering, GRATITUDE that our burden of care is over (there may be SHAME at these feelings too). Or else, we may find ourselves cracking bawdy jokes at the wake, or dissolving into inappropriate giggles during the cremation. For many, this bubbling over of emotion is a common, if sometimes a little frowned-upon, release. Among the Koma of northern Ghana, however, it is actually customary for grandchildren to laugh and joke during a grandparent's funeral, mocking the funeral rites — even attempting to kidnap the corpse — their behavior providing a moment of "comic relief" for the mourners.

But in truth, grief has barely started by the time the funeral is over. In *A Grief Observed*, C. S. Lewis wrote of his "permanently provisional feeling" in the months and even years following his wife Joy's death. Restlessness prevailed. "It doesn't seem worth starting anything. I can't settle down. I yawn, I fidget, I smoke too much." There are so many habits and expectations to be rearranged when a part of our life is kicked out from under us. Lewis hung around, waiting for something to happen. "I am beginning to understand why grief feels like suspense," he wrote.

It is a suspense, however, studded with harder feelings too: the anger and bitterness at having been abandoned; the way we might reproach ourselves for our contribution to our own misery — *if only we hadn't cared*, we think, or at least not *so much*. And then the sorrow is set off again by a sharp stab of remembrance. A flicker of a shadow in the mirror, an imaginary key heard in the door, the expectation of a phone call that never comes. In grief, the loss of the loved one haunts us. For the two years after the painter Chagall's wife Bella died, his canvases bear a repeated theme. The artist swims out from the murky background, hand in hand with his ghostly bride: he supports her flagging form, she reaches out to him. If others see such absorption as a stubborn refusal to "move on," even those in its grip might wonder if such ghosts will ever find rest.

Yet, for an emotion that can feel so peculiar and lonely, grief has conventions and scripts, whose stage directions, different from culture to culture, tell us how we should mourn. According to the *Sahih Muslim*, a book of precepts or *hadith* attributed to the Prophet Muhammad, collected in the ninth century, grievers may weep for their lost ones.

Convulsive shrieking, slapping one's cheeks and tearing at one's clothes, however, are strictly forbidden, for "the deceased is tortured in his grave for the wailing done over him." By contrast, in the weeks following the death of Princess Diana in 1997, British reserve was seen to give way to a new era of emotionality. Some of those who remained unmoved, or saw the displays of teddy bears and flowers as mawkish and sentimental, reported feeling self-conscious, as if theirs was a stubborn refusal to mourn. It was all, as Jacqueline Rose has put it, "so coercive — grief not only had to be done but had to be seen to be done."

Such rituals do not only dictate how we should experience grief, but also how it ought to progress. We commonly refer to different "stages" of grief. Denial comes first. Then anger, bargaining, depression. Finally comes acceptance — which is often glossed as "closure." This "five stages of grief" model can be traced back to work carried out by the Swiss psychiatrist Elisabeth Kübler-Ross in the late 1960s, although her research was based not on grief felt at the loss of another, but on her observations of people facing their own terminal diagnoses (see: EUPHORIA). We might increasingly wonder how helpful this rigid model with its progression of stages may be (Kübler-Ross herself wasn't so sure). For many of us, moving from denial to acceptance involves more of an ebb and flow. For others, grief is an endlessly circular process, something we never really "get over" — even if we do learn to live with it. "You don't come out of it like a train coming out of a tunnel," Julian Barnes has written. "You come out of it as a gull comes out of an oil-slick. You are tarred and feathered for life."

See also: SADNESS.

GUILT

Imagine Oscar Madison's predicament in Gene Saks's film of Neil Simon's Broadway hit *The Odd Couple*. He takes in his friend Felix Unger, who is suicidal after his wife threw him out. But Felix nags and whines, polishes and dusts. He insists on using coasters! He makes life intolerable for "divorced, broke and sloppy" Oscar, who snaps, and throws Felix out all over again. But Felix retaliates in his own infuriating style:

> **Felix:** *Remember what happens to me is your responsibility. Let it be on your head. [...] Either I'll come back and get the rest of my clothes, or someone else will.*
> **Oscar:** *[blocks the door] You are not going any place until you take it back.*
> **Felix:** *Take what back?*
> **Oscar:** *Let it be on your head. What the hell is that? The Curse of the Cat People?*

Felix's revenge infects Oscar with one of the twentieth century's most dreaded afflictions. Guilt. It's the modern-day curse.

It should be a simple transaction: we transgress the rules, and are left clammy with SHAME, fretting our punishment and experiencing the CLAUSTROPHOBIA that comes with visions of reproachful looks and veiled criticisms. This is an intolerable experience, so we rush to repair the damage. If we are lucky, our attempts to atone — clumsy or otherwise — are accepted and the guilt fades (or we might even experience the heady rush of absolution!). Compensation is at the heart of the matter. From the Old English *gylt*, usually traced back to the German, *geld* (to pay), guilt demands we repay our debts.

131

It's never that straightforward, though. Moral codes aren't universally agreed upon, much less the behavior required to make amends. In the past, guilt didn't appear on lists of the passions; the word described a fact of responsibility not a feeling—although contrition and REMORSE always figured highly. In our own age what counts for guilt is a ghoulish sort of stagnant feeling, a queasy sensation that keeps reappearing. It is haunted by a fear that it is excessive or unwarranted, so that we can speak of feeling guilty, yet in the same breath imply we've done nothing wrong (it's more a plea: "Don't make me feel guilty!" or an attempt to elicit reassurance: "But I feel so guilty!"). At the other extreme, there are those guilty feelings that can't be worked off because it's not clear how they've been earned in the first place—the guilt of being the sole survivor of a car crash, or receiving an award when your equally talented colleague did not; the guilt felt by children who imagine themselves responsible for their parents' divorce. Some people take too little responsibility, others too much. And some have responsibility foisted upon them.

This modern vision of guilt as an emotion capable of being distorted and passed around emerged at the very end of the nineteenth century in the writings of Sigmund Freud. It begins with a dream Freud had in 1895. That day, Freud had received a visit from his friend "Otto" (the doctor Oscar Rie), during which they had discussed a patient they were both treating named Irma. Freud had diagnosed Irma with hysteria, believing her symptoms psychosomatic, yet Rie had reported that Irma was making no progress. This left Freud uncomfortable. Was Otto insinuating his psychoanalytic treatment was not working? That night, Freud dreamt he was examining Irma's throat and found it full of white scabs. He suspected an infection caused by an injection Otto had given Irma. Clearly, Otto had been negligent, and not sterilized the needle properly. When Freud woke the following morning, he realized that in his dream, he had assigned the blame for Irma's failure to recover to Otto. He saw that his dream was a form of "wish fulfilment," and only then did he realize that somewhere in his mind he feared that Irma's ongoing illness was his own fault.

In Freud's later writing, guilt emerges as a feeling we are desperate to avoid—a feeling that the ego, so busy defending its fantasies of perfection, is always prone to hide. He argued that guilt itself is located in the superego, a punishing part of the conscious mind that has internalized the authoritarian—and often exaggerated—demands of one's parents, and replays them over and over again (Freud called this inner monologue the "voice of the Father"). Freud, then, took up the old model in which guilty feelings were the consequence of transgressing a powerful authority, but, in place of God, put the ogres of childhood fantasy: angry parents. As we grow older, our desires may compel us to reject or disobey this oppressive voice. Yet, it still breaks through, often in peculiar dreams, or in an excessive need to make amends. One of the behaviors it gives rise to is the practice of sending other people on guilt trips. We may be so eager to avoid the unpleasant demands of our own guilty consciences that we shift the blame onto other people, especially those we resent for pointing out our shortcomings—in Freud's case, his friend Otto; in Felix's, his friend Oscar.

Freud's ideas gave rise to a new way of talking about guilt. "A guilt complex" became a voguish diagnosis in the early twentieth century, and one that still shapes discussions of depression and anxiety. As Alfred Adler, one of the early architects of psychotherapy, put it in 1927, the guilt complex is a "combination of self-accusation and repentance," which "strives for superiority on the useless side of life." Even guilt itself, he wrote, with its whirring obsession with self-punishment and blame, was a kind of avoidance, a retreat from being useful: we feel guilty instead of doing what we know we ought. This Adlerian vision of guilt as a kind of stagnation or inhibition has been very influential in the modern self-help movement, in which guilt is seen to be the enemy of productivity, but also of personal fulfilment. When you're so busy trying to atone for guilt you haven't really earned, it's hard to find much room to enjoy life.

So can guilt ever be made to vanish? For Oscar and Felix in *The Odd Couple*, an impromptu ceremony captures the fantastical element of the desire for absolution. At the story's happy conclusion, Felix waves his hand over Oscar's head ("I remove the curse"), and Oscar curtsies in thanks. Oscar might mock it, calling Felix the "Wicked Witch of the North." But for a man who's spent the night driving round New York fearing the worst and fretting about the guilt that will inevitably haunt him, there is certainly relief on his face.

Most of us don't have this chance to return to the source of the guilt and ask to have it removed. Perhaps those responsible are dead. Perhaps we're too humiliated to make contact with them. Perhaps we fear a conversation would not bring a resolution anyway, but open old wounds and create even more guilt for the future. So instead, we find ourselves stuck in interminable conversations with ourselves. Was it our fault? Or theirs? Should we take more responsibility? Or less? Are the people we feel guilty about sort of angels ("How could I hurt her? She's never been anything but kind to me!") or shameless manipulators with impossible standards?

The truth usually lies somewhere between. Cognitive behavioral therapists suggest visualizing this balance by drawing a "responsibility pie chart," to demonstrate to yourself the extent of your responsibility for bad things happening. What is clear, however, is that though we may walk through into a therapist's office hoping for a priestlike absolution, or that they'll excise our uncomfortable feelings of guilt with a ceremonial wave of the hand, a good therapist will set their sights far lower. It's less a question of making guilt vanish than adjusting to its background hum.

For other emotions linked to debts *see:* ANTICIPATION; GRATITUDE.

See also: REMORSE.

H

HAN

According to the novelist Park Kyung-ni, the emotion *han* is deep within the Korean psyche. Attributing it to the country's long history of being colonized, she characterizes it as a collective acceptance of suffering combined with a quiet yearning for things to be different — and even a grim determination to wait until they are. "If we lived in paradise," she wrote, "there would be no tears, no separation, no hunger, no waiting, no suffering, no oppression, no war, no death. We would no longer need either hope or despair.... We Koreans call these hopes *han*.... I think it means both sadness and hope at the same time."

See also: LITOST.

HAPPINESS

He sits with his young daughter in a café near his city home in Sweden. She drinks lemonade, and asks questions about the sky and skeletons. He concocts fanciful answers. "Even if the feeling of happiness this gives me is not exactly a whirlwind but closer to satisfaction or serenity," writes the Norwegian author Karl Ove Knausgaard in his autobiographical *A Death in the Family,* "it is happiness all the same." But moments later, the old worries curl up around him and settle into their familiar routine. Is this all he is capable of, he wonders, this pale version of other people's exhilaration? If he hadn't chosen books over family, might his life be jingling with joyful laughter too? "We could have lived somewhere in Norway, gone skiing and skating in winter... and boating in the summer, swimming, fishing, camping... we could have been blissfully happy."

This is the thing about happiness. As the philosopher J. S. Mill put it, "Ask yourself whether you are happy, and you cease to be so."

Today happiness is a multimillion-dollar industry. Self-help books encourage us to track our emotional temperatures. There are apps that turn the effects of certain foods and exercise on our moods into graphs. This increased self-consciousness about happiness occurs on an international level too — since 2003, the EU has measured and compared the happiness of people in its member states, a barometer watched eagerly by politicians as happiness has become a shorthand for that other ubiquitous goal: "well-being" (*see:* EUPHORIA). And the stakes are high. You'd be hard-pressed to find a book on happiness that does not cite studies showing that a cheerful disposition makes you live longer, or that people who enjoy life are more successful at work. If something seems important, we want to control it; if we want to control it, we measure it first. But in our hurry to weigh and measure that most subjective, fleeting experience of happiness, we might be forgetting to check first what we're putting at risk.

The idea that happiness can be generated and controlled is relatively new. From the Old Scandinavian root *happ* (chance, luck or success), before the eighteenth century, the word "happiness" most often described feeling that God's grace was shining upon you. Though it described a state of pleasure and CONTENTMENT, it was connected more with good fortune than engineering: happiness was there when things went your way — a happy fit, a happy coincidence, happenstance. This link between happiness and chance seems to have subtly shifted around the eighteenth century. In 1776, Thomas Jefferson stated in the US Declaration of Independence that every citizen had a right to "life, liberty, and the pursuit of happiness," as if happiness was something that could be sought out, even captured. Meanwhile in Britain, making happiness one's life's ambition seemed to have become such a fashion among the educated elite that wits such as Alexander Pope ridiculed it: "O Happiness! Our Being's End and Aim! Good, Pleasure, Ease, Content! Whate'er thy name." Some historians have even linked the rise of interest in happiness with improvements in the period's dentistry and the subsequent willingness to flash a toothy smile (*see*: SATISFACTION).

The imperative to be happy was swiftly followed by attempts to parse and catalogue it — so as to work out what might stand in its way. One of the best-known examples remains the hyperrational philosophy Utilitarianism. In 1789, the same year as the American Constitution came into force, the British lawyer Jeremy Bentham put together his unintentionally louche-sounding "catalogue of pleasures." Arguing a moral decision was one that increased the total sum of happiness in the world, Bentham made an inventory of things that — according to an eighteenth-century male lawyer — produced pleasure (things like skill, power and piety), and things that caused pain (such as privation, awkwardness or having a bad reputation). If you needed to make a decision, for example whether to visit your elderly parents, you simply had to dig out your catalogue, tot up which pleasures the visit would produce, subtract the total pains it would create, and then if the pleasures outweighed the pains, you could plan your journey.

Bentham's felicific calculus has come in for quite a beating from philosophers over the years. What brings people pleasure is clearly subjective — and as a guide to behavior, it is clearly problematic, making no effort to exclude actions that are morally bad (such as torturing a cat) but that might conceivably bring someone pleasure. But was he so different from today's proponents of "the new science of happiness" whose goal it is to maximize happiness, and dedicate reams of paper to working out precisely how? One person who had a particularly violent reaction to Bentham's happiness agenda was his prodigy and godson, J. S. Mill. Raised on strict Utilitarian principles, Mill was able to spew out hedonic calculations along with his Latin verse aged nine. The only problem was that he wasn't happy at all. In his late teens, Mill experienced a period of prolonged mental anguish and melancholy. After his recovery (which he said was achieved by reading poetry), Mill came to believe that happiness was rather more complicated than Bentham had understood. Even if happiness was the goal of life, he believed it couldn't be pursued or grasped. Like luring a cat to sit on your knee, happiness had to be ignored rather than cajoled: he saw it as a shy sort of feeling, sneaking up when you least expected it. "Let your self-consciousness, your scrutiny, your self-interrogation exhaust themselves on [a different goal]," wrote Mill. "And if otherwise fortunately circumstanced you will inhale happiness with the air you breathe, without... putting it to flight by fatal questioning."

When someone asks if you are (a) very happy (b) quite happy or (c) not very happy at all, you might wonder whether all this "fatal questioning" might be putting us on the brink of a mental crisis of our own. Perhaps the idea that happiness is obligatory, or that we are entitled to it, or that we have failed if we can't achieve it, can make us anxious and dissatisfied. One response to this dilemma is to reject the term altogether. Many contemporary philosophers and psychologists, including Martin Seligman, one of the founders of the positive psychology movement, prefer to use the term "flourishing" rather than happiness. A rough equivalent of the Greek term *eudaimonia*, the most influential account of which appears in Aristotle's *Nicomachean Ethics*, it suggests that a meaningful life is full of pains as well as privileges. While happiness has come to be associated with a generalized positive feeling, to lead a flourishing life demands that you practice courage (which can be difficult), and compassion (which can lead to sadness felt on behalf of others), and deferred gratification (which means you might have to experience the frustrations of waiting). Leading a flourishing life might not be all swimming and fishing in Norway, but it might be, according to Seligman and his colleagues at least, a more satisfying way to live.

Perhaps the greatest consequence of replacing talk of happiness with talk of flourishing will be to restore happiness to its rightful place as an emotion. Over the last 200 or so years, happiness has come to mean more of a condition or state, of the happily-ever-after variety, than a temporary feeling that, like all emotions, may sometimes be present and sometimes not. It may not even always be desirable: as researchers in the *Journal of Happiness Studies* recently showed, not all cultures automatically desire happiness — their interviews suggested that New Zealanders are particularly nervous about happiness, subscribing to a "what goes up must come down" attitude; while in the Ifaluk culture of Micronesia, expressing happiness is "associated with showing off, over-excitement and failure at doing one's duties" (*see:* SMUGNESS). If we reclaim our happiness as a feeling that is as fleeting as surprise, or as complex as grief, we may find many shades and contradictions. Because while for one person, happiness is an uninhibited groan of contentment, and for the next an eerie sense of everything being "just right," and for a third a fluttering of EXCITEMENT, it's also an emotion that feels dangerous, and daring, a "perfect bridge over the crocodiles."

See also: CHEERFULNESS; JOY.

HATRED

A burned-out car. Police sirens wail in the distance. Abdel, a local youth from the *banlieues*, the poor, multiethnic housing estates on the outskirts of Paris, has been beaten unconscious by neo-Nazi policemen. In the unrest that follows, three friends roam the streets. Vinz and Said fantasize about taking revenge, while Hubert, the quietest and most thoughtful of the group, fears the effect of tit-for-tat violence. "Hatred breeds hatred," he says, summing up the CLAUSTROPHOBIA of their world, where hatred sticks in the throat, and then flares up in flashes of cruel and apparently random violence.

Mathieu Kassovitz's film *La Haine* (*Hate*, 1995) was released at a moment when hatred loomed large in the headlines. It was in the 1980s that American journalists first coined the term "hate crime" to describe a wave of attacks on people of marginalized groups, their homes and places of worship. In the 1990s, western Europe experienced a similar outbreak of violence fueled by intolerance and prejudice, and introduced its own "hate-crime legislation."

We might, when we get indignant or exasperated in day-to-day life, say that we hate something or someone ("I hate it when people leave food wrappers on the street!" "I hate people who don't replace the photocopy paper!"). We might speak of the line between love and hate being paper thin. Or the frustration that drives the "I hate yous" hurled in rage by teenagers at their parents (and sometimes right back at them too). But in the last twenty years the meaning of the word "hate" has also narrowed, describing a prejudiced attitude that can be objectifiably quantified, and even argued over in court. Hate has become a state of mind — part emotion, part attitude — for which it is now possible to be held legally accountable.

* * *

The link between hatred and prejudice is not entirely new. It can be traced back to Aristotle, who thought hatred was very different from an emotion such as ANGER or RAGE. Anger, he argued, was a painful, short-lived desire to inflict pain on an individual. Hatred, in contrast, was a more abstract concept, always felt toward groups of people, or types. "For if we believe that someone is *a certain kind of person,* we hate him," he wrote. It was also "incurable," and annihilation was its goal. So rather than simply wanting to hurt or argue with the person we hate, we wish simply that "he should cease to exist." One crucial difference between Aristotle's definition of hatred and our own, however, is that Aristotle believed hatred was an ethical emotion, one we are naturally predisposed to feel toward people who behave unjustly. "Everyone hates a thief and an informer," was Aristotle's example. It was for this reason that, according to Aristotle, hatred was not painful to experience. In fact, it left one with a rather pleasing feeling of moral superiority (*see also:* INDIGNATION).

The current language of "hate crimes" has flipped Aristotle's definition on its head. Rather than hating transgressors, it is the haters themselves who are now thought morally deficient. Many legal scholars think the word "hate" has no real place in the rhetoric of crimes motivated by prejudice. The word "hate" does not appear in the legislation itself; more neutral words like "bias" are used. It is governments, police spokespeople and journalists who speak of "hate-fueled violence." Some legal scholars say this emotive language is deliberately inflammatory, making it possible to give tougher sentences: it is, it seems, easier to punish someone for their irrational emotions than for their beliefs. Those who defend the terminology argue that it's precisely the emotional content of a prejudice that is most harmful. It's the hatred that is toxic and that inflames the desire to humiliate victims, not some reasoned belief. Can you punish an emotion? Is there even an objective measure for it? Hatred may be the focus of legal and philosophical argument, but in the meantime, for many, it has become a byword for all that is contemptible, intolerant and antisocial in our societies.

And yet, and yet...Even the most polite and respectful among us do continue to enjoy a certain kind of hating. The Victorian critic William Hazlitt characterized hatred as a rather refined enjoyment. In his essay "On the Pleasure of Hating," he describes how a shared hatred gives a frisson of camaraderie at a dinner party, bringing people together in the shared delight of tearing others apart.* Hatred draws clear lines around oneself in opposition to the disliked object, he wrote. It gives one a feeling of being temporarily much greater than we actually are. "We grow tired of everything," wrote Hazlitt, "but turning others into ridicule, and congratulating ourselves on their defects."

For more on emotions in court see: JEALOUSY; CONTEMPT.

See also: SMUGNESS.

HEEBIE-JEEBIES, THE

Like the jitters or the willies, the heebie-jeebies are a feeling of ghoulish apprehension.

See also: DREAD.

---

* Kingsley Amis realized he had met a kindred spirit in Philip Larkin when he discovered he also defined a bore as someone who "when he sees an unusual car in the street GOES OVER AND HAS A LOOK AT IT."

HIRAETH

The Welsh word *hiraeth* (pronounced *hir*-aeth, with a rolled *r*, and the second syllable rising) describes a deeply felt connection to one's homeland, and casts its woods and hills in an almost magical glow. But *hiraeth* is not a feeling of coziness or comfort. It is rather a yearning feeling, flecked with suspense, as if something is about to be lost and never recovered. Perhaps their long history of English occupation explains why the Welsh are so familiar with this combination of love for a homeland and sense of its vulnerability — the emotion now plays a key role in the rhetoric of Welshness, celebrated by its national poets and tourist brochures alike (*see also:* SAUDADE). Today, *hiraeth* is most commonly associated with émigrés, experienced most sharply on returning home — and knowing the time to leave again will come all too soon.

See also: HOMEFULNESS; HOMESICKNESS.

HOARD, THE URGE TO

One yellow sock, a lipstick-stained scarf, a handful of rose petals pressed in a bundle of letters. These are just some of the relics collected by the playwright, poet and Sapphic seductress-extraordinaire Mercedes de Acosta, mementos of her love affairs with some of Hollywood's leading ladies of the 1920s and '30s, among them Isadora Duncan, Marlene Dietrich, and Greta Garbo.

The ephemera we carefully store away for our future selves to inspect, sniff and trace with our fingertips are the repositories of our inner lives. "For it is invariably oneself that one collects," wrote the philosopher Jean Baudrillard. In the detritus of her often secretive love affairs, de Acosta amassed evidence of belonging, of loving and, more importantly, of having been loved herself.

If human relationships can be difficult and demanding, objects can be intensely reassuring. From old vinyl to pairs of shoes, gathering treasures around us can bolster our sense of self in an unpredictable world, giving a feeling of permanence, even achievement, and communicating who we want to be to the world. Jealousy and possessiveness can be part of the picture too, as when we covet a brand of sunglasses for status, or delight in hoarding trinkets so our rivals can't have them. As we grow up, collections may be monuments to our connoisseurship and give us important-sounding names — a deltiologist collects postcards, a numismatist specializes in coins, a collector of teddy bears is an arctophilist (*see also*: CURIOSITY). Such collections might testify to a need for order and control, but there is also something deliciously perverse about taking pleasure in a task that can never be completed.

Might the urge to hoard be outside of our control? Psychotherapists often link the desire to hold on to wealth at all costs to past experiences of deprivation and traumatic loss. Before he goes to bed each night, the famously parsimonious Ebenezer Scrooge of Charles Dickens's *A Christmas Carol* inspects his takings. As the psychoanalyst Stephen Grosz has suggested, this meagre obsession with profit and loss can be read as a kind of grief gone wrong, a compensation for the tragic early death of his mother and subsequent emotional neglect by his father. It is an attempt, through the acquisition of money, to retrieve the irretrievable.

At its most extreme, the urge to hoard can have catastrophic consequences. Towering columns of old newspapers and rooms piled dangerously high with unusable vacuum cleaners can present real hazards for those trying to live there. But though they may be risky, these collections are not without meaning. For some it's a way of barricading against a hostile world, for others, a way of fending off loneliness by filling the vertiginously empty space (*see:* PEUR DES ESPACES). Most of all, those objects that might seem like "old trash" to an outsider can have real emotional resonance for the collector. Even the misanthropic Muppet Oscar the Grouch knew this. He lists the useless items in the trash can he calls home: a broken clock, an abandoned umbrella, a rusted trombone. But though he hates everyone, and won't even risk talking to the other Muppets in case another Grouch sees him, Oscar's carefully amassed trash offers the warmth of emotional connection in a hostile world. Among his precious collection is a sneaker, worn through, that his mother gave him on the day he was born: he loves it, because it is trash.

See also: CURIOSITY; NOSTALGIA.

HOMEFULNESS

In July 1841 the poet John Clare escaped from High Beech asylum in Epping Forest to get home to his beloved Mary Joyce. For three and a half days he walked with broken shoes, sleeping in porches and eating grass from the roadside. In the letter he wrote to Mary Joyce describing the journey, he recalled that, exhausted and foot-foundered, he reached the point where the road forks to Peterborough and was suddenly restored: "I felt myself in home's way." The writer Iain Sinclair, who retraced Clare's journey, used the little-known word "homefulness" to describe Clare's feeling at this point. He became full with the feeling of home.

The feeling of homefulness surges up at the end of less arduous travels too: it's there when we step off the airplane after a holiday or turn into our road with shopping bags bulging. It spreads through us with its combination of relief, belonging and the satisfaction of a long journey's end.

But we all know that home has got less to do with a place than with the people there. In his madness, Clare had forgotten that Mary Joyce was long dead. When the woman who was actually Clare's wife found the bedraggled poet stumbling along the road to Northborough, she took him to their house and tried to school him in the ways of the sane. And there, he wrote, he realized there was nothing more lonely than feeling "homeless at home."

See also: HOMESICKNESS; WANDERLUST.

HOMESICKNESS

. I long for home, and to see the day of returning.
— *Homer, The Odyssey*

At Camp Bastion, the enormous military base that was sprawled across the Iraqi desert between 2006 and 2014, tents were festooned with family photographs, and parcels of homemade cookies arrived daily. Aching for home, as military psychologists are well aware, is as much a reality for soldiers as for six-year-olds at slumber parties. With symptoms including panic attacks, night terrors, dejection and concentration lapses, military psychologists recognize that homesickness in the desert can have fatal consequences.

There is a long history of military men pining for home. Odysseus, hero of the Trojan War, sits each day on the shore of Calypso's idyllic island where he has been trapped for seven years. The hero stares out into the wine-dark sea, great heaving tears staining his cheeks. It's only because Athena intervenes that he is cured of his stagnation, and builds a raft to sail back to Ithaca. In the early seventeenth century, the debilitating effects of being away from home attracted the attention of medical experts, when an epidemic of fatal homesickness broke out among Swiss mercenary soldiers (*see:* NOSTALGIA). By the American Civil War the idea that homesickness could create serious illness was so widely accepted that Union army bands were forbidden to play "Home Sweet Home" in case it exacerbated the problem. It was a reason for discharge, since its only known cure was to be sent home. By the end of the Civil War, at least five thousand men had been diagnosed with nostalgia, and seventy-four had died of the wasting and occasional suicides and desertion it caused.

By the end of the First World War, the idea that you could die from homesickness had faded into obscurity. Homesickness no longer appears on the list of medical grounds for discharge from the army. Adventurousness might be part of what makes men and women enlist ("Join the army, see the world!"), and talk of homesickness might seem at odds with the macho military culture, but psychologists also recognize that prolonged distance from home can help create the conditions for serious illnesses like depression and anxiety to thrive. It is expected camaraderie will pull most people through loneliness. But families and friends are also urged to write to help keep up morale, and Skype and Facebook are described in guides for the families of deployed soldiers as "lifelines." And unlike the early Swiss mercenaries who were banned from singing their national anthems for fear of triggering an attack of nostalgia, in Camp Bastion glimpses of home were built into the fabric of the army base, with franchises offering the sweet bite of a Burger King bun or the tang of a cup of PG Tips. Selling a brief moment of substitute HOMEFULNESS, these small triggers of home salve an ache for familiarity — and keep the desire for loved ones from tipping over into despair.

Homesickness is part of civilian life too, although perhaps it is less readily spoken about. Sufferers have described their fear of being seen as a bit of a wimp. Some psychologists have even called it a taboo, arguing that this further isolation exacerbates already painful feelings and depression-like symptoms. In part, historians believe that the status of homesickness began to decline at the turn of the twentieth century, around the same time that nostalgia began to fade as a medical diagnosis. At this time, a rapidly expanding railway network across Europe was giving people unprecedented opportunities for travel, while a burgeoning tourist industry promoted the desire for movement as both a natural instinct and a celebration of human curiosity (*see:* WANDERLUST). In this atmosphere, to be away from home and not actively enjoying the experience might well have seemed rather a personal failing.

However, in recent years, there are signs that homesickness may be beginning to be taken more seriously again. In part this is due to the many novels and films of the last twenty years that articulate the experiences of migration. For some, it is punishingly cruel: Edward Said, himself in exile from his Palestinian home, called it an "unhealable rift forced between a human being and a native place...the crippling sorrow of estrangement." Others experience life as a permanent outsider with more conflicted feelings, a new kind of homesickness. Never quite belonging to one place or another, in one breath they ache for some distinctive taste or smell of home, and in the next confess that they couldn't imagine — no, not even imagine! — going back there to *live.* As anyone who's ever gone home for Christmas knows, occasional bouts of sickening for home must be set against the reminder that going back might just make you very sick of it indeed.

See also: DÉPAYSEMENT; NOSTALGIA; HOMEFULNESS.

HOPEFULNESS

On Internet message boards, the dominant attitude was upbeat. People exhorted her to "stay positive." There were even pop-up ads when she clicked on to health advice pages, selling a teddy bear named "Hope." When the sociologist Barbara Ehrenreich was diagnosed with breast cancer, she was surprised how coercive she found the insistence — by medical professionals, by her friends — to keep optimistic. Her subsequent account *Smile or Die* describes how the positive psychology movement has co-opted hope. The movement insists on a link between a positive attitude about the future and improved well-being. Hope and optimism have become synonymous, both emerging as positive sorts of expectation that can, and should, be manufactured at will.

Can hope really press back the march of cancerous cells? There's probably no harm in finding out. Except that Ehrenreich also cites a 2004 study that suggests that continually looking on the bright side of a cancer diagnosis — "benefit finding," one of the techniques advised to stay positive — did not always help patients. A hopeful outlook might make life easier for carers and family members, but many of the patients themselves found it alienating, even guilt-inducing, and it prevented them from acknowledging and expressing the FEAR and ANGER they also felt.

In fact, the idea that hope can be constructed, and constructive, seems at odds with what hopefulness so often feels like. With its flickering promise of a happier ending, hope provides a glimpse of relief in a desperate situation. It can, much later and in retrospect, leave us feeling cheated and let down. We speak of our hopes being "dashed" or "destroyed." Sometimes we even lay the blame on our own shoulders, as if our foolishness, and not chance, caused the pain: "I should never have hoped" (*see also:* REGRET). In truth, hope is always a leap into the unknown. It's there when expectations fade, when we have reached the end of all we can practically do, and are left quietly willing, perhaps praying, for the best to happen — but knowing, too, that the worst might instead. To feel hope is to acknowledge how little control we have. It makes us vulnerable and strengthens at the same time. What is peculiar, then, is the idea that hope can be marshaled and put to work. As Ehrenreich found, we can't just conjure hope. Optimism may be a cognitive stance, a habit of mind we just might be able to train ourselves to fall into. But hope is an emotion, and our experience of it is not entirely in our hands.

See also: DREAD; VULNERABILITY.

HUFF, IN A

The weather plays an important role in our emotions. A muggy day oppresses, a glance of sun on a cold morning lifts the spirits. Rain, clouds and especially storms provide a storehouse of metaphors for teasing out hard-to-describe feelings.

Since the mid-eighteenth century, feeling huft or huffed — and later being "in a huff" — was to be swept up into a windy swell of petulance as a result of a real or imagined insult. Feeling puffed up with PRIDE and ANGER was an important part of it.

However, being in a huff, or something like it, stretches back much earlier than that. The ancients took for granted that the winds affected the insides of the body. The word for breath and wind in classical Greek was the same — *pneuma* — and the winds that whipped about the body were assumed also to travel through it, sustaining life but also raising whirlwind passions within. In Sophocles's tragic rendering of the ancient Greek myth of Oedipus, when Antigone learns that her brother's body is to be left to rot outside the city walls in punishment for being a traitor, she is swept up in righteous fury and demands the proper rites. The ill winds were no mere metaphor: "bitter-blowing winds from Thrace" had first brought death to

Oedipus's family, writes Sophocles, and now they whip up his daughter's defiant passions too:

> *From the same winds still*
> *These blasts of soul hold her*

For more on the relationship between wind and emotions, *see:* MELANCHOLY.

For other weather-related emotions *see also:* ACEDIA; GEZELLIGHEID.

HUMBLE, FEELING

See HUMILIATION (it's much more important).

HUMILIATION

In the spring of 1863 Abraham Lincoln officially proclaimed that April 30 should be set aside as "a day of national humiliation." America, he argued, had become "intoxicated with unbroken success...too self-sufficient...too proud." The civil war that had blighted the country had been God's retribution for this arrogance. Only penitence, prayer, fasting, all leading to a collective feeling of humility, could prevent similar atrocities in the future.

Few of us want to be humiliated on a regular basis — unless, of course, we're requesting it and latex is involved. For the most part, humiliation is something unwelcome, something punishing rather than actively sought out. Like EMBARRASSMENT, humiliation happens before an audience; like SHAME, it makes us want to shrink from sight. But crucial to humiliation is its CLAUSTROPHOBIA, its sense of being trapped in a diminished position. It's there when we are the object of another's CONTEMPT: as in the playground when all the other kids laugh at your braces, or when you discover that everyone in the village knew about the affair before you. So when we speak of feeling humiliated today, we are speaking of a feeling of degradation — and often the start of a cycle of dangerous retaliation. For Kofi Annan, Nobel Peace Laureate and former UN Secretary-General, "all the cruel and brutal things, even genocide, start with the humiliation of one individual." It's for this reason that humiliation has been called the "nuclear bomb of the emotions," fueling a desire for revenge at all costs (*see also:* RESENTMENT).

This is all a long way from Lincoln's "day of national humiliation" with its call to curb dangerous pride. At the time of his speech, ritualized acts of penance were encouraged in some Christian communities, and might involve wandering the streets wearing sackcloth and ashes, or eating morsels of stale bread while others dined on lavish meats. Humiliation made you modest and respectful, and reminded you of your final destination — in Latin, the prefix of *humiliare* (to humble) is *humus* (earth). The practice of humility is still part of many of the world's religions. For example, the Jains' commitment to extreme nonviolence is a daily reminder of their equality with all living things. To give up our elevated status isn't always easy, though. It was perhaps through bitter experience of trying to impose humility on his brethren that the twelfth-century French abbot Bernard of Clairvaux warned: "Many of those who are humiliated are not humble. Some react... with anger."

It's hard to pinpoint the exact moment humiliation and humility began to part ways. "All human beings are born free and equal in dignity and rights," is Article 1 of the 1948 Universal Declaration of Human Rights, and "No one shall be subjected to torture or to cruel, inhuman or degrading treatment or punishment" is Article 5. Deliberately humiliating a prisoner is seen as a gross violation of their human rights. But a request that we be humble? There is one sense in which this is back in vogue, though it still provokes anger. The demand made by some bloggers and on Twitter to "check your privilege" has been criticized for stifling debate. But perhaps in the spirit in which it was originally intended, it is a call to practice a kind of humility, to recognize the ways in which our own happiness and achievements can be the result of class, family, gender, race, global position and luck, as much as hard work. This is not the oily, ingratiating humility of Charles Dickens's Uriah Heep (he's "ever so 'umble") or the false modesty of a celebrity, but a recognition that the good things in our lives are not always all of our own making, but depend on other people too.

See also: GRATITUDE; *MALU.*

HUNGER

The doughnuts glisten. The smell of coffee — two sugars — curls under your nostrils. All you can think of is the crisp, salty snap of a pretzel, or the lemony tang of an ice cream. In the West, we are in the grip of an obesity crisis, and it is the lure of tempting foods that is most often blamed. But our emotions also lead us to overeat. Fat can be accumulated through a desire to defend oneself — against other people's demands, against being treated frivolously or only as a sexual object. Food can be a way of bolstering ourselves against an oncoming stress, or showing some kindness to ourselves when we feel overlooked.

The Baining people of Papua New Guinea take for granted this close connection between physical hunger and the desire to be cared about properly. So much so that their word for hunger (*anaingi* or aisicki) means both a rumbling belly and the fear that you have been abandoned. In a society where food binds people together, creating friends out of strangers, to be left hungry is to also feel stranded and alone.

For the Baining, hearing birdsong is a poignant symbol for hunger, and is an enduring theme of their songs. It is only when the babble of human voices recedes, and the noises of the forest creep in, that hunger is felt at its most intense:

The ambiowa [a bird] cries for me
The ambiowa cries for me
She cries for me and hunger is killing me
My parents and all of them, they went to Malasait

See also: AWUMBUK; LONELINESS.

HWYL

Literally the word for a boat sail, *hwyl* is a wonderfully onomatopoeic Welsh word (pronounced *who*-eel) that means exuberance or excitement, as if clipping along on a gust of wind. Used to describe flashes of inspiration, a singer's gusto or raised spirits at parties, *hwyl* is also the word for goodbye:

Hwyl fawr — Go with the wind in your sails.

See also: JOY.

IJIRASHII

Every night, somewhere in America, a parent is reading their child one of the country's most famous of children's tales: *The Little Engine That Could*. It's a 1930s story of an intrepid shunting engine. When the bigger locomotives refuse to pull a long train over the mountain, the little one gives it a try, chuffing, "I think I can I think I can I think I can," as it slowly grinds up the slope. The little engine's ultimate success is supposed to instill optimism (*see*: HOPEFULNESS) and COURAGE in children. Many of the adults reading it at their children's bedside, however, might just feel a catch in their throat.

The sensation of being touched or moved on seeing the little guy overcome an obstacle or do something praiseworthy has a name in Japanese: *ijirashii* (pronounced e-jee-ra-*she*). It's the feeling we might get watching an athlete, against all the odds, cross the finishing line, or on hearing of a homeless person handing in a lost wallet. Perhaps it might even make us weep, as did Churchill on seeing the dignity and resilience of the poorest Londoners during the Blitz. In some cultures its combination of pathos and vicarious pride might be dismissed as sentimentality. In Japan, however, this feeling is celebrated, considered the appropriate response to witnessing the immense fortitude of those who at first seemed weak and vulnerable.

* * *

For other reasons to weep, *see:* RELIEF.

For another example of vicarious pride, *see:* NAKHES.

IKTSUARPOK

When visitors are due to arrive, a fidgety feeling sprouts up. We might keep glancing out of the window. Or pause midsentence, thinking we've heard the sound of a car. Among the Inuit this antsy anticipation, causing them to scan the frozen Arctic plains for approaching sleds, is called *iktsuarpok* (pronounced *eet*-so-*ahr*-pohk).

Might the restless checking of our phones, waiting for an expected response to a text or comment on a status update, be a type of *iktsuarpok?* Constantly refreshing the screen to see if a hoped-for e-mail has arrived can feel like one of the most distracting aspects of contemporary life. Perhaps it's not the technology, however, as much as our desire for human contact in an isolating world, that is to blame.

For another feeling provoked by visitors to remote places, *see:* AWUMBUK.

See also: LONELINESS; RINGXIETY.

ILINX

There's a peculiar exhilaration in the idea of picking up a pile of loose papers, opening the window and flinging them all out. Or intentionally smashing a delicate china cup. Or in standing on a kitchen chair and tipping out a bag of marbles so that they crash, bounce and roll across the floor. According to the twentieth-century French sociologist Roger Caillois, the "strange excitement" of wanton destruction was one way of experiencing the feeling he named *ilinx* (from the Greek word for whirlpool). He defined *ilinx* as a "voluptuous panic," a sensation of spinning, falling and losing control — the sort of feeling that riding a roller coaster might produce. Callois traced *ilinx* back to the practices of ancient mystics who by whirling and dancing hoped to induce rapturous trance states and glimpse alternative realities (*see:* ECSTASY). Today, even succumbing to the urge to create a minor chaos by kicking over the office recycling bin should give you a mild hit.

See also: DÉPAYSEMENT.

IMPATIENCE

It was the upholsterer of the cardiologists Meyer Friedman and Ray Rosenman who first noticed how the chairs in the waiting room were fraying. There were strange patches of threadbare material on the arms (suggesting drumming fingers) and on the front edges (suggesting antsy wriggling), while the back was as good as new. No one relaxed in these chairs. No one reclined while they waited. The patients, mostly successful, busy middle-aged men with blocked arteries and soaring blood pressures, were intolerant of the unproductive time they were made to spend there.

It was these waiting-room chairs that eventually led Friedman and Rosenman to the idea of the Type A personality in the 1950s. Type As were patients whose sense of "time urgency" was a constant pressure.

They were always successful, ambitious and (literally) on the edges of their seats — and they were also much more likely to die of heart disease or strokes. (As it turned out, it was an immensely unhelpful nomenclature: despite the disadvantages, everyone ended up wanting to be Type A, especially the Type As...)

With its rushing and tutting and issuing of impossible demands, impatience might seem an inevitable consequence of our time-poor, irritant-rich lifestyles. The line in the supermarket or the stubborn elevator that won't arrive however many times we jab at the button seems only to mock the insistent demand that we use each moment productively, and live life to the max. Truth is, waiting has never been easy. This is why, wrote Friedrich Nietzsche, "the greatest poets did not disdain to make the inability to wait the theme of their poetry." From the Latin *pati* (to suffer), impatience means a "failure to bear suffering." It was a cliché in the sixteenth century as now that time slows down when we are waiting ("Time goes on crutches till love have all his rites," says the smug Claudio in *Much Ado About Nothing*). But as everyone knows, this hiatus before our desires are granted can also be a delicious kind of torment (*see:* ANTICIPATION).

The impatient patients in Friedman and Rosenman's office remind us that a "failure to bear suffering" is more than being unable to wait for gratification in this instant-hit world of ours. Those men in Friedman and Rosenman's waiting room were struggling with the part of themselves forced to be *the* patient — the weakened, uncertain part, temporarily required to cede control to another's expertise and schedule, and brought face to face with the UNCERTAINTY of their future in the process.

See also: ANTICIPATION; TORSCHLUSSPANIK.

INDIGNATION

She stood in the crowded hall, amid the astonished faces. Outside there were protests, and inside, a man spoke from a small wooden stage, eloquent with fury. He was, recalled the abolitionist and leading figure of the woman's rights movement Elizabeth Cady Stanton in 1895, "majestic in his wrath … wit, satire and indignation."

A former slave and entirely self-educated, the antislavery campaigner Frederick Douglass was perhaps the most important African American in nineteenth-century public life. His oratory stirred audiences on both sides of the Atlantic, his anger no blind RAGE but haughty, righteous and channeled into dignified debate. Douglass's crusade was not just an expression of the injustice done to him, but a response to the deliberate cruelties inflicted on all enslaved black men and women.

One might expect a history of indignation to be a tale of people rising up against oppression. Not so. In fact, in the earliest discussions of this emotion, indignation was more commonly felt by the elite busily protecting their advantage. Aristotle thought indignation — he called it *nemesan* — was most strongly roused when people below us in the social pecking order broke the rules. Thus the gods were most susceptible, their indignation fanned each time a mortal tried to seek out divine secrets or gain supernatural powers. For Aristotle, then, indignation was the outrage felt when someone else receives an honor they haven't properly earned, or wheedles an unfair advantage, toppling us in the process. In the seventeenth century, the political philosopher Thomas Hobbes offered a slightly different definition of indignation, as the "anger for great Hurt done to another" caused not by accident but by intentional "Injury." Indignation was most felt when others showed a contempt for justice, and in particular when the relatives or favorites of those in authority disregarded the rules. Indignation, wrote Hobbes, "carrieth Men, not only against the Actors and Authors of injustice, but against all Power that is likely to protect them." It was perhaps from Hobbes's definition that indignation became most closely linked not to those in authority, but to the disesteemed who live beneath it.

Today's political theorists hold indignation up as an emotion capable of playing a key role in political life. Unlike anger, which can overpower or alienate, undermining the principles of democratic debate, indignation comes, as it were, with an RSVP attached. Think of the pyrotechnics of the speech delivered by Julia Gillard before the Australian parliament in 2012. In an oration that made no attempt to disguise her personal outrage, she charged her opponent with a series of misogynistic comments. The speech expressed anger at the same time as it demanded a response. As footage of that day's events spread rapidly over social media, discussions and comments showed another side to indignation: there were hints of excitement, triumph, even glee (*see also*: CONTEMPT; SCHADENFREUDE). In his autobiography, Frederick Douglass described similar feelings on first reading the abolitionist newspaper *Liberator*, which he subsequently edited. Its "scathing denunciations of slaveholders — its faithful exposures of slavery — and its powerful attacks upon the upholders of the institution — sent a thrill of joy through my soul."

See also: INSULTED, FEELING; RESENTMENT.

INHABITIVENESS

The urge to settle permanently in one place can be felt as a quiet hum. Even wanting to stay in a job can bring some often much-needed reassurance and stability to our lives — even if we might worry we're being a bit unambitious. According to the phrenologists, a group of early-Victorian scientists who thought they could detect personality traits by examining a person's skull (*see:* PHILOPROGENITIVENESS), the urge to find a groove and stay in it was innate. They called it "inhabitiveness" and defined it as a "love of continuity, of endurance, of sameness, of permanency of occupation."

"Inhabitiveness" itself lacked staying power, and by the middle of the century had faded into obscurity, partly because phrenology itself lost scientific credibility. But perhaps this loss of a word for the pleasures of permanency can also be traced to the enthusiastic response — by some Victorians at least — to the ideals of dynamism and mobility, and the idea that humans are not only hardwired to nest, but also to discover and roam too (*see:* WANDERLUST).

For other ways of feeling at home *see:* HIRAETH; HOMEFULNESS; HOMESICKNESS.

INSULTED, FEELING

*You listen to me now.... The man don't hit hard ... he's slow,
he has no skill, no footwork, he's awkward.... This man have two
chances, slim and none.*
— *Muhammad Ali, interview with David Frost, 1974*

It's thanks to Muhammad Ali that trash talking has become such an important part of the art of boxing. His virtuoso insults flung at the world heavyweight champion George Foreman — in the buildup to the "Rumble in the Jungle" — are legendary. Today, months ahead of the fight, boxers continue to trade insults on social media, the wittier the better. And the fact they see it as an effective way of wrong-footing their opponents tells us a lot about what being insulted feels like.

Mostly, it's a SHOCK: a sudden and bewildering drop in status. One moment you feel respected, the next — bam! — an object of ridicule and CONTEMPT. It's the insults that come out of nowhere that sting most, leaving us flustered and confused.* But that's not only why boxers dole out the insults. They don't want just to rattle their opponents. They want to rile them too, make them blind furious till they're snapping out the punches, and tiring themselves on the way.

Boxing might look like a sport fueled by rage and aggression. But as any boxer will tell you, whoever is seeing red when the bell rings — because they're swept up in the fury of being put down — will be the fighter you can expect to lose.

See also: BEWILDERMENT.

IRRITATION

Their aim was to irritate the audience out of complacency. To scandalize them, to make them agitated and annoyed. "On the Pleasures of Being Booed" was the name of one of their manifestos. Another suggested sprinkling itching powder on the seats in the auditorium, till all the spectators were red with scratching. The Futurists, a group of anarchic artists based in Italy in the first decades of the twentieth century, wanted to set themselves among their audiences like a bag of fleas, to agitate them until something — anything — happened.

---

* It's this baffled feeling that causes what the French call *l'esprit d'escalier*, or "staircase wit": thinking of the killer retort only when you've left the scene of the argument and are on the stairs on the way out.

* * *

Irritation is a state of friction. Being rubbed the wrong way can be a cutaneous or emotional experience, but neither language nor experience distinguishes between the two. The rash that chafes against a shirt collar might create feelings of agitation and claustrophobia. The irritation that starts with frustrated and blocked desires leaves one uncomfortable in one's own skin and unable to bear the touch of another. When we are irritated, any kind of contact or intimacy seems too much, too *bristling*. Even the solicitous glance of a loved one may make us recoil.

Irritation might seem a rather minor feeling. It's common enough, of course, and to be caught under its fingernails is very unpleasant, but it lacks the gravitas of INDIGNATION or the glory of RAGE. The Futurists, however, did not see it as inconsequential. Far from it. Their work revived a much older sense, in which irritation was purposeful and important.

In the sixteenth century, to irritate simply meant to stir or incite to action. Courage might be irritated. Love, too. So might body parts. In 1753 the German physiologist Albrecht von Haller discovered that when he placed a candle on the hind leg of a decapitated frog, the leg twitched and moved away from the flame. Haller concluded that the power of instinctive movement lay in the "irritable muscles" themselves, rather than in some incorporeal "soul." His theory was disproved ten years later when Robert Whytt provided the first evidence of the simple spinal reflex, one of the key points around which the nineteenth century's secular account of emotional life was framed.

At around this same time the word "irritation" began to be used to describe a vexed feeling, usually brought on by someone else's contemptuous behavior: new taxes were irritating, so were people who reneged on deals. Irritation wasn't always justified, though. A hundred or so years later, some Victorian physicians saw a tendency to be easily irritated as the mark of weakness, attributing it to those they thought were congenitally oversensitive: alcoholics, the insane, artists and dandies. During the American Civil War irritability was further characterized as an emotion of excess and distortions, when doctors described a new condition they called "irritable heart." Its symptoms included palpitations, chest pains, fatigue and shortness of breath: all very similar to heart disease, but without physiological cause. The "irritable heart" suffered by soldiers was explained as a psychosomatic illness, neurasthenia — roughly equivalent to modern-day "stress." In medical literature, then, the easily irritated were those most susceptible to the fantasies of the fearful mind: those who had lost control.

Today this link between irritation and irrationality is alive and well. According to the American Psychiatric Association's *Diagnostic and Statistical Manual of Mental Disorders* (or *DSM*), being quickly roused to annoyance is a symptom of anxiety, sleep deprivation, and depression. It's there when we feel frayed around the edges, thin-skinned, stressed, or hungover. Fractious because a loved one is trying to help us, exasperated by the photocopier refusing to cooperate — conventional wisdom teaches us not to take our own and other people's irritations too seriously, in case by scratching we aggravate them further.

The Futurists thought irritation neither irrational nor meaningless. They saw it as an experiment in vulnerability, a gateway experience that made their audiences susceptible to more powerful emotions — like remorse, shame and anger. For them, getting irritated was a lofty endeavor. For the rest of us, a slammed door or a sharp remark will be as good as it gets.

See also: PIQUE, a fit of.

JEALOUSY

You have to trust. That's what you tell yourself. When you see the e-mail hurriedly closed down and a bright smile — is it too bright? — on the face. Or the door quietly closed on a phone call. Or a mumbled explanation for returning late and crumpled. You have to trust. But it catches you in a daydream. The flirtation, the kiss. The plans. Shake the thoughts from your head. Breathe. Stare at the bag (don't open it!). Stare at the coat (don't search it!).

We may dedicate a lifetime to avoiding the effects of jealousy. It is mostly a private agony, doing its work furtively in the dark. We know that suspicious accusations will make us look feeble and petty. They could cause problems that don't exist. So jealousy makes itself known in other ways, in little spites, muttered grievances. A slammed-down dinner plate. A refusal to have sex. It is even a motive for murder. His voice scratchy on the record player, John Lennon sings of losing control, of not meaning to hurt anyone: he's just a jealous guy.

Jealousy is the suspicion of a rival, a DREAD of being supplanted. In contrast to ENVY, which is defined as wanting a *thing* one does not have, jealousy involves the fear of losing a *person* or their affections to someone else. It is triangular: me (the victim), you (the traitor) and the other (the thief). Such treacheries are all the more painful for the feeling of having been discarded (*see:* HUMILIATION). It is this threat that makes jealousy so inflammatory — and intimacy such a risk.

We are heirs to a strange and conflicted history of jealousy, one that has almost entirely been shaped by gender. While a jealous woman has been historically regarded as meagre and quibbling (she is never the heroine, only ever the bitter rival to true love), a jealous man belongs to a more honorable tradition. In the courtly romances of medieval Europe, the idea of love became inseparable from the yearning felt for an unobtainable lover — unobtainable usually because he or she was married. The lover's jealousy inflamed desire, and was its true signatory: "He who is not jealous can not love," wrote the twelfth-century author Andreas Capellanus in *The Art of Courtly Love*, continuing, "jealousy, and therefore love, are increased when one suspects his beloved." But jealousy did not only thrive in the hearts of interlopers. Husbands could feel it too. Writers of medical treatises in this period described jealousy as the ANGER felt when one's honor had been compromised. It heated the body and energized it for the necessary violent retaliation (they believed men, who were thought to be already hotter than cold, damp women, would experience more powerful surges of jealous rage). In Shakespeare's *Othello* (1603/4), its tragic hero absorbs these complex attitudes to jealousy: Othello, the original "jealous guy," is at once hero and victim, an archetype of love's brutal possessiveness, and a man turned to "poison," his soul eaten away by the "green-eyed monster." Of course, the real victim is Desdemona, but somehow Othello's plight always seems more grand — as well as more poignant since it is without real cause.

The idea that jealousy was the natural response to infidelity was consolidated in that period, through a series of legal cases. In 1670 John Manning walked in on his wife with another man, and then beat him to death with a jointed stool. He was sentenced to be branded on the hand — though the court "directed the executioner to burn him gently, because there could not be greater provocation than this." Thirty-seven years later, a judge declared jealousy to be "the rage of a man, and adultery the highest invasion of property." With jealousy defined as a natural masculine emotion inevitably experienced when one's property (i.e., wife) was threatened, murder was downgraded to manslaughter, and some men who had murdered in jealous rages were acquitted altogether.

By the end of the nineteenth century the notion that jealousy was "the rage of a man" was further bolstered by a scientific-sounding claim that jealousy was an evolved impulse latent in all men — rather than women. Evolutionary psychologists still claim, based on little actual evidence, that in prehistoric societies jealousy became a "hardwired" trait so that men could protect their genetic inheritance, whereas women didn't need to. This idea is especially problematic because it first emerged among Victorian scientists who believed that some people — such as non-Europeans and the poor — were lower down the evolutionary ladder and therefore closer to their more "primitive" emotions like jealousy and RAGE.

The echoes of this conflicted history could still be heard in the 1970s, when many artists and activists questioned the link between possessiveness and love. Lennon was not alone in describing the dangers of being overtaken by a strange instinct of jealousy around this time. Feminist campaigners contested legal practices that saw women as property and excused the men who killed them. Some who experimented with alternative relationship structures questioned the idea that jealousy was natural at all (*see:* COMPERSION). Jealousy began to seem both petty and alarming rather than grand and justified. According to French philosopher Roland Barthes, writing *A Lover's Discourse* in the late 1970s, it gave rise to a quadruple dilemma. The jealous man suffers "four times over," he writes. "Because I am jealous, because I blame myself for being so, because I fear that my jealousy will wound the other, because I allow myself to be subject to a banality: I suffer from being excluded, from being aggressive, from being crazy and from being common."

Since 2009 in Britain — some twenty years after Canada and Australia — the provocation of infidelity is no longer admitted as a defense in court, although research has shown that judges still show sympathy to murderers who cite jealousy as a cause for the "red mist" that led them to kill. Of course, as long as people have relationships and wandering eyes, jealousy will be a fact of life. But what we can change is its unique status as an emotion that justifies violence. Not least because it's not just men who succumb to the low hum of suspicious thoughts, causing them to search e-mails and discover clues to their loved one's infidelities in the most innocent of glances. We all do.

For more on emotions and law *see:* HATRED and VENGEFULNESS.

See also: ENVY; INSULTED, feeling.

JOY

Although Bertha Young was thirty, she still had moments like this when she wanted to run instead of walk, to take dancing steps on and off the pavement, to bowl a hoop, to throw something up in the air and catch it again, or to stand still and laugh at — nothing.
— Katherine Mansfield, "Bliss"

Your breathing becomes shallow, as if the lungs are being squeezed. Your eyes gleam. The cheek muscles stretch the face into the hugest of smiles. There's the urge to fling open the arms, to clap them together. To sweep up the nearest person in a dance. The knees may buckle, there may be tears too. Either way, joy can be a kind of violence, and always a SURPRISE. From the Old French *joie* (a jewel), this is an emotion that dazzles us into submission. It feels, as Katherine Mansfield put it, "as though you'd suddenly swallowed a bright piece of that late afternoon sun and it burned in your bosom, sending out a little shower of sparks into every particle, into every finger and toe."

One of the great definitions of joy comes from the seventeenth-century philosopher Baruch Spinoza. A Jew banished from his religious community for believing that God could be found in trees and stones, he was condemned to wander around Holland without a family or home, earning a meagre living as a lens grinder. Believing the stories of our lives were fundamentally beyond our control, Spinoza linked joyfulness to the accidental and unforeseen. It surges up when something is better than we can possibly have imagined. "Joy is pleasure accompanied by the idea of something past, which has had an issue *beyond our hope*."

The philosophers of the eighteenth century were more interested in happiness than the joy of serendipity and accidents. They spoke of happiness as something one should orchestrate for oneself, something to be pursued consciously (*see*: HAPPINESS). Against this backdrop, joy managed to protect its links with the unforeseen, still something discovered rather than made. Humility, gratitude and wonder — rather than pride and satisfaction — were its closest companions. Joy also meant sexual pleasures, not least those that arrived unannounced: in the Earl of Rochester's poem "The Imperfect Enjoyment," a premature ejaculation earns the unforgettable nickname "the clammy joys."

What Bertha experiences in Katherine Mansfield's story is an accidental transcendence — which, we discover later, may be the efflorescence of a nervous illness, what today we'd call mania. The late nineteenth century saw all kinds of positive mental states turned into psychiatric diagnoses (*see*: EUPHORIA; ECSTASY), but Mansfield studiously avoids the terminology in the way she describes Bertha's mood. Instead, she leaves the experience uncategorized, intent on capturing some of joy's giddy unpredictability, its refusal to sit quietly within the bounds of the ordinary and understood. The flipside of this, of course, is how quickly joy vanishes. Its fleeting nature was what most fascinated Virginia Woolf about this emotion, a writer not remembered for her capacity for joy. Yet, her diaries reveal she stumbled across it in the most unexpected places — in a well-polished door knocker, in the gleam of a window. She gave this experience of a sudden, revelatory joy to Mrs. Ramsay in her 1927 novel *To the Lighthouse*. Amid the banality of serving a family dinner, Mrs. Ramsay is struck by a feeling that life is gloriously perfect. Everything seems possible and right:

> She hovered like a hawk suspended, like a flag floated in an element of joy which filled every nerve of her body.
> ... "This cannot last," she thought.

See also: HOPEFULNESS; VULNERABILITY.

KAUKOKAIPUU

Sometimes we feel homesick for a place, even though we've never been there. Sometimes we just want to be anywhere but here. From *kauko*—faraway, and *kaipuu*—a yearning, the Finns know the craving for a distant land as *kaukokaipuu* (pronounced *ka-oo-ko-kye*-poh).

See also: DISAPPEAR, the desire to; HOMESICKNESS; WANDERLUST.

LIGET

It's the fire in the chili and the rush in the rapids. It makes tempers fly, and drives people to work harder. Among the Ilongot, a tribe of around 3,500 headhunters living amid the gloomy jungles of Nueva Vizcaya in the Philippines, *liget* is the name given to an angry energy that fuels not just human bodies but inanimate ones too.

The American anthropologist Michelle Rosaldo first brought *liget* to the attention of Western readers in the 1980s. More used to thinking about ANGER as a negative emotion, Rosaldo was struck by *liget's* sense of optimism and vitality. *Liget* is certainly capable of stirring up pointless arguments and violent outbursts. But more usually it excites and motivates — makes people plant more seeds than their neighbors, or stay out hunting for longer. "If it were not for *liget*," the Ilongot told Rosaldo, "we'd have no life, we'd never work."

In 1981 Rosaldo died from an accidental fall during her fieldwork. Her husband, Renato, also an anthropologist living with the Ilongot, described his response to her death in terms of a further aspect of *liget*: the rage of grief. The *liget* that follows a bereavement is thought to spur the Ilongot on to a headhunting expedition. It's when they hunt down an enemy tribesman, decapitate him and fling the severed head into the jungle, that the Ilongot believe they can achieve catharsis, and banish the pain of their loss. In this way, the *liget* that grips the Ilongot when their loved ones die is a furious desire to act and avenge, and so wrest back some control.

See also: GRIEF; RELIEF; RIVALRY.

LITOST

Litost (pronounced *lee*-tost) is a Czech emotion that is notoriously hard to translate, though according to the Czech author Milan Kundera it's hard to imagine "how anyone can understand the human soul without it." It describes the whorl of SHAME, RESENTMENT and fury that lifts us off our feet when we realize another has made us feel wretched. Unlike the lingering hatred of grudges or the inertia of sorrow, *litost* is active. As Kundera puts it in his *Book of Laughter and Forgetting* (1979), *litost* is "a state of torment caused by the sudden sight of one's own misery…like a two-stroke motor. First comes a feeling of torment, then the desire for revenge."

What makes *litost*'s vengefulness even more distinctive is that it is often perversely self-destructive. Sometimes getting even is easy: if we're demeaned by someone weaker than us, a cutting remark might be enough to restore our wounded PRIDE. When we're hurt by those wielding power over us, however, revenge must take circuitous routes. In Kundera's novel, a child is belittled by his foul-tempered violin teacher for playing the wrong note. Blinded by *litost*, the child concocts an ingenious plan: he deliberately repeats the mistake until the teacher becomes so enraged that he snaps and throws the pupil out of the window. "As he falls," writes Kundera, "the child is delighted by the thought that the nasty teacher will be charged with murder." The goal of *litost* is to make the other person "look as miserable as oneself," your attention so focused on punishing your tormentor that your own destruction becomes far less important (*see also:* ABHIMAN).

Though he believes *litost* is an emotion common to us all, Kundera does suggest it emerged as a distinct concept in Czech language because of Bohemia's beleaguered history of oppression. When, in 1968, Czechoslovakia briefly broke free from Soviet rule, Russian tanks invaded Prague. Any outsider would have said an attempt to resist the Russian army was futile. Yet the graffiti on the city walls spoke of unyielding resistance: "We don't want compromise, we want victory!" This was, writes Kundera, "*litost* talking," a mixture of pride and perversity through which, even in defeat, Prague's residents could feel a mixture of defiance and hope.

See also: VENGEFULNESS.

LONELINESS

The passengers climb in and then out again, never making eye contact. They leave a purse or a magazine, occasionally spunk, on the seats. In Martin Scorsese's film *Taxi Driver*, it's the lack of human connection in bustling New York that fosters Vietnam veteran Travis Bickle's contempt of the city. He might not call himself lonely, but he knows he is alone, and it is this total alienation that ultimately provokes him to act out his violent fantasies.

There is a long tradition of suspicion toward those who choose to be alone. "Solitude produces ignorance, renders us barbarous, feeds revenge, disposes us to envy, creates witches, dispeoples the world," wrote John Evelyn in 1667, parodying his culture's excessive fear of the intentionally solitary. Worse still, it encouraged "mental fornication" and masturbation, since the lonely "have...no *passions*, save the *sensual*."

In the final decade of the eighteenth century, however, a rebellious group of Romantic poets and painters deliberately sought loneliness out. Today we might speak of loneliness as a feeling of dejection and disconnection, something we should avoid. What the Romantics called loneliness, however, described the physical condition of solitude, which could give rise to transformative spiritual and emotional experiences. In Caspar David Friedrich's paintings *Mountain Landscape with Rainbow* (1809) or *Wanderer Above the Sea of Fog* (1818), a solitary walker is absorbed by the vast craggy wilderness around him, his back turned to the viewer and in that way, isolating us too. Being "lonely" in nature, he surrenders to feelings of awe, wonder and terror at its sublime majesty — all the petty worries of ordinary life, and even a sense of an independent self, ebbing away.

In the middle of the nineteenth century, however, the meaning of the word "loneliness" shifted from a description of physical isolation, to depict a painful emotion. Characters in Victorian novels, uprooted from family and friends and forced to seek their fortunes in grimy, overpopulated cities, began to talk of their dejection. It was the first time people described themselves as "being lonely" while still being surrounded by other people. By the end of the century, the modern metropolis, rather than the countryside, had become firmly installed as the main source of loneliness, with sociologists such as Georg Simmel calling cities places of "utter lonesomeness" that produced a "feeling that the individual is surrounded on all sides by closed doors." Travis's isolation in *Taxi Driver* is a direct inheritance of this *fin de siècle* nervousness about the anonymous and rapacious city breeding the isolation that gives way to madness and DESPAIR.

In twenty-first-century Britain, politicians decry an "epidemic of loneliness" in our cities. Rising divorce rates, people choosing to live alone, increased use of computers, the supposed solipsism of our culture and a lack of community identity are all blamed. Social media, thought to replace in-person interaction with a poor digital substitute (it's hard to make eye contact even on Skype or FaceTime), is held up as a problem, so that according to a survey by the Mental Health Foundation, it's the young, rather than the elderly, who are most at risk of loneliness. And the stakes are high: in one study by the Chicago neuroscientist John Cacioppo, loneliness was found to increase the odds of an early death by 14 percent, twice the risk for obesity. His study found that extended isolation from family and friends caused feelings of desolation and APATHY. These feelings bring an urge to self-medicate with the warm hug of TV and sugary foods, causing other health problems; but they might also lead to mental health issues such as depression, anxiety and dementia too.

But there is another kind of loneliness, which neither the Romantics nor the neuroscientists talk about. It is the dark, cramped feeling of not being understood that can strike even in the midst of a busy family life. In Japan, *hikikomori* (withdrawn) is a condition afflicting mainly adolescent, middle-class males. The psychiatrist Tamaki Saito, who coined the term, believes around seven hundred thousand men in Japan suffer from it. The precise causes are not quite understood, but feeling alienated from your family's values or the career path they have planned for you seems to trigger a desire for sufferers to isolate themselves entirely, cutting off all contact with family and friends and refusing to leave their room, sometimes for several years. In *hikikomori*, then, one feeling of loneliness gives way to another. And reminds us that loneliness is not only a feeling that comes when we are lost in the great wilderness of the world, but also comes when we feel hemmed in by its expectations and desires.

See also: CLAUSTROPHOBIA.

LOVE

Oh that you were [here], my Susie, we need not talk at all, our eyes would whisper for us, and your hand fast in mine, we would not ask for language.
— Emily Dickinson, Letter to Susan Gilbert, June 11, 1852

Is there anything left to say about love? Reams of poetry and songs, libraries' worth of philosophy, are dedicated to trying to express it, to understand and define it. The very volume of words tells us not only how much there is to say on the subject, but also how little can be said with any certainty. This elusive emotion is so important that it grabs all the attention, and so slippery that no single attempt successfully pins it down. Even at the end of a life lived happily together, it's hard to say what precisely love is. We know it's there — it must be, how else can we still put each other first, survive the quarrels and the missed connections? Something keeps us together, but what, and how, and why? ... The words wriggle away just as we are trying to form them and what's left is a defeated shrug and a smile. "It's just, you know..." We may wax lyrical about love, but we are often struck dumb by it too.

Love's speechlessness begins when love itself does. One of the oldest examples of love's inarticulacy is a fragment of verse left by the poet Sappho, who lived around the sixth century BCE on the Greek island of Lesbos. Through the burble of conversation and singing, she glimpses her beloved across the room, talking — and she falls into a kind of paralysis:

My lost voice stutters,
Refuses to come back
Because my tongue is shattered.

This shattered tongue is not a throwaway metaphor, but part of a whole sequence of physiological responses that Sappho describes. A fire rages through her internal organs, sending smoke into her brain so that "all that I see is hazy / My ears all thunder / Sweat comes quickly, and a shiver / Vibrates my frame." Overcome with the intensity of her love, she says, "I am not far off dying."

"We ought to move on from this hackneyed expression," wrote the novelist Stendhal of the feeling of being lost in amazement or reduced to silence on setting eyes on our beloved for the first time. But, he admitted "it does happen." In the early medical tradition, not only were symptoms like Sappho's real, they were also part of a much bigger medical problem of lovesickness. It was the Arab physicians of the tenth and eleventh centuries who first formalized the concept of love-sickness as part of unrequited or as-yet-unconsummated love and a manifestation of the illness melancholia (see: MELANCHOLY). Ibn-Sina (his name is often Latinized as Avicenna) called the passion al-'ishq, or illishi, and described it as a kind of yearning for a perfect union with the beloved — both spiritual and sexual (see also: VIRAHA). Though it was a noble desire, over time its intensity could cause melancholic vapors to rise into the brain, bringing mental confusion and making the lover forgetful and withdrawn. When he or she did talk, the words tumbled out, inchoate and senseless.

The idea of speechlessness continued to haunt the European lovers, particularly those of the courtly love tradition emerging in the century that followed, perhaps one of the biggest outpourings of love in Western culture, and one to which many of our own conventions of love can be traced. The Occitan troubadours — and their female equivalents, the trobairitz — of the eleventh and twelfth centuries sang of their yearning for unobtainable lovers. Sometimes it was through the wordlessness of a breath that their love could find its best expression. Sighs were part of the language of the yearning lover. So too were yawns, a testament not to BOREDOM, or even CONTEMPT, as they would be today, but to long devotion, as one troubadour described in the late twelfth century:

> Day-long I stretch, all times, like a bird preening,
> And yawn for her.

These silences are still part of the way we love. You can hear them in the tacit forgivenesses, in the squeeze of a hand, or a shared look across a room. You can hear them in the word "love" itself. We know this word carries immense meaning. We accept it as an objective mark of another's feelings, even an incantation that seems to shift our relationships up a step (or knocks them back). "I love you," says Alec in *Brief Encounter*. "Please don't," replies Laura, knowing things can never be the same again. Yet, for all its gravitational pull, it so often fails to signify completely, needing to be qualified or explained. "I love you but I'm not in love with you"; "I love you, but not in that way." Can "love" really be so capacious and purposeful all at the same time? And can it really be the same emotion behind the tickling and flirtations as well as the cozy comforts of setting up a shared life? Is the feeling we experience toward a loyal friend over the years truly the same as the quiet hum between partners of five decades or more or the emotion felt for Gods or parents or pets? It feels as though we have lost some words along the way —

And have left only this one syllable — vague, open to misinterpretation. So we shrug our shoulders.

It's just, you know…*love*.

See also: DESIRE.

MALU

However accomplished, funny, loved or successful we may be, most of us feel flustered in the presence of someone we hold in high esteem. The brain fogs over. Sentences come out scrambled. We may feel the overwhelming urge to run away. In English there is no precise word to describe this excruciating feeling ("HUMILIATION" and "shyness" are too broad; "starstruck" is closer, but still not quite right). Among the people of Dusun Baguk in Indonesia, it's called *malu*.

Malu is all too recognizable: the sudden experience of feeling constricted, inferior and awkward around people of higher status than us. You might be experiencing *malu* if you clam up before your partner's parents, or a conversation with a former headmistress leaves you staring at the floor and sweating. For Indonesians, *malu* is, in itself, nothing to be ashamed of. Many in the West would feel a profound self-hatred if the CEO asked our opinion, and we blushed and gabbled in reply. However, in Indonesia *malu* is an appropriate response. Taught to children from a very young age, outward expressions of *malu* govern manners and appropriate conduct. In any given situation, *malu* distinguishes those who command respect from those who bestow it. Like saying "thank you," signs of *malu* oil the wheels of social life and reinforce hierarchies of power. There's even a small plant that

Indonesians believe exhibits *malu* tendencies — the indigenous putri malu (*Mimosa pudica*), the leaves of which droop and shrivel up when touched.

Like all emotions, the coy deference of *malu* can also be put on. When a person pretends to be too reticent and nervous to ask for something they secretly covet, they are *malu-malu kucing* — literally: behaving like a shy cat.

See also: EMBARRASSMENT.

MAN

Start a new career. Move to a different city. Become a writer or learn to play the violin. It's often hard to explain *why* we might want to do something like this, only that we experience a profound calling, a feeling that we must. In Hindi, this deepest level of wanting is called *man* (pronounced *mun*, it is a colloquial shortening of the Hindi word for intention or longing, *manorath*). Like the hunger felt before you know what you want to eat, *man* is always there waiting to form itself into a desire — and when it does, it brings a strange clarity. Sitting somewhere between head and heart, *man* is a visceral yearning backed up by the recognition that what we desire reflects our innermost self. And it is widely acknowledged to be nonnegotiable. According to writer Preti Taneja, "No one can argue with another's *man*." Sometimes what we desire is incomprehensible to our family and friends — but if it's your *man*? That's "a full-stop to any conversation," she says.

See also: DESIRE.

MATUTOLYPEA

The alarm clock trills, the dawn slips in through the curtains, and we wake up overcome with misery and bad temper.

It's not "getting out of bed on the wrong side." It's the much more important-sounding matutolypea (pronounced mah-tu-toh-leh-*pee*-a). No one seems to know quite when the word was invented, or by whom. But its meaning comes from the combination of the name of the Roman goddess of the dawn, Mater Matuta, and the Greek word for dejection, *lype*, to give us the dignity of "morning sorrow."

See also: UMPTY.

MEHAMEHA

Western psychologists have argued that fear is a universal emotion, that it boils down to a single response shared by all people across the globe. Tahitians, however, distinguish between two varieties of fear, each with its own physical response. The first is ordinary, heart-thumping, stomach-knotting fear for your life, which they call *ri'ari'a*. The second is the uncanny sensation experienced in the presence of spirits, ghosts and other dangerous supernatural phenomena. They call this feeling *mehameha* (pronounced *may-ha-may-ha*).

A Tahitian named Tano described *mehameha* to the anthropologist Robert Levy: "There are times when you go into the bush and suddenly your head begins to swell, and your body feels changed, and you hear something, a rustling, a noise.... You get gooseflesh, and you think 'there is a spirit'." An altered state, which often occurs while walking alone, at twilight, beyond the confines of the village, *mehameha* causes the head to expand as if being blown up like a balloon, the hair to stand on end and the skin to prickle. Like "getting spooked" or inexplicably shivering in a warm room, *mehameha* leaves those who feel it twitchy and unnerved.

Mehameha may snowball into terror, though it is quickly diffused if the strange noise is discovered to be merely a gecko scurrying after its dinner. However, if you must walk out at dusk, the safest remedy is to take a friend along with you: as the Tahitians well know, *mehameha* only ever strikes when we are alone…

See also: LONELINESS; TERROR.

MELANCHOLY

Let her voice curl drowsily through the rooms. Draw the curtains, wrap a blanket around the knees and feel the warm sting of tears filling up the eyes. You know it's foolish, that it will make others impatient and angry ("Stop moping around!"). Yet, when the mind drifts to everything we've lost, it can be hard to resist. If artists, students and blues singers are the ones most easily associated with melancholy, this is because it's an emotion that takes time to feel properly. Perhaps it's a little self-conscious, a bit pretentious; but most of all, it must be carefully unwrapped, each tissue-paper layer of SELF-PITY, NOSTALGIA and REGRET carefully studied. Billie Holiday was right to sing about a "sugarcoated misery." There might be loss at its core, but we savor it like exquisite confectionery: a rare indulgence, a little high. The only risk is we might get addicted.

The idea that melancholy might be both arty and dangerous has its feet firmly in the Renaissance, when feeling melancholic was at its most fashionable. According to the medical theories of the time, melancholy was a cold and clammy substance found in the body (the idea originated in the fifth century BCE with the Greek school of Hippocrates, who named the substance *melania chole*, or black bile). Renaissance physicians believed everyone had a bit of black bile in them. It was one of the body's four elemental humors, the others being blood, choler and phlegm. Each person was thought to have a unique balance of these four humors, a delicate ecosystem that would affect all kinds of things from one's health to one's personality. For instance those with excesses of choler in their body were, according to the Renaissance author Thomas Wright, "at every trifle...inflamed" and quickly reconciled (*see:* COURAGE). People with a greater balance of melancholy were the opposite. Since black bile was a thick and heavy humor, melancholics tended to be lethargic and solitary, and so were drawn toward sedentary and introspective lifestyles (*see also:* SADNESS). And though they were slower to take offense, they were "with extreame difficulty reconciled." As now, universities were one of their favorite haunts.

According to early modern medicine, maintaining good health was a question of keeping the delicate balance of the humors stable. Certain things could interfere with it, sending some humors spiking, and making others behave in peculiar ways. Dramatic events that roused strong passions were thought to impact most on the melancholy humor, turning a person's ordinary unhappiness into a more serious disease — melancholia. Anyone could succumb, but those who already had the most black bile swashing around in their bodies were most vulnerable. Falling in LOVE, the death of a parent, a great disappointment: such events were thought to raise the body's temperature, thus heating the thick melancholy in an organ called the hypochondries, and sending noxious fumes into the brain, fogging the mind and confusing the vital spirits. The victim of an attack of melancholia would be left plagued with self-doubt, and with an inexplicable feeling of sorrow and DREAD, which forced them to avoid company, and even wear wide-brimmed hats to keep out daylight. In many ways melancholia was much like the illness we call depression today, but there is one crucial difference. The melancholic vapors were also thought to produce visions. Robert Burton in his famous account of the illness *The Anatomy of Melancholy* called them "terrible monstrous fictions in a thousand shapes and apparitions." These visions, and the fumes that caused them, gave rise to the other names by which melancholia was known: hypochondria, from the organ in which the humor was heated; and "windy melancholy," so called because alongside strange visions, the fumes were also thought to produce flatulence.

Morose and farting, melancholics were unlikely candidates to kick off a fashion. Yet, by the fifteenth century, melancholy was considered a rather desirable disease in some circles. Aristotle had suggested that outstanding philosophers, poets and statesmen had larger amounts of melancholy than usual in their bodies. In the mid-fifteenth century, the Italian scholar Marsilio Ficino, believing himself to be of a melancholic disposition, enthusiastically took up this idea. Ficino argued that melancholy was linked to genius because of the visionary fumes, which he thought brought creative insights. It was partly as a result of this claim that a cult of melancholic genius flourished, and Renaissance scholars began to portray themselves as gloomy. Some even affected the pose — Hamlet is famously accused of wearing "but the trappings and the suits of woe." But the fashion for melancholy was not only for men. Born in 1623, some twenty years after *Hamlet* was written, Margaret Cavendish, Duchess of Newcastle, was a prolific writer on natural philosophy, as science was called at the time. Samuel Pepys attacked her for being "mad, conceited and ridiculous" for such pretensions. However, on the cover of her *The Philosophical and Physical Opinions* (1655), she is not so much defiant as baleful, staring out at the reader from hooded eyes, her mouth sullen, her features sunken, oblivious to the fat cherubs who float happily about her. She published her work under her own name, rather than anonymously as did other women writers at the time, and her melancholic pose is her attempt to be taken seriously as a scholar.

Even if melancholy was the mark of the thinking man or woman, it could bring tortures, the price paid for genius. For Burton, an hour of "sweet" melancholy musings during a solitary walk could give way to the more severe version of melancholia, and leave him cowering from invisible terrors from which it was very hard to recover. In the twentieth century we might still fear that an innocent melancholic affectation could tip over into something more painful and lasting — and some of our own cures have a surprising amount in common with those of the seventeenth century too. In the Renaissance, the recommended cures for melancholia were not pleasant: purgatives thought to reduce the volume of black bile included hellebore, which induced vomiting, and leeches, which sucked blood. Burton, instead, made writing about melancholy his life's work ("I write of melancholy by being busy to avoid melancholy," he wrote), and in the end he saw his studies as both the cause of, and the cure for, the illness.

See also: SADNESS.

MIFFED, A BIT

There are no odes to it. No concertos, or paintings depicting its haughty little sniff. Yet for all its apparent insignificance, feeling a bit miffed occupies a special place in the British psyche.

To feel a bit miffed is to be a little put out, somewhat offended. It happens when we temporarily lose our place in the pecking order — as when we are expecting a nice present and find we've been palmed off with a hand-me-down, or when some teasing goes awry and we are left feeling INSULTED, or a conversation turns contentious and INDIGNATION ensues. Miffed, a bit, feels serious, albeit temporarily: but to an outsider, the miffee, lips pursed and expression haughty, just looks a bit silly.

In fact, feeling miffed has an impressive family tree that can be traced back to at least the seventeenth century, when having a "mifty" or "miffy" manner was to appear peevish or put out. Although it might seem quaint, feeling miffed should be acknowledged for its subtle depths: on the outside, a crust of bristling defensiveness; inside, layers of bamboozlement and the confusion of DISAPPOINTMENT. Most of all, it is blessed with what the French deconstructionists call *jouissance*, a playful ambiguity of meaning that leaves the reader plenty of room for interpretation. Because, while the British may say they feel "a bit miffed, actually," they may in fact mean that they are extremely miffed indeed.

See also: AMBIGUPHOBIA; HATRED.

MONO NO AWARE

At the waning of the Japanese Heian period (794–1185), Murasaki Shikibu, a poet and lady-in-waiting, crafted what is often described today as the world's first novel, *The Tale of Genji*. It recounts the political intrigues and complex and numerous love affairs of an emperor's illegitimate son, giving an insight into life at the imperial court. The book is infused with a quiet feeling for life's transience, the way all living and even inanimate things fade and disappear, which produces a feeling called *mono no aware* (pronounced moh-*noh* noh ah-*wah*-ray).

Mono no aware is literally translated as the pathos (*aware*) of things (*mono*) and is often described as a kind of sigh for the impermanence of life. This is a feeling awash with many shades: the sorrow and serenity that come with recognizing the inevitability of change; the anticipatory grief of losses to come; and the piquancy added to pleasures by the knowledge that they must end. Rooted in the Zen Buddhist concept of *mujo,* or impermanence, *mono no aware* is also linked to an aesthetic sensibility: *wabi-sabi.* The principle of *wabi-sabi,* though complex and much debated, evokes a special beauty found only in unfinished or imperfect things, beautiful not least of all because their imperfections are signs of decay and transience. So *wabi-sabi* is a sensitivity to the beauty of the crack in a porcelain vase, for example, or the wilted edges of a fallen maple leaf.

The Tale of Genji's tenth chapter "The Sacred Tree," captures the wistful feeling evoked by transient beauty. Dressed in rare and expensive silks, Genji picks his way across a gloriously decaying reed plain to visit his lover the Rokujo Lady before they must part ways forever, he to marry another, she to the seclusion of the Ise shrine. "The autumn flowers were gone and insects hummed in the wintry tangles. A wind whistling through the pines brought snatches of music," and the following morning, Genji departs with "his sleeves wet with dew and tears."

See also: RUINENLUST.

MORBID CURIOSITY

Why do we find it so hard to keep our eyes on the road when we pass a crash on the highway? Or stumbling across a dead animal on a country walk, find ourselves both compelled and disgusted by the sight of its spilled guts. When the British construction worker Ken Bigley was executed in Iraq in 2004, the video of his beheading was reputedly one of the most searched-for terms on Google the next day. Why do scenes of pain, mutilation, death and decay exert such an irresistible attraction?

There is no real consensus among contemporary psychologists about the reasons for morbid curiosity. Some say it's because we live in a sanitized age: when death and suffering are hidden behind hospital curtains, they become all the more fascinating. But morbid curiosity isn't just a modern phenomenon. In *The Republic*, written almost 2,500 years ago, Plato recounts the tale of a young Athenian nobleman, Leontius. Walking outside the city walls, Leontius comes across a pile of freshly executed criminals. Though he clamps his hands over his eyes and knows he ought not to look, he is quickly overcome and runs up to the corpses, drinking in the gruesome sight.

Though Plato himself didn't venture to explain why Leontius was so eager to gawp at dead bodies, many philosophers since have tried to understand this phenomenon. There are, broadly speaking, three main theories.

The first, and most common, is that witnessing other people's suffering is cathartic. The eighteenth-century German philosopher Immanuel Kant, for example, noticed that people raced to the sites of live executions "as to a theater play," with great whooping excitement. He thought it wasn't because they were inherently interested in the tension of watching the condemned kick and writhe in agony but rather because, once the sorry spectacle was over, they'd be left with a "feeling of relaxation." Kant based his theory on the much older, and more famous, theory of catharsis outlined by the Greek philosopher Aristotle (*see*: RELIEF). His idea was that by arousing intense feelings of terror and pity, we purge them too. Though he was famously sketchy on the details, some kind of release of pressure may explain why on leaving the cinema after a fist-in-mouth gorefest, we can feel lighter and oddly refreshed.

The second theory argues that morbid curiosity is an inbuilt reflex and serves some purpose. Around the same time Kant was formulating his "feeling of relaxation" theory, the English moralist Adam Smith argued that witnessing the suffering of others helped foster the bonds of what then was known as sympathy (see: EMPATHY). When we cringe at another's pain, we're not simply enjoying the drama but are also experiencing a faint echo of their suffering in our own body. Such vicarious winces, wrote Smith, are evidence of an inbuilt instinct for putting ourselves in another's shoes. Smith's argument, or versions of it, remains very influential. Today's psychologists speak of it as an evolved impulse, so that when we rubberneck at the stretcher being loaded into the ambulance, or crane to see the blood on the tarmac, we're not shamefully exploiting another's misery for kicks but taking the opportunity to empathize with their pain and strengthen social bonds. Some psychologists also suggest that we gawp to familiarize ourselves with disaster and prepare ourselves for threat. Either way, the idea that morbid curiosity is innate in us, more a reflex than a choice, might explain why it feels irresistible, like the tickle that makes you shriek with laughter or the terrible urge to yawn.

Perhaps, though, these explanations are too sanitized. The third cluster of theories is concerned with our darker instincts. The early-twentieth-century psychoanalyst Carl Jung believed that deep in each of our minds is a thick black reservoir in which our erotic desires, murderous rages and feelings of suicidal despair swim. According to Jung, we are both drawn to and repelled by this "shadow aspect" of ourselves. One reason its pull can be so powerful is that the mind craves to complete itself, to become fully integrated, rather than fragmented and partly repressed. For Jung, therefore, when we stumble across opportunities to indulge our macabre impulses — by looking at pictures of tortured prisoners, for example — we may experience the relief, even euphoria, of completion. It's the pursuit of this feeling that might explain why characters like Dr. Robert Vaughan and his group of symphorophiliacs (car-accident fetishists) in J. G. Ballard's novel *Crash* are aroused by collisions and their mangled aftermaths.

Still, for many of us, morbid curiosity remains a furtive, guilty pleasure. We may allow ourselves to glance rather than gaze; desire to touch the corpse but keep our hands rooted in our pockets. A visit to Auschwitz or Ground Zero might leave us filled with DISMAY and sorrow for what occurred there, but also with SHAME and BEWILDERMENT at our own prurient interest. Perhaps we may be compelled to watch someone die, yet feel conflicted by the knowledge that we are violating their privacy, and later wonder if it was only the transgression itself that appealed. Perhaps the only people with the right to view extreme images of illness and suffering, wrote Susan Sontag, are the doctors "who could do something to alleviate it." "The rest of us are voyeurs," she concludes, "whether we mean to be or not."

See also: SCHADENFREUDE.

MUDITA

The sight of another's smile is not always simple. We may walk around their gorgeous new house, or hear about that perfect afternoon spent with the grandchildren at the zoo, and sense our hearts lifting up to meet theirs, echoing with their joy. But beneath our congratulations there might also be a little knot of envy, something shriveled and beaten. Sometimes, as Gore Vidal realized, "it is not enough to succeed. Others must fail."

For Gautama Buddha, who lived in the fifth or sixth century BCE, joy was not a scarce resource to be competed over, or parceled out to only a lucky few. He saw it as boundless. For him the word *mudita* (pronounced moo-*dee*-ta) captured an experience of JOY, rather than ENVY or RESENTMENT, on hearing of someone else's good fortune. And he suggested that the fact *mudita* could be felt *at all*, is evidence that someone else's pleasure doesn't diminish your own store, but increases it.

See also: GLADSOMENESS; COMPERSION; EMPATHY.

Or alternatively, see: SCHADENFREUDE.

NAKHES

"I didn't know they made Ninth Place ribbons," observes Robert De Niro's all-American patriarch Jack Byrnes as he skeptically examines the Wall of Gaylord, a shrine to his Jewish son-in-law's "accomplishments" in the parental home. Jay Roach's comedy sequel *Meet the Fockers* pokes fun at the cultural divide between the ultra-supportive atmosphere of Gaylord Focker's upbringing and the rugged frontier spirit Jack represents. Excessive parental PRIDE might be a worn trope in Jewish humor. But really, everyone recognizes the DELIGHT and SATISFACTION felt at a child's — or even younger sibling's — accomplishments. Perhaps your youngest has just crawled for the first time, or your oldest has cooked a quiche. Seeing a child achieve something — anything! — can make the heart feel like it's about to burst with joy.

In Yiddish there's a special word for this feeling: *nakhes* (pronounced: *na*-khez, with the *kh* pronounced like the *ch* in loch). It makes parents *kvell* (crow with delight) over even the littlest achievements of their squirming offspring, binding the generations together in a shared feeling of success.

See also: MUDITA.

NGINYIWARRARRINGU

Certain emotions end up such an important part of how we experience the world that we unpick their subtle variations, christening each one. In the West in the last ten years, we have named many types of anger (*see*: RAGE). For the Pintupi, whose homeland is the deserts of Western Australia, there are fifteen different kinds of fear. Among them, *ngulu* is the dread you feel when you believe another person is seeking revenge; *kamarrarringu* the tense, frozen feeling when you sense someone is creeping up behind you; *kanarunvtju* a terror about bad spirits visiting in the night, so pervasive that it stops you sleeping; and *nginyiwarrarringu* is a sudden spasm of alarm that makes people leap to their feet and look about, trying to see what caused it.

See also: FEAR; MEHAMEHA.

NOSTALGIA

A song might instantly transport you back to an old love affair. Perhaps looking through photographs brings not just wonder — look at that wallpaper! I was so thin! — but also sorrow for lost connections and faded hopes. The pleasures of reminiscing are both warm and melancholic, and often called bittersweet.

Less than a hundred years ago, however, nostalgic reverie could actually kill you.

In 1688 a medical student named Johannes Hofer wrote a treatise on a mysterious disease that had broken out among Swiss mercenary soldiers fighting abroad. It began with the soldiers being distracted by thoughts of home — often, wrote Hofer, brought on by hearing cowbells chiming in the distance. Then it would progress to lethargy and sadness, "frequent sighs" and "disturbed sleep." Strange physical symptoms followed — lesions, heart palpitations, and from there a "stupidity of mind" — a kind of dementia. Some soldiers died of the illness, wasting away from a refusal to eat. Others attempted to return home — the only known cure — and were executed for desertion. Hofer invented a new word to describe the disease, nostalgia — from the Greek *nostos* (a homecoming or return) *algos* (pain). By the nineteenth century, nostalgia had become one of the most studied medical conditions in Europe, and the last person to be diagnosed and die from the disease was an American soldier fighting in France in 1918 (*see also:* HOMESICKNESS).

In the early twentieth century the meaning of nostalgia began to drift, connected not so much to sickening for home but with yearning for things past. Today, nostalgic reveries are wistful but rapturous travels in time, to smells and songs and images that send us spinning off down rabbit holes into our former lives. Too much nostalgia can leave you stuck between a dissatisfying present and an alluringly unavailable past (*see:* REGRET). But often making a sudden connection with a long-lost memory creates welcome feelings of belonging, identity and continuity. As Virginia Woolf put it in *To the Lighthouse*, these involuntary glimpses of how things used to be bring a "coherence in things, a stability" that shines through the chaos of our lives like a precious jewel.*

---

* Advertisers and businesses capitalize on these warm fuzzies. Cupcakes, vintage-clothes stalls, the craze for eighties revival....Has it gotten out of hand? According to a report by the American satirical paper *The Onion*, it might have: "US Dept. of Retro Warns: 'We May Be Running Out of Past.'"

A surprising number of psychological studies have recently emphasized the benefits of indulging in nostalgic reflection, suggesting it increases our sense of existential meaning and social connectedness. Psychologist Clay Routledge has even proposed "nostalgia workouts," such as reading old letters or making a list of cherished memories, to combat ANXIETY, LONELINESS and rootlessness. Our surroundings and physical sensations can help. Olfactory recall is the most powerful and immediate — neurologists say this is because odors pass directly from our nostrils to the limbic system, where our emotions and memory reside. A team of researchers in southern China have even noticed that nostalgic feelings are more common in colder weather, arguing that reminiscing may serve an evolutionary purpose by raising our body temperature — it is, quite literally, heartwarming.

From deadly disease to health-giving pastime in less than a century: nostalgia ain't what it used to be.

See also: MELANCHOLY; REGRET.

OIME

In Japan, where the pleasures of being cared for by others are celebrated (*see*: AMAE), there is also the word *oime* (pronounced o-*eh*-meh). It roughly translates as: the intense discomfort of being indebted.

See also: GRATITUDE.

OVERWHELMED, FEELING

Of all the worries that preoccupy us in the early twenty-first century, the threat of "information overload" seems the most exclusively modern. We bob along above a seething, swirling mass of digital information, reassuring ourselves with an illusion of control. But one false move and we'll be tipped out, thrashing and gasping for air. The watery imagery — to feel "out of one's depth," the "digital deluge" — is not surprising: to feel overwhelmed comes from the Middle English word *whelme* or *quhelm* (to capsize). We may start by trying to get to the surface, but before long, there will be a sinking feeling — the defeated sensation that comes from surfeit (*see*: DISGUST).

* * *

In fact, though the technology is new, the fear of being overwhelmed by information is not. At the end of the fifteenth century, following the invention of the Gutenberg printing press, cheap books began to swamp the market. And complaints about "too much information" swiftly followed.

Before that time, one might have believed it possible to know everything there was to know. The tenth-century scholar and book trader Lubna of Cordoba worked in the great library at the Umayyad palace of Andalusia, one of the great centers of learning of the medieval Arab world. She was a highly regarded polymath: according to her contemporaries, she "excelled" in poetry and had "mastered" mathematics and science. This was not simple hyperbole. From her work copying the Islamic Hadith, and traveling to and from Baghdad's book markets to buy copies of the ancient texts of the pre-Socratic philosophers, Lubna was thought to have most of the world's knowledge stored in her head.

In the decades that followed the invention of the printing press, writers began to express their feeling of being unable to cope with the flood of new information. "Is there anywhere on earth exempt from these swarms of new books?" asked Erasmus. As is the case with our own information overload, readers worried about whether they could entirely rely on this published material. Important ideas, once mixed up with all the rest, would, as Erasmus put it, "lose all their goodness." Others shared his fears. Calvin complained about "that confused forest of books," Descartes of the BEWILDERMENT caused by what was then known as *copia*, an excess or richness of detail, after the Roman goddess of abundance. It left them facing a very recognizable predicament. How do you know what's important? Should they try to train their focus on reading a canon of classics and ignore everything else? (And even then, how would you choose what to include in that canon?)

Or perhaps, they should just give up reading altogether, and hope for divine inspiration to strike.

One more practical response to this early "information overload" was the invention of techniques for selecting, processing and storing ideas. Alphabetically organized reference books had existed for at least 1,500 years since Pliny created his *Naturalis Historiæ*, but now they became immensely popular. One of the mightiest was the Dutchman Lawrence Beyerlinck's eight-volume *Magnum Theatrum Vitae Humanæ* (*The Great Theater of Human Life*, 1631), which ran to 10 million words. New "best-bits" genres also flourished, such as the Florilegium — which collected quotable sayings and organized them under subject headings so that time-poor speech makers or letter writers could add a learned edge to their words. Note-taking techniques were taught in universities, and filing systems for these notes (a wooden cupboard with rows of hooks from which pages could hang, organized under themes or ideas) were invented so that no one would have to read a book twice.

Today we try to navigate "information overload" with similar tools. Search engines scope out the territory, while research students are taught to break down their program of reading into SMART (specific, measurable, assignable, realistic, time-related) goals to make things feel more manageable. Though it is easy to become discouraged, one of the effects of the threat of being overwhelmed is that we have been forced to become more adept at how we read. The image of Lubna in her library, painstakingly copying out Latin and Greek texts, is a long way from anything we can imagine for ourselves now.

We might, instead, take heart from Samuel Johnson. He seemed to have accepted quite cheerfully that the proliferation of new books required readers to move between different levels of attention. He modeled four different modes: "hard study, perusal, mere reading and curious reading." The first required intense concentration, the last was a cursory skim done amid the chatter of a coffeehouse. It was only with this kind of pragmatic approach that Johnson could keep his feelings of overwhelm at bay — knowing, as he did, that "writers will, perhaps, be multiplied, till no readers will be found."

See also: BAFFLEMENT.

PANIC

Frenzied stampedes at the emergency exits, deadly crushes at the lifeboats and on the football terraces. Yell "shark," warns the mayor in *Jaws*, and "we've got a panic on our hands." Restraint and rationality disappear, replaced by a wild instinct for self-preservation making us clutch and kick and scream.

The word "panic" has its origins in Greek mythology, describing a sudden, inexplicable terror felt by travelers in wild, uninhabited places. Only later did they realize they had stumbled across the feral half-man half-goat deity, Pan, disguised as a tree or a rock. Pan was the overlord of clamorous rites, and those who followed his cult celebrated him with ecstatic parties. Panic therefore became linked with a hard-to-explain feeling of dread, and the sensation of being taken over by the force of a dangerous, collective irrationality (*see also:* ECSTASY).

At the end of the nineteenth century, panic was a much-studied phenomenon among a new school of thinkers who called themselves "crowd psychologists." Gabriel Tarde and Gustave Le Bon held up panic as an example of contagious emotions at work. They believed that when individuals became part of a crowd, they regressed to an earlier primitive state where the boundaries between individuals were less stable and emotions could fly back and forth like germs. These ideas still form part of the way we speak about panics today as a kind of "primitive" experience, though it's worth noting that these late-nineteenth-century ideas came out of a way of thinking about human emotional life that we'd find untenable today: thought to be lower down the evolutionary ladder, it was members of the so-called lower races, the hysterics and those labeled "degenerate," who were believed least in command of their own emotions and most likely to succumb to those of others.

Today we do not just catch panic from other people. We also stir it up in ourselves. First named in the 1960s, the solitary "panic attack" may be one of the most terrifying things possible to suffer. You inhale, but there's no air. The heart hammers as the room closes in. You feel your chest constrict, and realize you're sweating profusely, and fear a heart attack is imminent, making the panicked feeling worse. Panic attacks are common symptoms of post-traumatic stress disorder and are often experienced by people with extreme phobias, though anyone might experience one quite unexpectedly.

And in the meantime, we remain more vulnerable than ever to the panic of the mob. Physical proximity — the smell of fear, the cry of "Fire!" in a crowded theater — is no longer necessary. Conspiracy theories and rumors can break loose over Twitter, causing a rush on bottled water, or spooking the stock markets. Security guards still diligently use code words for "fire" and "unattended bag" when they speak over PA systems. But perhaps more dangerous still may be the panic that could spread between smartphones and laptops, bouncing from satellite to satellite and leaving a tangle of chaos and confusion behind it.

Panicking yet? If not, then *see*: TORSCHLUSSPANIK.

For more on contagious feelings *see*: EMPATHY.

PARANOIA

The room goes quiet as you enter. Schoolkids at the bus stop laugh as you go past. That important envelope has been opened. There are strange clicks on the phone. The heart thumps, the palms sweat and the world shifts a gear. Someone is out to get you.

Or are they?

Everyone, at one time or another, has suspected they're being undermined, or that some innocent comment has a veiled meaning. When we speak of feeling (rather than being) paranoid, it's this double uncertainty we're trying to capture. It's not just that we might feel suspicious of other people's motives. We're not sure whether we can trust our own either.*

The word "paranoia" first came into medical literature in the fifth century BCE, when the Greek physician Hippocrates noted that patients suffering from fever often became delirious. He used the word — from the Greek *para* (beside) *nous* (the mind) — to describe their outbursts. In the mid-eighteenth century, as the old diagnosis of melancholia faded away, doctors revived paranoia to describe the misperceptions and hallucinations of an "alienated mind" (*see*: MELANCHOLY). It wasn't until the late nineteenth century that paranoia took on its modern meaning, which linked it to frequently ingenious persecutory fantasies. Inspired in part by the memoirs of a German judge named Daniel Schreber, who believed that God, in league with his psychiatrist, was trying to turn him into a woman using special rays emanating from the walls, a new generation of psychiatrists recategorized paranoia from a temporary neurotic (or emotional)

---

* And even paranoiacs, as the old joke goes, have enemies.

illness to a permanent psychotic disorder characterized by severe delusions.

Many words originally used to describe extreme psychiatric conditions have made their way into our workaday emotional vocabulary: we talk of our feelings of depression or ANXIETY or CLAUSTRO-PHOBIA. Within a few decades of its invention as an illness connected with fantasies of persecution, the word "paranoia" began to be used more widely. Those who were unduly suspicious, or quick to assume others were trying to undermine or humiliate them, were called paranoid. Some writers thought it evidence of a suffocated and conventional mind: "There is nothing," wrote Vladimir Nabokov in 1957, "more banal and more bourgeois than paranoia" (see also: JEALOUSY). As tensions between America and the Soviet Union escalated into the Cold War, it became common to speak of paranoia exacerbating hostility on a global scale. In newspapers, leaders were characterized as twitchy and defensive, their emotions obscuring reason and making them quick to oppress or attack. Paranoia might have seemed petty and suburban to Nabokov, but at one stage it looked like it might be responsible for blowing up the entire world.

Today, paranoia is believed to be on the rise. We live in one of the least dangerous epochs in human history, far less likely to die from being bludgeoned by a neighbor or eaten by an animal than our ancestors. Yet we appear to be more suspicious than ever that others are out to hurt us. The psychologist Daniel Freeman, who has studied the rise in paranoia among passengers on the London underground since the bombings of July 2005, believes our "fear culture" has contributed to an unjustified nervousness about threat (see: FEAR). He's probably right. But does reminding oneself that you're being irrational and deluded always soothe paranoid thoughts? Sometimes it makes them worse, eroding our ability to trust in other people and ourselves. What would happen if we took the content of our paranoid fantasies not less seriously, but more?

The two illnesses now most associated with paranoia are schizophrenia and dementia. It might, however, be rather too simple to dismiss patients' reports of persecution as merely the disordered efflorescence of a diseased mind. Psychoanalysts tend to credit paranoiac fantasies with more meaning, often seeing them as a way of managing aspects of our own lives that we cannot tolerate. If you're aging and live alone, and your children rarely visit, it may in fact be preferable to believe the FBI is screening your phone calls than the alternative — that no one cares very much about you at all (see: LONELINESS). Perhaps it's more bearable to think that someone at work is deliberately holding you back than that your efforts aren't good enough, or easier on you to believe your partner is having an affair than confront the loss of intimacy in your relationship. Instead of reproaching ourselves, and each other, for "just being paranoid," taking our fears seriously might help us tease out what's really bothering us.

This more open attitude toward paranoia has been embraced in a range of pioneering medical treatments. If your grandmother confides in you that the nurses are stealing her photographs, it might simply be that her hearing aid is broken. Most of us feel more paranoid when we can't quite understand what is being said, for example in a foreign country where we don't speak the language. But sometimes there might be something more complex going on. Penny Garner, who became interested in dementia after caring for her own mother, has argued that some of the apparently paranoid stories people experiencing dementia relay to their carers are better understood as the patient's attempt to use past experiences to make sense of their disorienting present ones. Garner suggests entering into the spirit of some of these stories rather than disputing them, in order to create a gentler, more supportive experience for both patients and their carers.

To be suffering from the early stages of dementia is to experience frequently alarming confusion. But all of us have to deal with ambiguity in our daily lives, and this is where suspicion really thrives (*see:* UNCERTAINTY). Perhaps our tendency to flesh out half-heard whispers with double meanings and malign intentions is evidence of a poor self-image. But perhaps paranoid feelings most remind us of the continual challenge that we all face living in a world that won't always reveal itself clearly ("only the paranoid survive"). This, and one of the most extraordinary aspects of human imagination: apophenia — being able to see meaningful connections where there are none, as when a person can make links between random words, or sees weeping faces in the clouds.

See also: AMBIGUPHOBIA; DÉPAYSEMENT; PRONOIA.

PERVERSITY

The more reason deters us from the brink the more impetuously we approach it.
> —Edgar Allan Poe, "The Imp of the Perverse"

It's senseless. It's bloody-minded. To ignore our bank statements, or let the dishes fester, or go out drinking when a deadline looms. We know we're the only ones who'll suffer for it. Yet, in that moment of perverse triumph, it's hard to miss the swagger in our step.

Fifty years before Freud would trace such wayward desires to the murky depths of the subconscious, the American master of the macabre Edgar Allan Poe came up with an even more tantalizing idea: a mischievous demon called the Imp of the Perverse. It's this imp who lures us into the most self-destructive of acts, tempting us to ignore our responsibilities, or tricking us into confessing our crimes, or leading us to the edge of the precipice and urging us to jump...

For other imps who implant emotions, *see*: ACEDIA and TERROR.

For other reasons to leap, *see*: *L'APPEL DU VIDE* and LITOST.

PEUR DES ESPACES

Madame B cluttered up her apartment with furniture. She found nestling into the little hobbit holes made by chairs and wardrobes soothed her. On those occasions she was forced to go outside, Paris's grand squares and boulevards brought a feeling of tightness in her throat. Worst of all was the prospect of crossing a bridge: imagining herself caught in the flow of people and traffic from one side to the other, she felt dizzy, began to shake, and became convinced that everyone was staring at her.

The late nineteenth century was the era of the phobia. Each week, psychologists seemed to diagnose a new form. By 1914 the list numbered over a hundred, from the entirely understandable thanatophobia (fear of death) to the downright peculiar triskaidekaphobia (fear of the number 13). Being struck with a terror of public spaces was the most well known of them all. In the late 1870s the French psychologist Henri Legrand du Saulle diagnosed his patient Madame B's condition as *peur des espaces*: a fear brought on by open, public spaces. In German, the same symptoms were termed *Platzangst* (literally: "square fear"); Freud called them "locomotor phobia"; and around the same time the psychiatrist Carl Otto Westphal came up with the name that is now the most widely used: agoraphobia (literally: fear of the marketplace).

Part of what made these fears of public spaces surface in the late nineteenth century were new visions of city life. With their arcades and grand railway stations, Europe's new modern cities were much-vaunted symbols of progress, supposed to create feelings of awe and freedom in those lucky enough to live in them. Yet, for writers such as Georg Simmel and later Walter Benjamin, the new cityscape brought loneliness and alienation — and also the disorientation that is aroused when we are given too many choices. Since feeling panicky around junctions and bridges, but safer in residential areas, was a particular feature of *peur des espaces*, the illness seems most of all a response to modernity's restlessness (*see also:* WANDERLUST).

Our understanding of *peur des espaces* has changed little since it was first described a century ago, though various additional theories have been suggested. Evolutionary psychologists have argued that our ancestors were primed to avoid open spaces where they could not hide from predators, and so believe agoraphobia is a kind of glitch, a no longer serviceable instinct bursting through. Researchers at University College London and Southampton University have linked agoraphobia to problems of the inner ear — the vestibular system that helps control our sense of spatial orientation and balance. They argue that people whose vestibular systems are weak become quickly disoriented when visual cues are lacking — for example in empty airports, or amid swarming crowds — and this may account for a feeling of dizziness in open spaces. Feminist critics have drawn attention to the fact that agoraphobia is diagnosed more frequently in women than men (approximately 85 percent of known sufferers are women). They have reminded the medical profession that some women continue to experience public spaces as intimidating — feeling uncomfortable because you are being stared at, or threatened because you are the target of sexually aggressive comments, may well give rise to a fear of public spaces. In such a context, agoraphobia may be not so much a delusion or illness as a reasonable reaction to a hostile world.

Alternatively, *see:* CLAUSTROPHOBIA; HOARD, the urge to.

PHILOPROGENITIVENESS

In the early nineteenth century there was a fashion for divining personality traits by examining the lumps and bumps on a person's skull. The new science was called Phrenology. In drawing rooms up and down the country, Victorians felt their own and each other's heads, hoping to unlock the secrets of their souls. One of the qualities phrenologists thought they could detect was the peculiar-sounding philoprogenitiveness. Early exponents of the science, such as Johann Gaspar Spurzheim and George Combe, defined it as "the glowing impulse of parental love." Others spoke of it as a desire — part emotion, part instinct — to nurture small and vulnerable creatures, whether family pets or bawling babies.

Here's how to find yours. Place two fingers in the hollow where the skull meets the back of the neck, and move them about an inch upward and to the right. Is there a ridge or a bump there? If so, you have a pronounced organ of philoprogenitiveness. And if the lump is large and you happen to be a parent? Then the phrenologists advised restraining yourself from the urge to coddle your children — not, to be clear, for their sake, but for your own, lest you become "a slave to maternal duties."*

See also: AMAE; NAKHES.

---

* In case you were wondering, phrenology has been completely debunked.

PIQUE, A FIT OF

A sharp anger caused by a wound to one's pride, leading swiftly to a dignified response such as threatening to resign or stomping off the playing field.

See also: HUFF, in a; INSULTED, feeling; MIFFED, a bit; VENGEFULNESS.

PITY

The courts of classical Athens were not much like our own. Judges and juries expected to be reduced to tears. In *On Invention*, a manual on rhetoric, Cicero advised plaintiffs on the arts of arousing pity. He suggested striking a "humble expression" and "weeping as you remember your lost loved ones," reminding the jury "that they have children too." But a moved judge and jury was no guarantee of going free. "Nothing," warned Cicero, "dries more quickly than a tear."

While COMPASSION entails the willingness to become involved in another's suffering, pity is more of a spectator sport. For the Greeks, pity implied an asymmetry of power: those who pitied also had the capacity to release or pardon, to offer charity (the Greek word for pity, *eleos*, gives the English "alms"). The philosopher Aristotle also thought pity rather enjoyable, its tears giving a pleasant feeling of being cleansed and drained (*see:* RELIEF). In medieval Christian Europe, pity became an important part of devotional practice (in fact, pity and piety were at this time the same word, variously spelt as *pieté*, *pietie*, *pyete* and so on). From around the 1000s, artists began to represent the Son of God not as a heroic figure, but as torn and skeletal, hanging on the cross. These altarpieces and icons were an important part of worship, with the devout encouraged to "beholde him with sorrowe of herte," and be filled with grief for his suffering and sorrow for their own wrongs (*see:* REMORSE).

The superiority and capriciousness of those weeping Greek jurors, however, was not altogether forgotten. For philosophers in the eighteenth century such as Kant, pity was a way of looking down on the needy, fixing them in a lowly position, a kind of CONTEMPT. In the twentieth century, Stefan Zweig's novel *Beware of Pity* offered an important critique of the emotion. Its heroine, who uses a wheelchair, describes being pitied as stifling, suffocating, pinning a person into a position of inferiority: "How well you're looking today, and how splendidly you're walking..." But most of all, it is temporary, a kind of theater: "Do you think I'm so stupid that I don't understand that you're bound to get bored here playing the Good Samaritan?"

Though it's not usual to talk of compassion being repressed — DESIRE and ANGER are the more familiar candidates — the historian Theodore Zeldin has argued that "since the world began, compassion has been the most frustrated of emotions, more so than sex." Another's suffering can be difficult to witness, one reason why so many of us draw up short at pity, keeping ourselves safe at a distance. Perhaps we might feel overwhelmed by the extent of practical support required, and so console ourselves with a tear and move on. Perhaps too, we might feel revolted by another's vulnerability or physical illness, unable quite to endure in them what we can't face in ourselves. Pity becomes a way of protecting ourselves, a kind of inhibition, releasing us from the discomfort of responsibility, or the pain of a deeper emotional connection. Or, as Zweig put it, it is a "compassion which is not compassion at all, just the instinctive fending off of alien suffering from one's own soul."

See also: SELF-PITY.

POSTAL, GOING

In the shadow of a series of deadly mass shootings by disgruntled postal workers in the 1980s, the expression "going postal" began to be used across America to describe a fit of workplace rage.

Some psychiatrists see mass shootings in America — of which going postal was an early example — as a type of culture-bound syndrome. There are other examples of such illnesses, all with their own distinct patterns and recognizable behaviors. Among the Gurumba tribe of New Guinea, *guria* (literally: being a wild pig) only afflicts young men between twenty-five and thirty-five years of age, and is thought to be caused by a bite from a spirit ancestor. It makes the men sweat and tremble, and run through the village, stealing valueless objects and threatening women and elders with knives (though no one is hurt). The victim of *guria* then runs off into the forest, and three days later returns, with all traces of the wild pig — and all memory of what happened — gone. Compare this to *amok*, or *amuk*, which in Malaysia is a delirious and violent episode, giving the phrase in English "running amok." Also imagined to be caused by spirit possession, an episode of *amok* is usually precipitated by some insult or humiliation, followed by a period of intense brooding, and finally erupting into a rage-filled rampage where the afflicted person kills anyone in their path, finally either killing themselves, or regaining sensibility with no recollection or understanding of what has happened.

For another culture-bound syndrome, *see:* WANDERLUST.

See also: RAGE; DISGRUNTLEMENT.

PRIDE

You can visit the head of Queen Idia in the British Museum. Cast in brass, in the old Kingdom of Benin (which lay in present-day southwest Nigeria), in the early sixteenth century, the likeness is astonishingly beautiful. There's stillness and dignity to her. Her eyelids are lowered. Her chin and lips are set firm. Hers is not an expression of desire or even triumph. It's neither needy nor smug. Instead, it shows a woman who appears contained, even demure, but with an unwavering sense of her own accomplishment. Idia was the mother of Oba Esigie, who ruled Benin from the late fifteenth to the early sixteenth centuries. She was one of the most powerful people of her society, honored for her prowess as a military strategist and for presiding over the ritualistic life of the court at a time when Benin cultural life was flourishing. No surprise that she should have such a powerful sense of her own value.

For most of us, pride must come and go in waves. It's a feeling of fullness, of form and outline, that surges up when we overcome an obstacle or master something difficult. Pride can fill us up so much that we burst, and tears follow, as when we are recognized with an award, or see our children flourish (see: NAKHES). But even in these watery moments, our insides — which can often feel incoherent — seem to be colored in, every hidden corner glistening with reds, oranges and blues. Where SHAME makes us want to hide from view, we feel pride when we allow ourselves — even if only momentarily — to be seen.

Strange, then, that we have also come to think of pride as an emotion that blinds us too. Philosophers distinguish between false and true pride — and even if such moralistic tones can be off-putting (who's to say which is which?) there's something useful in this distinction. There are many reasons why even the pride that philosophers call "true" has been treated with caution, and why it is considered a sin in most of the world's religions. Pride might blind us to our limitations, make us overreach and commit the sin the ancients called hubris, which comes before a fall. It can be intransigent, leaping to attack at the slightest scratch (*see:* ABHIMAN). But the "false" pride, known by some as "false-friend pride," is different. It's there when we think we're backing ourselves, but are in fact, being defensive and brittle. This is the pride that makes us refuse help, or resist the urge to apologize. This is the pride that can't admit lack and loss, and that therefore makes it very hard to acknowledge one's truer self — the self that is partial, and dissatisfied and needy. This is the pride that is most common and least trusted of all. In Alice Munro's short story "Pride," the unnamed narrator is overcome with fury when his only friend suggests, quite casually, that a quick operation would fix his hare lip. Is it INDIGNATION he feels? A sense that he is being asked to correct some "flaw" about himself? Later in the story the real dilemma comes into view: "She was right. But how could I explain that it was just beyond me to walk into some doctor's office and admit that I was wishing for something I hadn't got?"

In 2010 the director of the British Museum interviewed the Nigerian poet and playwright Wole Soyinka about the Benin Bronzes, a collection of metalwork to which the head of Queen Idia belongs. Soyinka spoke movingly about his experience of seeing the bronzes: it "increases a sense of self-esteem because it makes you understand that African society actually produced some great civilizations, established some great cultures." So powerful has been the colonial propaganda depicting Africans as backward and uncivilized, that even the British soldiers who entered Benin Palace in 1897 and found it lavishly decorated could not countenance that the ornate sculptures and panels had been made locally. They thought they were stealing something already looted from Europe by the Benin army. In the face of such cultural dismissal, the undertaking to develop a sense of pride in one's own history and identity might seem a tall order. This is the pride that the twentieth century's various consciousness-raising fiestas — gay pride, black pride, disability pride — have their sights trained on. Soyinka's response to seeing the Benin Bronzes simultaneously describes an experience of lack and of pride: because it's sometimes only when we are able to admit what has been taken from us that we can feel ourselves to be whole again.

For more on self-esteem, *see:* CONTENTMENT.

PRONOIA

A strange, creeping feeling that everyone's out to help you.

See also: GRATITUDE.

RAGE

A fit of rage is wild and twisted. The eyes bulge, the limbs flail. We spit and shout. We cannot hide it in the way we conceal jealousies or nurse resentments. We fly into rages. Boil over. It comes in paroxysms and bursts. ANGER can be justified, and INDIGNATION righteous, but rage is an irrational frenzy.

The last twenty years have witnessed a proliferation of types of rage. There are violent clashes on the roads (ROAD RAGE) and tantrums in planes (air rage). Spluttering, swearing frenzies erupt in supermarket aisles (shopping cart rage), in offices (mouse rage; *see*: TECHNOSTRESS) and even while opening groceries (wrap rage). They may have jokey nicknames (*see*: POSTAL, going, for example), but the fact we've bothered to identify these many different rages at all suggests our relationship with our uncontrollable fury is not straightforward. We don't make a similar effort to differentiate types of HOMESICKNESS, for instance, or doubt. Our capacity for flying off the handle fascinates and terrifies, all at once.

Perhaps the stresses and frustrations of modern life are giving rise to increased levels of ferocity: the more sources of rage, the more sorts we can distinguish. But at least part of what drives this desire to parse and label fury is that in Britain and America this emotion has become increasingly unacceptable. American psychologists have created a new umbrella diagnosis: intermittent explosive disorder. One needs only three episodes of impulsive aggressiveness, each "grossly out of proportion" to the person or thing that has irritated, to be diagnosed. To qualify as an explosion, the angry outburst should be a sudden and complete loss of control, involving breaking or smashing something "worth more than a few dollars," or hurting, or trying to hurt, someone. By this reckoning, intermittent explosive disorder may be a lot more widespread than even current figures suggest. And the cure? Attributing outbursts of rage to low serotonin, the current advice is to dull anger with antidepressants.

But what would a society without rage look like? The political theorist Hannah Arendt, who famously coined the phrase "the banality of evil," found the idea fearful. In her essay *On Violence*, she argued that "only where there is reason to suspect that conditions could be changed and are not does rage arise. Only when our sense of justice is offended do we react with rage." More than the fiery articulacy of indignation, the foaming, libidinal intensity of rage was, for Arendt, a natural response to injustice. To attempt to "cure" a person of it would be almost to dehumanize. It would deprive the sufferer of a capacity for defiance, and society of an opportunity for change.

It may seem ridiculous to lose your rag because your teenager hasn't tidied up, or your partner has said that thing AGAIN, or you've waited in all day for a delivery that never came. These might *feel* like injustices at the time (though probably not the kind Arendt had in mind), but though they are petty and trivial, and we almost always regret them later, such rages are an important part of being human and involved in the world. If we can't have the occasional flare-up of mouse, or shopping cart, or wrap rage, then we can't have revolutions and riots either.

See also: EXASPERATION.

REGRET

Brooding. We all know it's not allowed. We know that way stagnation lies. (Let it go! Live in the Moment!) Yet, there's something so seductive about regret. The way it paints an aura of possibility around what has been broken — even seeming to mend it momentarily with "what ifs." It takes us on a journey through the fantasies of alternative outcomes ("If only I had phoned her back"; "If only I had saved the money"). It tantalizes us with the possibility of reversing our decisions or preventing our accidents. It's for this reason that, though regret is rarely a comfortable state of mind, it also contains a flicker of pleasure and a strange, if temporary, sort of RELIEF.

The regret of the past was not the same as our own. From the Old French *regrés* (sorrows or disappointments), the word seems to have first entered the English language in the 1400s, and described grief felt at the loss of a person, or of one's place in the world. One distinctive difference was that regret was also a kind of performance, an often-heightened expression of sorrow. The "making of regrets," or *regrettes*, was a pious yet clamoring affair: the lamentations at a wake, the weeping at funerals. In the sixteenth century — the moment historians associate with the birth of the modern concept of an interiorized self — regret began to harden into its contemporary meaning as a self-reproach, a private anguish felt looking back at some action you wish you'd not committed — or that you wish you had. It was at this time that the threat of this hidden torture, rather than punishment in the hereafter, became a deterrent favored by parents and preachers alike. "For this deed thou shalt for anguish fret," warned the Calvinist parliamentarian Francis Rous in 1598, and "feed thy wombe with woe and deepe regret."

Today, regret remains firmly entrenched as a private emotional experience. Yet, look closely and its earlier links with loss still linger. As psychologist Alice Haddon suggests, the regrets we feel most sorely are often the ones that jar hardest with our sense of self. The person who believes herself to be brave sorely regrets not speaking out. The skilled stock-market trader cannot be reconciled to the gamble that cost his client so dear. This is a loss — a painful one too — since those parts of ourselves that we cling to hardest are usually the ones created in defense of some much earlier failure or criticism. For many of us, there'll be some stupid, throwaway comment made by a parent or teacher that jangles at the back of the mind: the joke that made you sound lazy, or the story about how you were never good at making friends. If you've made the effort to prove it wrong, seeing the evidence stack up in its favor can be painful. For this reason, regret is often tangled up in the ways we can be deprived of those roles we are appointed to, or design for ourselves (see: DISAPPOINTMENT).

Regrets are often described as pointless. What's the use of looking back? It's true that sometimes regret, like GUILT and SELF-PITY, can stultify and stand in the way of the longer, harder process of making amends (see: REMORSE). But this is not to say that regret is always a bad thing. Researchers from Stanford University's School of Business have shown that people who are more inclined to self-reproach make better managers: it comes with the territory of having a heightened sense of personal responsibility and the ability to learn from one's mistakes. Trying to understand why we regret some mistakes bitterly while shrugging off others may also be valuable, since it highlights the beliefs we hold about ourselves, and our sometimes impossible standards. Regret — and moving past it — can therefore help us emerge with a more flexible, and resilient, vision of ourselves. Most of all, recognizing when we regret a decision reminds us of the ambivalence that haunts all our lives. Should we have predicted the outcome? Perhaps. But none of us is omniscient, and anyway, who knows what dragons might have been lurking down the path we didn't take (*see:* UNCERTAINTY)?

More often than not, what at the time seems an inconsolable loss is not the end of the story. Perhaps we'll adjust ourselves to our regrets. Perhaps we'll learn from them. But unlike resignation or acceptance, regret is ultimately a kind of desire for something different to have happened. It makes the mind waver, it gnaws. And by allowing us to imagine the possibility of things ending differently, it contains, rather peculiarly, a little germ of hope.

See also: MELANCHOLY; NOSTALGIA.

RELIEF

"Would you mind if I cry a little?" she asks.

It's 3 a.m. on Christmas night, and everyone has gone to bed. Helena, an aging and wealthy actress, and her philosophical friend Isak, sit together on a damask sofa, drinking cognac. Isak is nodding off. But Helena, a little drunk, a little sentimental, wants to talk — about her children, and their debts and infidelities. About time passing. About getting old. She asks if she might cry.

Isak nods sagely and puts his arm around her. They sit poised for a moment in this familiar tableau, waiting for the tears to flow. She looks upward, blinks rapidly, sighs. She makes a little pushing noise, as if she's trying to squeeze a droplet or two out of her stubborn tear ducts. She heaves her body up and down as if pumping a gas canister, but no moistness appears.

"No, upon my soul, I can't. The tears won't come. I'll have to have some more cognac."

She drinks. And then laughs at her own absurdity — and it's this laughter in the end that brings the relief she craves.

This scene in Ingmar Bergman's *Fanny and Alexander* taps into an old idea about crying. That, in the words of Ovid, "it is some relief to weep: grief is satisfied and carried off by tears."

When we speak of a feeling of relief, we're often describing one of two different experiences. One is the relief of a pure bodily sensation, discharging a tension that has uncomfortably built up. Sneezing, belching, defecation and orgasm are all examples. The other, the relief felt at near misses and narrow escapes, that comes with another sort of whistling discharge: "Phew!" Examples of this are finding your keys after thinking you've locked yourself out, or an all clear from the doctor after a worried week. This second type of relief is part of a group of feelings psychologists call "prospect-based emotions" (DISAPPOINT-MENT and SATISFACTION are others). They depend on our ability to imaginatively launch ourselves forward and backward through time to compare alternative realities. Studies of relief argue that the two forms of relief (bodily relief and near-miss relief) share the same basic structure: a pleasure felt when an actual or anticipated pain subsides (*see also:* EUPHORIA).

Weeping plays its role in both. Many of us will cry on receiving good news after a long and anxious wait, making tears part of the relief felt with a near-miss. But if crying leaves you not only sore eyed, but also quieter inside and oddly lighter, then you might also think that weeping itself has refreshed you — and that therefore, like a belch or an orgasm, tears are a sort of physical discharge of tension in their own right. That tears bring relief is an old idea, stretching back to Aristotle's theory of catharsis (*see:* MORBID CURIOSITY). "What soap is for the body, tears are for the soul," states one Jewish proverb. A much proffered modern version of this idea holds that when liquid flows from our tear ducts it flushes hormones or toxins away, leaving us feeling relaxed or released. But since when we weep we discharge little more than a milliliter of fluid, this actually seems unlikely. As neuroscientist Robert Provine put it, "If tears reduce stress, drooling and urination may be cathartic Niagaras." There must be something more complex at work than simple hydraulics.

In fact, relief rarely comes as a pure feeling of relaxation or reassurance. The moments following a close call on the highway are a heart-thumping adrenaline rush. At the end of a long project, the relief of having finished may be spiked with disappointment. As an emotion, it flickers and is diffuse, appearing in all sorts of guises. Perhaps it's in this more complex experience of relief that its true meaning lies. Think of the feeling of unburdening yourself by telling a secret or confessing to guilt. Or the way that a friend's agreement to help us prepare for an interview or accompany us to the doctor's can lessen the weight of worry. Such experiences might make us feel lighter. But this may be less because we have simply vented or expressed our anxieties (better out than in!) than because we experience the solace of being listened to and understood. In this sense, relief might be less about something being flushed away than about our feelings finally being seen.

For more on weeping, see: EMPATHY.

See also: GRIEF.

RELUCTANCE

Commitments. We're told to make them. Magazines and self-help books urge us to take the plunge. Be decisive. Be clear about what you want and communicate it.

No space for the little voice that wants you to squeeze the brake just a little bit, hear the whir of rubber pad brushing against steel rim. No space for heel dragging, or forgetting your passport, or putting off the phone call. No space for an emotion as noncommittal as reluctance.

This ambivalence is what the aviator Amelia Earhart felt on the morning of her wedding to George Putnam on February 7, 1931. "You must know again my reluctance to marry," she wrote. This was no jangle of last-minute nerves. This was a conversation the couple had had over and over and over again. She didn't want to try to perform the role of a dutiful wife, which would tighten around her like shrink-wrap. She wanted to fly.

Theirs was a happy marriage, by all accounts. Her reluctance served the couple well, an early warning system. "I want you to understand I shall not hold you to any midaevil [sic] code of faithfulness to me nor shall I consider myself bound to you similarly," she wrote. And she put in a parachute, extracting a promise that "you will let me go in a year if we find no happiness together." She died only six years later, five years after becoming the first woman to cross the Atlantic, her bones resting somewhere at the bottom of the Pacific Ocean, her marriage still intact.

For the other benefits of ambivalence *see*: UNCERTAINTY.

REMORSE

A young man sits on a carpenter's bench, blood pooling on the floor beneath him. Overcome with emotion after kicking his mother, he has cut off his own leg. In the painting by the Venetian artist Antonio Vivarini, dated to the 1450s, now hanging in the Metropolitan Museum in New York, Saint Peter kneels over the severed leg attempting to heal it, while two women — perhaps one is the boy's mother — wring their hands anxiously in the background.

The realization that we have hurt another person is one of the most painful we can experience. Remorse arrives when the initial flare of ANGER calms, when the reality of what we've said or done clumps in the throat. Unlike the whirring and suffocation of REGRET, remorse is urgent and wild. Full of TERROR, flecked with LOVE, it's a desire to preserve our bond with the person we've hurt. It is in childhood, according to the psychoanalyst Melanie Klein, that remorse takes on its most desperate shape, when we fear we've hurt our parents — who in our childhood fantasies seem more easily wounded than most, and more capable of cruel retribution. Remorse, then, is most clearly defined as an urgent desire to *do* something. To make amends, to attempt to heal the one we've harmed. Because, unlike SHAME, which is a horror of something we *are*, remorse involves something *done*, and urges us to correct it. In this sense, remorse is both extremely painful and full of striving and HOPEFULNESS too.

Remorse may be an old-fashioned word, but in fact it has rarely been more under the spotlight. We live in what has been dubbed an "Age of Apology." From politicians such as Tony Blair and Kevin Rudd making formal apologies for atrocities committed by their predecessors, to South Africa's Truth and Reconciliation Commission, the idea of a public apology is rooted in the notion that a display of remorse has an effect on the victims, helping them heal. We seem so committed to the belief that remorse soothes suffering that we clamor for contrition when a scandal breaks and feel some satisfaction to see a politician resign or a celebrity dab away a tear on a talk-show sofa.

Yet, in each of these cases, apologies also seem inadequate. It's probably the "performative" aspect of remorse that makes this emotion so vulnerable to questions about its sincerity. An apology, to use the philosopher J. L. Austin's theory, both expresses something and *changes* something. As children we are instructed to "say sorry like you mean it," and so learn that a theater of remorse can stand in for the real thing. Did Tony Blair really feel remorse for the actions of a nineteenth-century Conservative government, or was his apology just a clever move in the Irish Peace Process chess game (and does it even make sense to feel remorse for a crime you personally didn't commit or weren't responsible for)? Did the dangling carrot of immunity from prosecution in the South African Truth and Reconciliation Commission encourage contrition expressed where none was felt (and if not, why was a process required for perpetrators to come forward)? We want sincerely felt remorse: "He showed no remorse" is the chilling summation of the criminal led to the cells, his incapacity to feel, or even feel the need to show, remorse evidence of an inhuman mind at work. But what if remorse isn't really an emotion at all?

The question of whether remorse was a passion or an intellectual position — or both — was much debated between the thirteenth and fifteenth centuries in Europe. The medieval culture of remorse was intensely passionate, a tear-strewn display of sorrow and abjection. The devout were exhorted to weep before Christ's dying body, to scourge their flesh and join in with the misericordia cries of plague and famine processions to show God the depth of their contrition (*see also:* PITY). Passionate remorse was also an important part of medieval legal process. On November 7, 1497, Christopher and Isabella Wryght were brought up before the judge at Durham after their child died in a fire, charged with child neglect — as serious a crime then as it is now. Court records reveal the pair "*confessatum cum dolore non modico ymmo clarmore & lacrimis effucionem*" ("confessed with no moderate sorrow, but on the contrary with outcries and a flood of tears"). Their extreme anguish was regarded by the judge as evidence of a sincere desire to repent, and moved him to mercy. Instead of imprisonment, the pair were sentenced to penance: dressed only in their shifts, bareheaded, barefoot, and carrying a halfpenny candle, they processed around the church of Alverton on four consecutive Sundays, being whipped throughout.

Yet in this highly emotional popular culture of remorse, there were those in the scholarly elite who thought it best considered not a passion, but an intellectual attitude. Medieval theologians such as Albert the Great and his student Thomas Aquinas argued that true remorse (*contritio*) was a special spiritual virtue, a voluntary desire to make amends and a willingness to go through a painful process of penitence in order to cleanse the guilt. They were also impatient with the idea that wearing hair shirts or being whipped was an important part of remorse. For them, it wasn't wailing or crying that showed true contrition, but a reasoned attitude that led a person to make amends. Crucially, it was only in a quiet state of mind that the penitent could calculate the correct level of penitence required to neutralize the sin. For this reason, powerful emotions, such as those displayed by the young man in Vivarini's painting, had no place in true remorse. Just as today we might end up digging a hole or making others feel worse with desperate attempts to make amends, medieval theologians feared excessive remorse would lead to disproportionate acts, causing more grief, rather than less.

For medieval scholars, then, remorse was a subtle calculation, done not in the heat of the moment but in a quiet and restrained way. In which case, perhaps the next time we examine the glistening eyes of a celebrity or politician our question should not be whether remorse is being truly felt, but whether it is being genuinely thought.

See also: GUILT.

REPROACHFULNESS

There are those who are brave enough to tell a stranger off for a throw-away racist comment, or for refusing to give up their seat to an elderly traveler on a bus. One imagines this is rather satisfying, inflating them with self-righteousness (*see:* SMUGNESS).

But in a world where moral rules can seem hard to agree on, and where feelings can be hurt and things taken the wrong way, even the desire to correct may be quickly followed by premonitions of instant regret. So we may find ourselves having to be content with expressing our reproach in censorious little squibs. A cold look. Tuts and sighs and mutterings.

Such exchanges rarely produce the contrition or immediate change in behavior of one's fantasies. Instead, our best efforts go unnoticed, or worse, are met with reproaches of their own. ("If you've got something to say, come say it to my face!") Little is more irritating than the reproachfulness of others. No one likes their faults pointed out, or the idea that someone thinks they're entitled to judge us.

And so we walk through the city itching to upbraid, bursting with censoriousness. We become the creators of eloquent rage-filled inner monologues, experts in the little cough, and seething with unexpressed fury.

See also: MIFFED, a bit.

RESENTMENT

It's the consequence of our own agreeableness, anger stuck in a loop. It's the hatred we suppress when forbidden to give voice to the ways we are hurt or humiliated or frustrated, a wound caused by our own dependency. In time, our hidden anger becomes compacted, sinking into the darkest places of the soul, till it glimmers in little acts of spite and pique, goading, competing, punishing.

Resentment is one of the quietest, and most ugly, emotions we have.

The idea of resentment as a voiceless feeling is an old one. Its medieval forebear, rancor, was understood as bitterness, and unsatisfied VENGEFULNESS. It brought the wasting of inertia, poisonous cancers and foul smells (the Latin *rancore* gives us our modern word "rank"). In Cesare Ripa's *Iconologia* — an enormous handbook for artists published in 1593, which described how over 1,250 passions and personality types should be represented — the rancorous type was pale and thin, his retained anger creating an "ulcer in the soul," and fistulas on his skin bursting with infectious poisons.

The fear that resentment will leave traces on the body still haunts us. The psychosomatic school of medicine, which came to prominence in 1950s America, linked resentment to digestive problems and stomach ulcers. Its members argued that it was only through unleashing the buried fury in a safe therapeutic relationship that the disastrous effects of resentment could be remedied — and their ideas have lingered ever since.

Yet what makes resentment so very unappealing today isn't just nervousness about its physical symptoms. Resentment has also come to seem bitter and meagre. An emotion that "seethes" and is "buried." And is harbored by lurkers and keyhole listeners, who aren't brave enough to show their true feelings, but take a perverse sort of pleasure in feeling hard done by, not wanting to tell others what the problem is lest it be resolved.

This vision of resentment as a pinched and petty emotion found its clearest expression in the work of the German philosopher Friedrich Nietzsche, and in particular his 1887 book *On the Genealogy of Morals*. He developed a concept of resentment — he used the French term *ressentiment* — to explain all that was obstructed and petty about modern life. He argued that the origins of European civilization lay in a heroic, golden age that celebrated noble rage and swift vengefulness (he called this the "master morality"). At some point during the Roman Empire, Nietzsche thought, this "master morality" began to die out, and in its place a different kind of attitude took hold — the "slave morality." Nietzsche argued that the slaves of the Roman Empire suffered under the contemptuous treatment of their masters, but were unable to express their indignation for fear of reprisal. Instead, they buried their urge for vengeance, occasionally unleashing it in small doses of PIQUE and spite.

According to Nietzsche, it was this attitude of hidden anger and denial that characterized *ressentiment*, and that Jewish, and later, Christian, religious teachings perpetuated with their vision of patient suffering on earth and redress in the hereafter (for Nietzsche the Bible was the ultimate expression of *ressentiment*). As a historical claim, it's based on almost no evidence. But as a description of an emotion obsessed with compensation rather than action, it has been very influential. One well-known contemporary exponent is the philosopher Slavoj Žižek, who has provocatively argued that terrorism is motivated by the "perversion" of resentment. Rather than granting suicide bombers access to emotions that, on Nietzsche's terms, might seem more "heroic" — an expression of rage, or an urge for others to share in a burden of pain, or even a desire for revenge — Žižek pins them back into the low-status, morally suspect response of resentment (*see also:* DISGRUNTLEMENT).

In the long term, resentment might become twisted and gnarled, but keeping anger buried temporarily can sometimes be the wisest option. In contrast to the immediate violence of anger, resentment is settled and deliberate. It waits, putting the brakes on an escalating situation. There are some cultures — those with long experience of oppression in which overt acts of retaliation could have catastrophic consequences — that recognize this long-held resentment and the strange effects it can produce as a distinctive part of their emotional life (*see:* HAN; *also:* LITOST). And those long and patient years of suffering and fantasizing about revenge, hoping for payback and being disappointed, etch scars into our emotional landscapes. This is why Nietzsche, though he disliked resentment intensely, believed it was only by developing it that "the human soul became deep."

See also: ANGER.

RINGXIETY

A phone trills in a crowded train carriage, and you frantically rummage for yours. Out on a country walk you whip out your phone like a gun from a holster, convinced you've felt it vibrate, only to discover a pathetically blank screen. According to the psychologist David Laramie, who coined the term, ringxiety is a feeling of low-level anxiety causing us to think we've heard our phones ring, even when they haven't. Evidence — as if we needed any more — that in this age of instant communication, being in a state of readiness for human contact is fast becoming a default setting.

See also: ANTICIPATION; DREAD.

RIVALRY

He infuriates you with the effortless way he steals your place. With his casual put-downs, the way he siphons off the attention. You feel your cheeks flush, your palms stick to the table. An urgent need to interrupt as everyone congratulates him on his recent success. You start boasting. You lie! You hate him for his scheming. But you hate him more for being better at it than you, leaving you flustered and bamboozled, with tears of frustration pricking your eyes. The only thing worse than this imposter is the fact that you're related to him.

Is rivalry an inevitable part of being human? Are possessiveness and jealousy, the desire to overtake, and the fear of being left behind all facts of our psychology? The seventeenth-century political philosopher Thomas Hobbes thought so, arguing that human nature was essentially competitive, and life a "warre of every one against every one." In the nineteenth century, the intellectual harbingers of evolutionary theory seemed to cement this vision of life as a battle over scarce resources. The most extreme thought those weakened by illness or poverty, unable to live unassisted, were simply its inevitable casualties: "It is best they should die," wrote Herbert Spencer, who first coined the phrase "the survival of the fittest." The term is often wrongly attributed to Charles Darwin, though he himself took a more measured view, arguing — with tales of gallant monkeys and loving crustaceans — that COMPASSION and altruism were just as important for survival as one-upmanship.

At the end of the nineteenth century, one of the effects of the new evolutionary theory was an interest among child psychologists in the competitiveness and jealousy of children. The idea that animosity might exist between siblings runs back to Cain and Abel. But when child psychologists began to investigate the phenomenon of "sibling rivalry," as it was dubbed in 1893, they treated it as a natural instinct — the great sharp-elbowed race for survival in microcosm.

In the first decades of the twentieth century, perhaps in part due to anxiety about family breakdown (see: JEALOUSY), nervousness about sibling rivalry caught on. Writers of child-rearing manuals portrayed children as envious and Machiavellian in their plotting, and advised parents to restrain them lest the next generation should grow up emotionally disfigured by resentment. Smaller family sizes exacerbated the problem, since as fair distribution of resources (attention, love, food) became theoretically possible, their lack was all the more obvious. In his 1949 play *Death of a Salesman*, Arthur Miller questions the idea that competition will ultimately bring rewards. Happy and Biff Loman are incapable of speaking to one another without sparring, while their father, Willy, despairs of life in the overcrowded city: "The competition is maddening!"

Today's child manuals give sibling rivalry less attention. Perhaps we have come to see it as less of a problem. Since the fall of the Soviet Union, most Western governments have come to accept — rightly or wrongly — that encouraging private commerce and a free market will make society more efficient and prosperous. Child psychologists seem to have followed suit, arguing that a little rivalry might help a child flourish. Claire Hughes from the University of Cambridge has suggested that children display ingenuity and creativity in figuring out what will most irritate their siblings. She links rivalry to increased motivation and flexibility, and even to emotional intelligence since one-upmanship requires us to understand how our own behavior affects other people's feelings.

The great Renaissance humanist Michel de Montaigne would not have been surprised. In his essay "Of the Disadvantage of Greatness," he argued that elbowing one's way to the top tests strategic thinking, helps cultivate virtues such as COURAGE and resilience, and allows us to taste the extremes of our emotions — JEALOUSY, TRIUMPH, ANGER and VENGEFULNESS. Those who have the "ease and slack facility of making everything bow beneath" them, he wrote, are "sliding not walking; sleeping not living."

The paradox, of course, is that in this case it really is the taking part that counts. As Montaigne knew, once you get to the top, life becomes insufferably dull.

See also: LIGET; SMUGNESS.

ROAD RAGE

Refusing to wait for the lights to change. Sneakily stealing a parking space. It was the idea that other road users were disrespecting the rules that made drivers bristle with INDIGNATION and start to retaliate. There were tales of motorists cutting each other off, ramming vehicles in front, even climbing out of their cars wielding crowbars.

Road rage was first named in the late 1980s by news pundits, alarmed at a sudden outbreak of violence on America's highways. Today, on both sides of the Atlantic, such frenzies are widely accepted as one of the hazards of the roads.

Driving on busy roads is undeniably stressful, but is this the only cause of aggression? A more important factor may be the way we become temporarily disinhibited behind the wheel. Inside our cars, we feel as if we are hidden and protected, as though wearing a mask or a suit of armor. It's the same when we roam about in Internet chat rooms or contribute to comments threads: without eye-to-eye contact, we're less able to pick up emotional cues. This makes us less likely to recognize drivers as other humans, and, further, allows paranoid or hostile feelings to fill the void. An embarrassed wince, apologetic smile — and, significantly, a moment of eye contact — goes a long way to making feelings of indignation evaporate. But driving inside our separate cars, we rarely have the chance to make these connections.

In a now classic study on prosocial behavior (or acting in a way that promotes social cohesion and friendship), first published in 2005, the psychologists Kevin Haley and Daniel Fessler found that subtly displaying images of eyes caused the participants in their experiment to behave in a more generous and conscientious manner. Subsequent experiments have confirmed that when eyes were displayed on a cafeteria honesty box, near recycling bins, and even on a charitable website, people behaved more responsibly. Could something as simple as decorating cars with pictures of eyes reduce aggression on the roads too?

See also: INSULTED, feeling; PARANOIA; RAGE.

RUINENLUST

Feeling irresistibly drawn to crumbling buildings and abandoned places.

See also: MORBID CURIOSITY; *MONO NO AWARE.*

SADNESS

Someone takes you by the hand: "Something terrible has happened."

After the SHOCK, something else sets in — a sunken, exhausted feeling. The mind sags. The limbs crumple. There is no need, not anymore, for energy: getting angry, attempting to change things, that time is over. Sadness may silence us — what else is there to say? — or we may seek out consolation with talking and tears. However it appears in our lives, sadness is one of the emotions that comes closest to resignation and acceptance. It's there when the irreversible happens: when we lose something or someone, and nothing can be done to get them back.

From its earliest incarnations, sadness — from the Old English *sæd* (sated), and with overtones of the Latin *satis* (satisfied) — has been associated with having had one's fill. "I am a lonely thing," confesses the weary battle shield who narrates one of the Riddles in the tenth-century *Exeter Book*, "wounded with iron / smitten by sword, sated (*sæd*) with battle work." In this sense, sadness was not understood as a depressed or lowered emotional state, but as an excess that edged toward BOREDOM.

Sadness was a very popular topic in the Renaissance, as popular as happiness is today. It was the relationship between sadness and weight that most intrigued the period's doctors and philosophers. Physicians argued an excess of a dense substance, or humor, called black bile caused sadness, weighing the body down and making the sorrowful clumsy, their faces drooping and gait slow. But this physical heaviness was also thought to make one's character weightier — so that sadness equated with being more sober, resolute and steadfast. Protestant theologians argued that since sorrow literally weighed a person down, it humbled them — from Latin *humus* (earth) (*see:* HUMILIATION). They delineated a particular category of sadness called "godly sorrow," a beneficial grief that came with recognizing one's spiritual failings and unworthiness before God.

A familiarity with gloom was also widely thought of as an emotional training, a lesson in resilience. In his *Castell of Helth*, a medical treatise and early self-help manual written in 1539, English lawyer Thomas Elyot urged readers to familiarize themselves with other people's sorrow to better tolerate their own. He offered lengthy descriptions of the causes of sadness — from the ingratitude of children to the failure to be promoted. In this sense, among early moderns, familiarity with normal sadness was regarded as a protective factor against its more serious manifestations — the illness of melancholia (*see:* MELANCHOLY), or suicidal DESPAIR.

It's hard to imagine Elyot's *Castell of Helth* being taken up too enthusiastically by today's self-help publishers. A list of reasons to be somber is unlikely to make the best-seller list. Yet, the idea that we might have to *learn* the art of sadness — how to experience its many flavors, and how to endure it too — does have a resonance today. Among those who fear we are forgetting how to be sad are the psychiatrists Allan Horwitz and Jerome Wakefield, authors of *The Loss of Sadness* (2007). They discuss the widely acknowledged "epidemic" of depression. Dismissing the claim that this is to do with the greater pressures of twenty-first-century living, they argue that the stratospheric rise in the number of people diagnosed with depression is the result of overdiagnosis. And this overdiagnosis is itself the consequence of an inadequate description of major depressive disorder in the widely used American Psychiatric Association's *Diagnostic and Statistical Manual of Mental Disorders* (or *DSM*). They are not arguing depression does not exist: it does, and from its sluggish apathy to blank, annihilating despair, it is truly debilitating. Their contention is that some people are being diagnosed as depressed when, in fact, they are sad, and this overdiagnosis is the only thing able to account for the startling jump in cases.

The first edition of the *DSM* was published in 1952, amid growing criticism of the lack of continuity in mental health diagnoses. To avoid theoretical wrangling about the causes of mental illness — was it the result of brain chemistry, social injustice or family trauma? — the *DSM* spoke only of symptoms, leaving out context altogether. However, this meant the old distinction between pathology and passion, which had traditionally distinguished illnesses like melancholia from ordinary sadness, was erased. Anyone who had experienced five out of the nine symptoms for at least two weeks, could be diagnosed with major depressive disorder — even if their depressed mood, decreased appetite, insomnia and so on had a reasonable explanation, such as the loss of a job or the end of a relationship. The earlier editions of the *DSM* did include a "grief clause," which meant that people could not be diagnosed with depression within two months of losing a loved one. But controversially the *DSM-V*, published in 2013, has dropped this exclusion too, and in this way, the old distinction between understandable and unwarranted sadness has been erased — in the diagnostic classification, at least. This is not just a matter for the consulting room: the *DSM*'s description of what constitutes depression trickles down into health education in schools, and appears on publicly funded health websites and in magazine articles. With opportunities for self-diagnosis rising (*see*: CYBERCHONDRIA), and our GPs pressed for time,

the desire to find a clinical diagnosis seems to be growing. And with
this emphasis on providing an answer comes a failure to accept sadness
as a natural consequence of being alive.

Is there anything inherently wrong with wanting to make bad
feelings go away? Perhaps not. But the antidepressants of choice
today — Prozac and the other SSRIs (selective serotonin reuptake
inhibitors) — do have side effects, and don't always work. More importantly, seeing sadness as a problem to be medicated away might leave
us poorly equipped to manage in the future. For the psychotherapist
Susie Orbach, overprescribing has a corrosive effect, sending a message that "pain can't be borne, lived through and tolerated," and rob-
bing us of an ability to recognize sorrow as an enriching part of life. "It
is our responses to adverse circumstances that make us human, and
our capacity to survive these feelings and grow through and from them
is part of what constitutes maturity," she writes. Crucially, when sadness is eclipsed by the diagnosis of depression, we become even less
willing to acknowledge that we're feeling sad at all, fearing it will
impede our success in the world, or that we'll be tainted by the stigma
that still surrounds mental illness. And this repression of sadness may
well make it worse.

With its feelings of satiety and acceptance, its quietness and even APA-
THY, sadness, as distinct from depression, is an important part of our
lives. It's the process through which we gather up ourselves to adjust to
a new version of ourselves after loss or DISAPPOINTMENT. It protects
us while we rest, and gives us strength. At the very least, as was well
known in the sixteenth century, if we see sadness as an unfamiliar,
strange creature, we will be less resilient in the face of it — and far
more vulnerable to its more serious manifestations as a result.

See also: GRIEF.

SATISFACTION

Sandy flings down her pom-poms: "You're a fake and a phony and I wish I'd never laid eyes on you!" Danny is crestfallen — but Rizzo, who has orchestrated the stand-off, is thrilled. Her eyes sparkle, her face lights up. The bonfire scene in *Grease* contains one of the best smiles in cinematic history: gleeful, contemptuous and entirely self-satisfied. Rizzo has had her revenge.

We smile for all sorts of reasons: delight, mirth, incredulity. There are wry smiles. And grins like the Cheshire Cat's. But one smile has a particularly intriguing history: the smile of satisfaction. It can be full of TRIUMPH or CONTENTMENT, irritatingly smug or ironic and wry (the smile that is part of the look the Italians call *il sorriso di chi la sa lunga*, the expression of someone who knows the whole story). But whichever form these satisfied grins take, they seem to have enjoyed a moment in the sun in eighteenth-century France, when Parisians learned — briefly — how to smile.

The origins of this "smile revolution" can be traced back to a group of natural philosophers active in the mid-century. They believed themselves to be living in an "Age of Lights," liberated from the gloom and oppressiveness of Church-sponsored knowledge. These philosophers presented themselves as free, inquiring and happy. And for them, a smile was the ideal emotional attitude with which to greet the world. "One must laugh at everything," said Voltaire. In fact, the statue of him that sits in the foyer of the Comédie Française has a slightly mischievous expression (though he himself thought it the grin of a "maimed monkey"). This is not a man plagued by desire or tormented by doubt, but one curious and quietly confident. It betrays a sense of what today's self-help gurus call "self-actualization," but that those *philosophes* who created, under the editorship of Denis Diderot and Jean d'Alembert, the great bible of the Enlightenment, the thirty-five-volume *Encyclopédie* dedicated to scientific and secular thought, called "satisfaction" or "interior contentedness."

From the Latin *satis* (enough) *facere* (to do), satisfaction originally meant the payment of a debt or fulfilment of an obligation. In particular, it meant the appropriate amount of penance required to balance out a sin (*see*: REMORSE). At least, this is the primary sense given in the *Encyclopédie*, but its authors also included discussions of satisfaction as a sentiment (their word for an emotion). They believed a feeling of satisfaction, which they sometimes called "contentment," came from using one's skills in the appropriate manner, and that discontent or restlessness came from having certain abilities or interests, but not being able to give them free rein. In this way, these eighteenth-century discussions foreshadow today's preoccupation with "job satisfaction." For these Enlightenment authors, the satisfaction of using one's faculties (we'd call them skills or capacities) was a "secret joy," and "the most pleasant sentiment of all."

Amid the social upheavals that led to the French Revolution of 1789, some French aristocrats began to move away from the stiffness of the court and embraced the attitude of the *philosophes*. Previous generations of the upper classes had been depicted in portraits with their mouths enigmatically clamped shut — perhaps they feared exposing the rotten and yellowing stumps of their teeth, perhaps they worried about being thought indecorous, since only farm laborers and servants appeared in paintings with their mouths agape. In the 1780s, however, smiles began to light up the walls of Versailles. They were a symbol both of progressiveness and of wealth — since only the richest could enjoy the prestige of the latest porcelain smile, a consequence of the period's advances in dentistry. Whether *philosophes* or aristocrats, however, Parisians didn't enjoy their self-satisfied smiles for very long. By the time of the September massacres of 1792, when mobs of Parisians killed thousands of suspected royalists, they were more commonly depicted wearing violent screams instead.

A hundred and fifty or so years later, in the 1950s and '60s, a person could walk down the street in any American town and see encouraging smiles beaming down from the billboards above them. Further improvements in dentistry no doubt fueled a willingness by advertisers to sell products with a smile — and America's celebration of CHEERFULNESS probably played its role too. Smiling housewives promised a vision of a satisfied — and importantly, a sexually satisfied — life. And it's this particular satisfied smile that we see in the original poster for *Grease*. While Danny (John Travolta) smolders with a pout, Sandy (Olivia Newton-John) appears dressed up in her rebellious, "bad girl" outfit, her lips parted in a smile, a row of perfect pearly whites for all to see — and envy.

See also: SMUGNESS.

SAUDADE

It is thought that the Portuguese first learned to speak of an emotion *saudade* (pronounced sow-*dahd*, or sow-*dah*-jee in Brazil) in the fifteenth century, during the Age of Discovery. Ships set sail from the port of Lisbon on their way to Africa and South America. Those left behind lived out their days scanning the horizon, longing for the return of their loved ones. Female troubadours sang of their *soidade* (the older spelling) in their *cantigas d'amigo* ("songs about a boyfriend"), their wistful lyrics expressing an ache for distant lovers, and the happiness of the past. Today, people speak of feeling *saudade* not only for distant people, but for far-flung places, and even misplaced objects as well.

Saudade: a melancholic yearning for someone, or something, that is far away or lost. It's always there, pulsing below the surface with its HOPEFULNESS tinged with GRIEF. There is a vague yearning, yet it is interlaid with resignation and the pleasure of remembering past joys.

Some emotions are so intimately tied to a particular artistic form that it's impossible to think of them without it. Melancholy and the blues. National pride and anthems. In the early nineteenth century, *saudade* found its modern form in fado music. Meaning "fate" or "destiny," fado was born on the cobbled alleys of Libson's Alfama district, home to sailors and prostitutes. Influenced by the Afro-Brazilian music brought back to Portugal by the royal family and their entourage on returning from exile in Brazil in the 1820s, fado's sobbing guitars and yearning voices evoke the experience of poverty, loss and the unfaithfulness of lovers. Fado is supposed to cleanse the singer of *saudade's* bittersweet melancholy too.

So to sing fado is to *matar saudades*. Literally: to kill *saudade*.

See also: NOSTALGIA.

SCHADENFREUDE

The unexpected thrill we feel at another's misfortune is a deliciously clandestine human pleasure. Sure, we put on our best sad face when our infuriatingly attractive friend gets dumped. But behind the commiserations, there's just a little pulse of excitement, making our eyes gleam and the corners of our mouths twitch. Admitting that they too could occasionally feel a stab of pleasure on hearing of other people's suffering, the Greeks called it *epichairekakia* (literally, rejoicing over evil), and the Romans, *malevolentia*, giving our own word "malevolence". Today, schadenfreude — from the German *Schaden* (harm) and *Freude* (pleasure) — is most widely used. It refers to an illicit enjoyment of another's bad luck, as opposed to the more forthright scorn or gloating.

The Roman poet and philosopher Lucretius believed our delight in another's struggle was not a sign of moral bankruptcy. We enjoy standing safely on the shore watching a boat tossed about on a stormy sea, he wrote, not because we inherently enjoy the spectacle of another's misery, but because "it is sweet to perceive from what misfortunes you yourself are free." Other people's bad news — divorce, a layoff — can leave us feeling relieved it's not happening to us. It's the sort of high we get with a narrow escape of the "there but for the grace of God go I" variety. As Iris Murdoch recognized, even the death of a distant acquaintance could produce feelings close to EUPHORIA, a burst of enthusiasm for one's own aliveness, "a glow of excitement and pleasure...a not yet diagnosed sense of all being exceptionally well with the world" (*see also*: RELIEF).

But in truth, we hungrily devour other people's misery for a ragbag of reasons. RIVALRY is one. And then there's ENVY, RESENTMENT, amusement, distraction.... Many of us would admit to feeling an ignoble rush of delight when our effortlessly successful work colleague is scolded by the boss. Seeing our competitors fall flat on their faces is gratifying because we think, probably wrongly, that our own stock goes up when that of others goes down. We love to read about celebrity gaffes for similar reasons. If the sales of magazines are anything to go by, it seems we relish the bodily imperfections of the rich and famous, their cellulite and collapsed nostrils, their man boobs and thick ankles. And we can barely contain our GLEE when pompous politicians are caught with their trousers down — oh, how the mighty fall! — because, for once, the tables are turned and it is we who feel superior. It's not just that we're jealous and covet their power and success. We're also resentful of the importance we've given them; part of us wants to see them punished, so our *own* status can be restored.

Schadenfreude might be seen as the opposite of EMPATHY, but even feeling vicarious sadness for another's misfortune can slide imperceptibly into the pleasures of PITY or even SMUGNESS. And we all know people who just love a good catastrophe, so long as it's not happening to them (often they're the ones who end up being most helpful in a crisis, because they're not paralyzed by awkwardness or an excess of COMPASSION). All that excited, gossipy drama, the endless phone calls, the boxes of wine and tissues, and the opportunity to rummage around in someone else's dirty laundry, which distracts them from looking too closely at their own. Misery, as the old saying goes, loves company. It's reassuring. Few of us care to admit it, but we get a kick out of hearing about other people's bad decisions and errant spouses and ungrateful children. It reminds us that it's not only our own hopes that get dashed. Everybody else's do too.

See also: CURIOSITY; MORBID CURIOSITY.

SELF-PITY

He mopes. He sulks. He slumps in the corner, head hanging between gleaming brushed-metal knees. Marvin the Paranoid Android in Douglas Adams's *The Hitchhiker's Guide to the Galaxy* is programmed with the latest in Genuine People Personalities (GPP) technology. His irritation at his fellow space travelers is outweighed only by the fierceness of his conviction that he is being mistreated and misunderstood.

* * *

The philosopher Max Scheler wrote that self-pity demands an imaginative tour de force: we must stand outside ourselves in a fantastic doubling. The person — or android — who feels sorry for himself "regards himself 'as if he were someone else,'" wrote Scheler, and looks down upon this helpless being, shedding a tear for the unfairness of *their* pathetic situation. By splitting ourselves in two like this, self-pity seems rather a beneficial emotion: when things don't go our way, one half of us gets to feel superior to the other, enjoying the RELIEF that pitying someone else can bring.

Sometimes self-pity is little more than a short and pleasurable indulgence, one that we are all entitled to enjoy. We get bored. We move on. But sometimes, like Marvin, we become stuck with our feelings of unfairness. And isolated by them too, since self-pity brings our horizons so claustrophobically near that other people's viewpoints, and even the fact that they might be struggling too, become impossible for us to imagine. It's here that the contempt that is at the heart of pity really makes itself known: not only do we loathe ourselves, and see no hope of things improving, but we can't bear anyone else either.

Frustrated families and friends have used all kinds of techniques to try to snap their loved ones out of the absorption of long-lived self-pity. Usually, they are variations on the "look how lucky you are" theme, which frankly just makes everyone feel worse. One technique that might work is suggested by recent research on altruism. Encourage your own beloved paranoid android to perform small and random acts of kindness toward strangers (or aliens) and they might just rediscover their compassion muscles — and find some kindness for themselves too.

See also: COMPASSION; PITY.

SHAME

The Greek philosopher and biographer Plutarch called it "one of the greatest shaking cracks that our soul can receive." For the French philosopher Jean-Paul Sartre, it felt like an "internal hemorrhage." We feel contempt for ourselves when we fall short of our own standards — as we all must do from time to time. None of us is flawless. We crumple at the thought of facing family or friends after being arrested or caught cheating, or surprised having sex in a way no one knew we enjoyed: "How shall I behold the face / Henceforth of God?" howls Adam in Milton's *Paradise Lost*, "Cover me ye pines! / Ye cedars, with innumerable boughs / Hide me." Where GUILT is usually thought to be an internal experience, characterized by *hearing* the voice of conscience, shame is more often linked to a feeling of social condemnation and the horror of being *seen*. We know we feel shame when we want to disappear from view — our own, as well as other people's. It turns us into talented escapologists. In private we grimace and fold ourselves under the duvet. In public we soldier on, half meeting other people's eyes, and hoping we can conceal our distress under a bright, waxy smile. Little is more shameful than shame itself.

In the 1940s the cultural anthropologist Ruth Benedict made a distinction between "guilt" and "shame" cultures that has remained very influential. The phenomenon of Catholic guilt is well known, but Benedict argued that all Christian societies were typically "guilt cultures," whose members were encouraged to feel an internalized private guilt when they transgressed moral codes. By contrast, Benedict believed "shame cultures" — she thought Japan was exemplary — maintained their status quo through the threat of public humiliation and ostracism. In a "shame culture," she argued, the interests of the group were put above those of the individual, and those who fell short of expected behavior were thought to bring dishonor not just on themselves, but on their whole family. Today's anthropologists rightly point out that it is too simplistic to reduce an entire culture to a single emotion. Yet, journalists and others trying to comprehend the mind-set that can lead to an honor killing, or a ritual suicide, still reach, sometimes too quickly, for the concept of a "shame culture." As a consequence, shame itself is made to appear to be something foreign and peculiar, as if it were felt, or only felt strongly, by immigrants with a slim grasp on their unruly passions. But this is not a true reflection of shame's place in Western culture. Feeling ashamed, as Salman Rushdie put it, "is not the exclusive property of the East."

In fact, Benedict was wrong to characterize Christianity as a religion dominated by guilt: in both Britain and America there are long traditions of punishment by shame. In nineteenth-century Puritan New England, for instance, those who flouted the community's strict moral codes were publicly punished, exacerbating their disgrace. A couple caught having extramarital sex in 1867 were both taken to the marketplace; the man was whipped and the woman made "to be present at the whipping post...that she may in some measure bear the shame of her sin." Shame is still used as a punishment. Check your e-mail online and it's hard to resist the "click-bait" flickering in the corner of the screen: cowering and tearful celebrities slapped with the headline of "My Drugs Shame!" or "Exposed!" In a culture where photographs can be broadcast almost instantaneously to the world, it's possible that shame — and its related public event, the apology (*see*: REMORSE) — is becoming more important than ever for reining us in.

Of course, you don't need to get caught taking a fiver from your flat mate's purse or *in flagrante* with your married next-door neighbor to be made to feel shame. Some of us fit neatly into the way we think we're supposed to be. But most don't. Most of us carry some sense of not quite living up to standards, of being not quite right — and so we feel contemptible, and learn to hide our so-called flaws, as well as the shame we feel about them. Over the last thirty years, the importance of recognizing and valuing difference has become a key theme in policy debate in much of Europe and America. It has led to a shift, by no means total, in attitudes toward gender, sexuality, race, physical ability and other aspects of our lives that can be subject to tacit, and sometimes overt, disapproval. Since the Stonewall Riots of 1969, women and men have marched under the banner of "gay pride." Its premise is clear: in the face of intolerance, it's only by being seen that we can feel whole.

More recent theorists of sexuality have questioned this emphasis on PRIDE, wondering if it might bleach out other parts of homosexual life that might seem rather more embarrassing, even undignified. They have initiated a "gay shame" movement. One of its legacies may be a willingness to talk about shame as a valuable emotion, rather than the damaging, toxic one we've come to think of it as. It might be that to forge identity in the face of disapproval, the existence of shame must be recognized — even celebrated. Because it's probably only when we let ourselves pay attention to our shamed feelings, and follow their twists and turns, that we can see ourselves most clearly. And discover the surprising number of ways the person we expect ourselves to be crashes up against the one we really are.

See also: HUMILIATION.

SHOCK

In September 1914 the first soldiers displaying the symptoms of what later became known as "shell shock" returned from the Front. With their "stammering and disconnected talk" and their twitching faces and stumbling gaits, these men left physicians groping for an explanation, and a cure. According to pioneering psychologist Charles Myers, the strange symptoms were caused by the impact of shells exploding nearby that rattled the brain around the skull, studding it with microscopic lesions. Other military psychologists thought the stress of life in the trenches — with its relentless fear and constant traumas — had eroded the soldiers' resilience so that they had succumbed to hysteria, an emotional condition with psychosomatic symptoms. Either way, shell shock threatened to reduce a generation of young men to stumbling, stuttering shadows of themselves.

To be shocked — from the French *choquer*, meaning to be knocked about or jolted — is to be brought up short by something sudden and unwelcome. Collisions, assaults, unexpected news: all may overturn one's view of the world as a safe place. Shock can quickly turn to speechlessness and numbness, as disbelief and incomprehension set in. Some say this is a sort of psychic anesthesia, helping us survive a terrible experience. But even when the pain relief wears off, what shocks us still reverberates, appearing in our dreams, our habits, even the way we expect other people to respond to us — sometimes for the rest of our lives.

The idea that a bad shock can lead to a deep and lasting psychic wound is relatively new. When the word "shock" was first used in English around 400 years ago, it was a military term, describing a collision of charging jousters, or the clash of armies: in Shakespeare's *Richard III*, a forthcoming battle is described as a "shocke of armes." It was only in the eighteenth century that people started to talk of their minds being violently assaulted, as if on a battlefield. What used to be called being "struck with WONDER" or "frighted almost to death" began to be spoken of as shock. And, as it turns out, for some at that time being easily shocked was something to be proud of.

The eighteenth century witnessed a revolution in our medical understanding of the human body and mind, in part due to the pioneering work of the London physician and anatomist Thomas Willis. He had carefully dissected the corpses of hanged criminals and argued that the body was not animated by the strange liquids of the humors, but by a delicate lattice of nerves and fibers found under the skin. This network carried vital spirits back and forth from the brain, and animated the rest of the body in turn, making the eyelids spring open in terror or the cheeks grow pink in delight. The outside world impinged on the inner one through these fibers too: the nerves — and in particular, those cordlike structures surrounding the heart, which were known as "heartstrings" — were imagined to quiver in a state of tension, vibrating and resonating on the slightest touch.

As a result of Willis's work, doctors began to speak of strong emotional responses not in the language of imbalances of the humors, but in terms of the condition of a person's nerves. Women, artistic men and the upper classes, whose bodies were untouched by hard work, were thought to have particularly delicate or sensitive nervous systems — a desirable trait in this period. For this reason, they were thought to possess a superior aesthetic sensibility, a more refined moral sense, and the ability to divine the feelings of others (see: EMPATHY; DISGUST). But these sensitive types had to be cautious too: the shock of a bit of unexpected news or the spectacle of something gruesome might reverberate so powerfully on the instruments of their bodies that madness might follow. In Johann Wolfgang von Goethe's 1774 novel *The Sorrows of Young Werther*, it is the shock of hearing his beloved is engaged to another that spins the hero into a mental chaos. He compares the experience to the violent assault of an electrical storm, all the worse for coming in the midst of a joyful occasion: in such situations "our senses have been opened to feeling and so take in impressions faster."

Doctors today have long dispensed with the term "shell shock" to describe a psychological injury, and speak of post-traumatic stress disorder instead. Today, the most common medical use of the word "shock" describes a life-threatening condition caused by blood loss or an allergic reaction: the blood pressure drops, the breathing becomes rapid and shallow, the skin cold and clammy. This consolidation of shock as a pure physiological response in the twentieth century has left us today much freer to talk of emotional shock as more ordinary. It's even become a faintly cosseted feeling, associated with the suburban and uptight. The rudeness of a fellow driver or next-door neighbor can shock us into baffled indignation (*see*: INSULTED, feeling). It's the sensation of being scandalized, the incomprehension when one's expectations are violently confounded: *How could they do that?* The mouth opens and closes like a fish's; the mind attempts to process the news. To the artists and intellectuals of the eighteenth century, so proud to be easily shocked, this reaction might have seemed even desirable. Today's artists, by contrast, might hope to shock their audiences — but show themselves to be quite unshockable as a result.

For other military emotions *see*: HOMESICKNESS.

See also: FEAR; GRIEF.

SMUGNESS

There are few characters in English literature as smug as Emma Woodhouse. "Handsome, clever, and rich," nothing gives her greater pleasure than her own impressive achievements. She is particularly delighted with her recent success in matchmaking. "So many people said Mr. Weston would never marry again," she says, but "I made the match" and was "proved in the right." On she goes with the gloating, "I planned the match," "success has blessed me." Until Mr. Knightley can take it no longer: "You made a lucky guess; and *that* is all that can be said." But Emma's self-congratulation knows no bounds: "And have you never known the pleasure and triumph of a lucky guess? I pity you."

The pink-cheeked gleam of self-SATISFACTION. Ding! The TRIUMPH of a won argument. Ding! The DELIGHT — with its extra twist of CONTEMPT — of feeling one's own superiority when a competitor falls. Ding! Ding! Ding! No wonder smugness is so irresistible a feeling. With its flash of triumphant grin, it's an oasis in a world of mistakes and apologies, a little moment of perfect being-in-the-right-ness, a smart, smooth, polished button of a feeling ("smug" or "smugge" originally meant having a neat, spruce appearance; it was only in the mid-nineteenth century that it started to mean being conceited too). Feeling smug is so irrepressibly lovely, you'd think we'd all want to walk around all day dressed head to toe in it. What a shame, then, it's universally disliked.

See also: HAPPINESS; HATRED.

SONG

Is any slight felt as keenly as unfairness? A smaller piece of cake, or portion of the will, can breed quietly seething resentments. The wails of "it's unfair" that lead beleaguered parents to carefully monitor the distribution of M & M's among siblings with the precision of physicists engaged in nuclear fission, might seem childish. But taking umbrage on discovering we've received less than our fair share is an all too common feature of adult life too (*see also:* MIFFED, a bit).

Those who live on the Pacific island of the Ifaluk are only too happy to acknowledge their feelings of righteous indignation. *Song* is their name for the specific feeling of anger aroused when someone breaks one of the cardinal rules of the Ifaluk value system and refuses to share properly. If a turtle hunter does not distribute the fruits of his hunt in exactly equal portions, or a woman smokes a cigarette but neglects to offer others a toke, those overlooked will make no attempt to hide their dismay, or restrain their condemnation. For those of us who live under free-market capitalist economies, feeling angry because you've been overlooked can seem petty, or worse, entitled ("Go and hunt your own turtle!") (*see also:* DISGRUNTLEMENT). Among the Ifaluk, however, *song* is accepted as an entirely justifiable response — one that plays an important role in ensuring things run smoothly in a culture which, above all, relies on mutual dependency and cooperation for its day-to-day success.

See also: RESENTMENT; RIVALRY.

SURPRISE

In 1872 Charles Darwin, by then an eminent Victorian naturalist acclaimed for his theory of evolution, described conducting a curious experiment on himself in the reptile house at London Zoo. Standing before a glass tank containing a deadly puff adder, Darwin thrust his nose up against the glass plate "with the firm determination of not starting back if the snake struck." Of course, no sooner had the angry puff adder lunged at the glass than Darwin skittered several paces backwards.

Later he admitted that the incident had "amused" him. Like the early-twentieth-century theorist of laughter Henri Bergson, Darwin knew that our bodies can be ludicrous when they misbehave despite our best intentions. According to Bergson, it is when our body's automatic processes are at work that we become ridiculous, even to ourselves.

* * *

Surprise is one of the most sudden and fleeting of emotions. Triggered by some startling occurrence for which we are entirely unprepared, it flares up, and then disappears almost immediately. No one can stay surprised for very long (although sometimes they *say* they are: "What surprises me about your behavior…"). Surprise proper seizes us, and sets off clattering reactions: the eyes ping open and the pupils dilate; the eyebrows shoot upward and the jaw drops. It's a reflex response that we're born with — even babies in the womb respond to loud noises with a "moro," or startle, reflex. If SHOCK silences us and roots us to the spot, surprises are often far noisier. They make us spring backwards, knocking over the furniture, or drop whatever we're holding, or let out gasps and excited shrieks. We might feel surprised (and delighted!) when our friends jump out from behind the sofa to celebrate a birthday; flabbergasted (and disgusted!) by an unexpected tax bill.*

When the philosopher René Descartes created his list of the "primitive passions," any sudden and overwhelming attack of emotion was called "a surprise." WONDER, he wrote, was a "sudden surprise of the soul." JOY, HATRED, even LOVE could be felt as surprises, convulsing the limbs and seizing the heart. It's the sense of one's whole body being taken over by an outside force that makes feeling surprised so disorienting. Some relish being swept off their feet (*see:* ILINX). But there are others for whom being surprised can feel undignified, embarrassing, even enraging. Perhaps what's most peculiar about being surprised is the dislocated sensation it brings — and the sneaking sense that we're not as in command of our bodies as we might like to imagine. The body's automatic responses make us ridiculous, as Bergson thought. But our lack of control is unnerving too.

---

* Some languages acknowledge this difference: in Ifaluk, *rus* is a nasty surprise, *ker* a nice one.

All emotions include an involuntary aspect. The fact that so many of our feelings of anger, joy and disgust rise up without our permission — usually at inopportune moments — is part of what makes them both exasperating and alluring. It was these moments of emotional disobedience that particularly intrigued Charles Darwin. Why do we jump back in surprise from a snake stored safely behind glass? Or shut our eyes when frightened in the dark? He wondered if these unnecessary emotional responses were vestiges, emotional habits left over from much earlier times. It was as if our bodies had learned to feel in a certain way a very long time ago, and were simply compelled to act out these earlier scenarios. Darwin's theory called into question the cherished idea that our emotions express some innermost part of ourselves, replacing it with a picture of human feelings shaped by vast forces, which stretched far beyond the margins of our individual lives. He showed us that our emotions don't entirely belong to us. And that though we might fondly imagine ourselves to be the drivers of our bodies, we are more like passengers, along for a ride.

See also: FEAR.

SUSPICION

Are you sure you don't mean PARANOIA?

TECHNOSTRESS

The Greek philosopher Aristotle observed that we're more likely to fly into a violent rage when slighted by someone we perceive to be inferior to us. In fact, he went even further, arguing that if you've been insulted by someone lower down in the pecking order, you are thoroughly entitled to shout, curse and even hit them: it's the only natural response.

We're less likely to see anger in these hierarchical terms today, but perhaps we should. It may be precisely why computers and other electronic devices rouse such murderous reactions. They are supposed to be making our lives easier, these wilful electronic slaves of ours. But mostly it feels as if they're in charge, forcing us to negotiate with them, cooperate, read their manuals...

Aristotle would have been furious.

For an emotional machine *see:* SELF-PITY.

See also: DISGRUNTLEMENT; RAGE; RINGXIETY.

TERROR

"It's when the lights go out and you feel something behind you, you hear it, you feel its breath against your ear, but when you turn around, there's nothing there…"

This was Stephen King's answer when he was asked to characterize terror. More violent than feeling spooked, more immediate than dread, less connected to gore and disgust than horror, terror is felt in the presence of an elusive, unseen menace and leaves us rigid, rooted to the spot. The nineteenth-century Italian physician Angelo Mosso, who dedicated much of his life to studying the physiological responses of various types of fear, observed among soldiers that "in terror, even the most intrepid men do not think of flight; it seems as though the nerves of defence were severed and they were left to their fate."

The Romantic poets and philosophers of the late eighteenth century were intrigued by terror. The Swiss painter Henry Fuseli thought it the aim of any serious artist. "The axe, the wheel, sawdust and the bloodstained sheet" merely made the gorge rise, he wrote. Terror, by contrast, like the medieval concept of a "wondrous fear," was an ennobling, even purifying emotion (*see:* FEAR). His painting *The Nightmare* (1781), in which a goblin squats on the chest of a lifeless woman, its round eyes staring out from the canvas, was thought to leave those who gazed upon it fighting for air. But it wasn't only imps and demons who terrorized. According to the philosopher Edmund Burke, vast mountainous landscapes could assail walkers, provoking the violence of "terror and wonder" in their hearts. As Wordsworth put it in *The Prelude*, these "huge and mighty forms, that do not live / like living men" brought "trouble to my dreams."

At first glance, much of this rich poetic inheritance has been bleached out of our contemporary political rhetoric, in which terror plays such a central role. "It is natural to wonder if America's future is one of fear," said George W. Bush addressing a joint session of Congress following 9/11. "Some speak of an age of terror." It is a stark contrast to Franklin D. Roosevelt's first inaugural address in 1933, when he warned that "the only thing we have to fear is fear itself." Talk of a "war on terror" inflames the menace. Perhaps this was the intention of the speechwriters who came up with the phrase. Learn that a terror, rather than a fear, threatens you, and you might feel cowed and overwhelmed. In the face of shadowy, elusive forces — a virus in an envelope, or on a website — self-defense seems futile, and terror petrifies us.

It's then that, like Mosso's terrified soldiers, we become voiceless and rooted to the spot. And might find ourselves incapable of arguing when someone else seeks retribution on our behalf.

See also: DREAD; FEAR.

TORSCHLUSSPANIK

Torschlusspanik describes the agitated, fretful feeling we get when we notice time is running out. The heart pounds, the nape of the neck prickles, as the deadline approaches. Yet, we're stuck, bewildered by choices and terrified we're about to make the wrong one. Life, and all its abundant opportunities, is passing us by.

Literally translated from the German as "gate-closing-panic," *Torschlusspanik* was coined in the Middle Ages. Seeing a rampaging army approach, and knowing that the castle gates were about to close, travelers and shepherds flung their belongings aside and stampeded across the drawbridge to safety.

Nowadays, the closing gates we rush toward are metaphorical. But the blind panic can be no less grim. Germans most often use *Torschlusspanik* to describe the feeling some women experience of being terrorized by the tick-tick-tick of a biological clock. Heightened by the scaremongering of newspapers and fertility ads, baby panic can rattle even the sanest of minds (*see also:* BROODINESS). But *Torschlusspanik* can also refer to any of those reckless, heart-in-mouth decisions we make because a deadline is looming, or because things seem scarce, whether impulse buying a pair of shoes just because the shop is closing, or putting a last-minute bet on a horse race. This is why the Germans remind themselves that *Torschlusspanik ist ein schlechter Ratgeber. Torschlusspanik* is a bad adviser.

See also: FEAR; PANIC.

TOSKA

So much of our emotional life is linked to the landscape. The craggy wilderness of the mountains gave the Romantics their love of loneliness and terror. Many of the inhabitants of northern Europe celebrate a feeling of coziness, the antidote to the flat ground and damp air (*see:* GEZELLIGHEID). In Russia, the emotion *toska* (pronounced *tas*-ka) is said to blow in from Europe's Great Plains, which sweep from the Pyrenees to the Ural mountains, and brings a maddening "unsatisfiedness," an insatiable searching. For Vladimir Nabokov, *toska* was a distinctly Russian emotion, "a dull ache" of the soul, "a longing with nothing to long for, a sick pining, a vague restlessness." As with so many of these emotions, there are several shades of *toska*. Over the centuries, philosophers and poets have linked *toska* to grand metaphysical anguish, but the word is also part of everyday spoken Russian too, capturing the distracted fog of the daily commute, or the yearning of a broken heart.

See also: ACEDIA; BOREDOM; *VIRAHA.*

TRIUMPH

There are some human noises that sound more like animal cries: whoops, hoots, screeches. To the pirates, the "dreadful screech" that wails through the ship sounds strange and ghoulish, "more eerie" than a cat-o'-nine-tails, or Davy Jones's death rattle. But to the Lost Boys, it's instantly recognizable as the crowing sound their leader Peter Pan makes, each time he sends a pirate to a watery grave.

The heart rises and the chest swells when we defeat an opponent. We leap up from our desks, flinging our arms skywards. Or sweep up loved ones in an elated hug. At a sports match, little is more contagious than the roars and whistles erupting in the winning crowd. The passion to conquer, and the thrill when we do, is what distinguishes humans from machines, world chess champion Garry Kasparov from IBM supercomputer Deep Blue.

Yet, there's an aggression about these cheers, too, with their echo of the *triumphus* processions of the ancient world, in which it was not enough to win; you had to heap violent HUMILIATION on your opponent too. In the ninth century BCE the Assyrian king Ashurnasirpal II commissioned friezes to be built around his palace at Kalhu (now Nimrud, on the banks of the Tigris in modern Iraq), celebrating his military conquests. They depict people from the invaded countries being dragged from their hiding places. Officials oversee shackled prisoners working in mines, or else count the severed heads of the slaughtered. And all of this carved by the captured citizens themselves. The friezes — like the Roman victory — depict the cruelest part of triumph: the desire to degrade the loser even further.

Perhaps, though, it came at a price. Triumph is not without its risks. "I can't help crowing...when I'm pleased with myself," confesses Peter. His sudden glory leaves him feeling invincible. So when Peter rescues Tiger Lily from the pirates, Wendy sensibly claps her hand over his mouth. If he crows, he'll give them all away...

See also: SMUGNESS.

U

UMPTY

Perkin Flump is in a very bad mood.* The quiet tune his grandfather is playing on the flumpet is just too loud. The water he's supposed to wash in is too cold. The floor he walks on every day is too bumpy, and it's hurting his feet. His breakfast porridge is too lumpy and too sticky.

"Are you feeling all right?" asks the mother.

"No I'm not feeling all right," he snaps back. "I'm feeling all wrong. I feel sort of yuck, all horrible. I feel umpty."

"What's umpty?" asks his mother.

"I'm umpty," he tells her. "It's a too-much morning. I'm just fed up and I'm going out to the yard to be umpty on my own."

When he gets there, his sister Posie and little brother Pootle spot a little gray cloud hanging stubbornly over his head. They try hiding from it, blowing at it, even singing to it, but nothing shifts it. It's only when an unlikely accident involving the flumpet and a carrot reduces Perkin to giggles that the little cloud lifts higher and higher, and finally floats away.

---

* The Flumps was a 1970s animated children's TV series, presenting the home life of a family of round furry creatures who lived in northern England. Perkin feels umpty in an episode called "The Cloud."

Umpty: a feeling of everything being "too much" and all in the wrong way.

Its only known cure: laughter.

See also: MATUTOLYPEA.

UNCERTAINTY

All things are so very uncertain, and that's exactly what makes me feel reassured.

— *Tove Jansson,* Moominland Midwinter

Getting lost is no longer a problem. Suspect you've wandered off down the wrong street, and you might whip out a smartphone, tap a screen and find your location via satellite. There are apps that tell us whether a train is delayed. Websites that predict which films or books we'll enjoy. With a proliferation of new technologies, it may seem as if there's less and less need to leave things to chance. But sometimes we might wonder what we're missing out on.

Uncertainty is often characterized as an unpleasant emotional experience, one we are motivated to avoid. Feeling doubtful at life's biggest junctions can be hard to tolerate. No amount of Googling can tell us whether to quit our jobs or have a child (*see:* TORSCHLUSSPANIK). Instead, we're flung back and forth between scraps of advice, our indecision leaving us claustrophobic and irate. No wonder that a desire to overcome uncertainty, by creating dependable structures, is thought to give humans an evolutionary edge.

Yet, though predictability temporarily salves us, hesitations and doubts are part of the architecture of our lives. At some time or another all of us will struggle with the fact that our future is uncertain. Even the most advanced theoretical physicists can't give us answers. According to Heisenberg's uncertainty principle, it's impossible to know both the size and mass of a particle at any one time, since each time you try to measure one, the other changes. If this is the condition of our sub-atomic universe, you can bet it's the condition of our day-to-day lives too: "Should I buy the tomatoes? But then I'll have to have the cauliflower too. But does she like cauliflower?" etc.

Freedom, serendipity, whimsy, creativity: these are the delights of uncertainty. Not knowing an outcome can be immensely pleasurable — it's why we keep reading murder mysteries, and why the first rush of a love affair is particularly intense. According to many artists, the desire to find out must be resisted: it's *not* knowing that is more valuable. Only those "capable of being in uncertainties, Mysteries, doubts, without any irritable reaching after fact or reason," wrote the poet John Keats, are truly free to create and explore.

Allow yourself to get lost, and you might glimpse that freedom too.

See also: ANTICIPATION; CURIOSITY; TERROR.

VENGEFULNESS

The brilliant retort that slices the smug back down to size. The shiver of nasty pleasure that comes from seeing someone floundering and speechless who only moments before was bulging with REPROACHFULNESS. Yes, there's glorious satisfaction in tit for tat. It's when our PRIDE is wounded by an insult, or some oversight has left us baffled or stunned, that vengefulness gives us a chance to restore lost dignity. Even if the revenge only happens in the mind's eye — the more baroque and excessive the better — it can still achieve this restoration. "Dishonor," wrote the philosopher Jeremy Bentham, "consists not in receiving an insult but in submitting to it."

An idea once popular among historians is that vengeful feelings used to be much more acceptable in the past than they are today. According to the influential historian and sociologist Norbert Elias, who wrote in the 1930s about the "civilizing process" of medieval Europe, people of the Middle Ages were "wild, cruel, prone to violent outbursts": private feuds and vendettas simmered among the nobility, while "the little people, too — the hatters, the tailors, the shepherds — were all quick to draw their knives." Today's historians paint a different picture. They argue that even though inflicting punishments was often a matter of individual honor in twelfth- and thirteenth-century England, it was still a tightly regulated process. The rules around private vengeance required that the punishment be carefully matched with the crime (a version of the much older *lex talionis*; an eye for an eye…) so that victims could achieve satisfaction without setting off a cascade of further retaliations. Against this backdrop, the passion of vengefulness was a two-part process; it involved both an urgent desire to right a wrong, and also the rational task of weighing up appropriate punishment (*see also:* REMORSE).

However, by the sixteenth century, judges and courtiers were quick to portray vengefulness as unruly and dangerous. With the expansion of the legal system across England, it was no wonder that the official methods of state punishment were being held up as morally superior — and private vendettas frowned upon. Philosophers followed suit. "Revenge is a kind of wild justice," wrote Francis Bacon, "which the more man's nature runs to, the more ought law to weed it out."

Did these efforts to discredit vengefulness work? The "revenge tragedies," so popular in the late Elizabethan and early Jacobean theater, cast doubt on the law's capacity to provide a reasonable alternative to private vengeance. In Kyd's *The Spanish Tragedy*, first performed in 1592 and one of the earliest of this form, the law is impotent and untrustworthy: the knight marshal, Hieronimo, "tears the papers" when he meets petitioners who want help with their cases, literally ripping up the letter of the law. So when Hieronimo's own son is murdered, it's no surprise that he takes matters into his own hands, plotting a complicated vengeance. Like so many of the plans concocted by wronged characters in revenge tragedies, his is long-winded and complex. The thinking — and often, procrastination — which went into these revenge plots is the opposite of an angry outburst. The revenge ultimately might be bloody and messy, but the vengefulness is not — it is much more deliberate, and its end result is served cold.

Conflicted attitudes toward vengefulness still linger. Of course (of course!) we ought to rise above our desire to get even. We all know the conventional wisdom is that we're the ones who suffer most from our own vengeful feelings, or, as Bacon put it, "A man that studieth Revenge keeps his owne Wounds greene, which otherwise would heale." We are suspicious of retaliatory urges — but sometimes, quietly impressed by them too. Why else do we so gleefully recount those urban legends — the prawns sewn into the curtain hem, the immaculate collection of Savile Row suits with the arms scissored off? Perhaps there is a strange admiration for those who daringly act on their vengeful impulses, while the rest of us dutifully submit, if not to the insult, then to the due process — and perhaps feel a little paler as a result.

For another outlawed emotion, *see:* HATRED.

See also: RESENTMENT; INSULTED, feeling; SATISFACTION.

VERGÜENZA AJENA

A contestant on a TV talent show swaggers onto the stage, brags about their singing voice... and then launches into "I Will Survive."

The face clawing! The toe curling! You want to throw your TV out of the window ("I can't watch it!") but you can't help glancing back.

The Spanish call this exquisite torture *vergüenza ajena* (literally: *ajena,* other person, *vergüenza,* shame and embarrassment, pronounced ver-*gwen*-tha a-*hay*-na). It is a vicarious humiliation, usually felt toward strangers.* You might experience it when a politician mispronounces an important name, but insists he's said it right, or a

---

* When we witness a friend or loved one (and especially, parent) dancing or singing badly, we might feel a twang of embarrassment, but of a different kind — that shudder comes because we fear being caught up in their orbit, shamed by association.

smug comedian cracks a joke at an audience member's expense, and is met with stony silence. When someone realizes they've made a mistake and blushes, we take it as a kind of apology (*see:* EMBARRASSMENT). The most intense *vergüenza ajena* is therefore reserved for the thick-skinned and the self-important. They don't seem to feel the shame they ought — so we supply it by the bucket load on their behalf. And then treat them with derision for this double failure: both for the mistake, and for failing to acknowledge it as one.

Vergüenza ajena is a paradox. It's a ruthless punishment for transgressing the codes of expected behavior. It mocks and excludes (*see:* CONTEMPT). But it also is empathetic: to feel the embarrassment of another's situation, we must put ourselves in their shoes. These apparently contradictory impulses both point to the importance of the group over the individual — which is why linguists have suggested that the Spanish have named this emotion. In Spain, the fear of losing one's *dignidad* (dignity) or *orgullo* (pride) is thought to be particularly pronounced — even the last piece of food left on a sharing plate is called *el de la vergüenza*, since it is a source of shame to whoever takes it. But it is also a culture where the bonds of *simpatía* (sympathy or kindness) run very deep. In this way, *vergüenza ajena* highlights sensitivity to propriety and disgrace, but the pleasures of solidarity too.

Spain isn't the only country with a word for this feeling. Germans call it *Fremdschämen* (external shame); the Finns, *myötähäpeä* (a shared shame); and the Dutch *plaatsvervangende schaamte* (place-exchanging shame). Among English speakers, though we may cringe and howl at the TV, *vergüenza ajena* remains a nameless pleasure — perhaps all the more agonizing for not being easily described.

For another reason to keep watching, *see:* SCHADENFREUDE.

See also: EMPATHY.

VIRAHA

I was shy at our first union; he was obliging with hundreds of skilful flatteries; I spoke with sweet and gentle smiles he loosened the silk-garment on my hips; O friend! Make him make-love to me passionately, I am engrossed with desire for love.

In the late-twelfth-century Indian kingdom of Orissa the poet Jayadeva composed the epic *Gita Govinda*. Its twelve chapters were not intended to be read, but sung and danced by torchlight, the centerpiece of bhakti temple worship. The song expresses the core principles of bhakti, from the Sanskrit *bhaj* (to share, to love), a path of religious living in Hinduism, and a heightened, feverish devotional style that spread across the Indian subcontinent between the fourth and the ninth centuries. The bhakti concept emphasizes a striving for spiritual intimacy with the divine, often expressing spiritual devotion in the language of erotic lust.

The *Gita Govinda* recounts the relationship between the amorous goatherd Govinda (an incarnation of the god Krishna) and Radha, a cowherd. When Radha discovers that Govinda has been unfaithful, she hides herself among the creepers in the forest, and implores her friend to help win the god back. Her verses are exquisite and sensual, recalling the sexual intensity of their first meeting and the yearning she now feels for the absent deity. They encapsulate a feeling that in Sanskrit is called *viraha*, usually translated as "longing" or the particular kind of love felt during separation or abandonment. An aspect of *sringara rasa* (erotic and romantic love), one of the nine *rasas*, or themes, that shape human experience, *viraha* is a feeling of incompleteness without a loved one, and a fixation on the ECSTASY of the longed-for reunion.

Viraha recalls other formulations of romantic infatuation, not only the erotic — the poetry of the Occitan troubadours, or the inconsolable longing expressed in Portuguese fado music (*see:* SAUDADE). The difference is that *viraha* is also a religious feeling, and ultimately an optimistic one. The full twelve chapters of the *Gita Govinda* — in which Krishna realizes the mistake of his infidelity, experiences *viraha* for Radha, and the pair reunite — symbolize the soul's quest to find its spiritual home.

Viraha is often contrasted with Christianity's separation between "carnal appetites" and higher spiritual love (*see:* DESIRE). But in truth, even Christian writers have made the union with God decidedly racy. "Batter my heart," implored John Donne in one of his sonnets addressed to the Holy Spirit; "ravish me."

See also: LOVE.

VULNERABILITY

Tread softly, because you tread on my dreams.
— W. B. Yeats, "He Wishes for the Cloths of Heaven"

It's the desire to connect that makes us most vulnerable. Those moments we stumble onto a perilously bright stage and, with all our imperfections exposed, whisper the truth about what we really want: sex, forgiveness, a child. Vulnerability is there when we pluck up the courage to ask for something we need, when we say, "I care about this, and I want you to care about it too." It's there when we make a commitment — "I love you"; "I trust you" — or confess to feeling tender, joyful, terrified. It feels like the wind whistling through the rib cage. It can be unpleasant. Exposing. Vulnerability is laying out the dreams of Yeats's poem, and hoping no one will stomp all over them.

* * *

In the last ten years, psychologists and social scientists have become interested in vulnerability. Their research has found that those moments when we experience ourselves as naked and defenseless are crucial to developing intimacy, building a sense of identity and cultivating self-worth. This is not a new idea. Medieval scholars spoke of finding the bravery required to live with integrity and speak from the heart, and thought it was a cardinal virtue (*see*: COURAGE).

Perhaps this twenty-first-century interest in vulnerability has been driven by dissatisfaction with the self-esteem movement, and its brittle, narcissistic displays of achievement. Or perhaps vulnerability has piqued the interest of researchers because of its centrality in twenty-first-century life. Entering bank details online, e-mailing personal information: there's a wheedling voice in our heads that wonders how protected our secrets are. And in the workplace? Being robust enough to withstand the vulnerability of our positions may be a critical factor in our ability to navigate life as "precariat" workers, bounced from one short-term contract to the next (for what happens when we fail, *see*: DISGRUNTLEMENT). Even precariats working in the creative industries, held up as exemplars of the entrepreneurial spirits that emerge when we are denied job security, may struggle with managing vulnerability. They have to learn to be audacious enough to lay out fledgling ideas before clients, and resilient enough to cope when they say "no."

Being able to "lean in" to the discomforts of vulnerability may be emerging as a particular emotional virtue, but it's not a straightforward good. The euphemism "a vulnerable person" is often used to describe all those marginalized and dispossessed in our society, at risk of manipulation or abuse. And for every person who walks into a therapist's office rigid with defenses, there are those whose extreme openness has become self-defeating. For the "oversharers" and desperate lovers who make themselves too vulnerable, full disclosure can alienate the people they want to draw closer. Their behavior may look like a desire for greater intimacy and authenticity. But repeatedly, it emerges as a strange way of pushing people away. Trust is what is at stake in both these cases. For those whom society designates "vulnerable," and those for whom vulnerability has become an unhelpful habit, a readiness to expose oneself is partly a question of being too trusting — and therefore of being too quickly hurt.

If vulnerability is replacing self-esteem as the emotion we should try to develop in our lives, what we should talk about is balance. An optimal in-between. Saying "I love you" is a risk worth taking. But a whole life lived on the precipice? To have value, vulnerability does not have to be terrifyingly transformative, or a constant background hum. It can be knowingly practiced, in careful measures too.

For more about emotions in the workplace, *see:* CHEERFULNESS.

On having the courage of your convictions, *see:* BASOREXIA.

WANDERLUST

Its first victim was Jean-Albert Dadas, a gas fitter from Bordeaux who was admitted to hospital in 1886 with exhaustion. His documents revealed he had traveled across France on foot, but he himself could remember little about it. Later, Dadas would walk to Moscow and Constantinople too, and those who met him on the way told of a man with a slim grasp of who he was, or the purpose of his journey.

A medical student, Philippe Tissié, wrote up Dadas's case, and coined the word "dromomania" (from *dromos*, the Greek for racecourse) to describe it. The diagnosis quickly became a medical sensation, and other cases followed. It was characterized by an insatiable urge to walk, sometimes for years. The walking was purposeful yet without a practical aim, and seemed to take place in an altered state of consciousness. When the dromomaniacs eventually rested, they had no memory of their journeys or why they had taken them. It was, wrote Tissié, a sort of "pathological tourism," and within only twenty-five years it had faded into obscurity.

Perhaps it begins with a restless twitch. Perhaps with a fascination with a distant country or landscape, a kind of yearning, even homesickness, for a place you've never visited but have seen pictures of in books (*see:* KAUKOKAIPUU). We may long to leave a footprint on a

275

glacier, or hear an echo of our voice across a lake at dawn. We know time slows down in strange lands. That other people's ways of thinking shake up our own, and make the world new again (*see*: DÉPAYSEMENT).

The German word *Wanderlust* (originally: the pleasure of hiking) first came out of a defiant Romantic tradition of solitary walking (*see*: LONELINESS). But today, we take it to mean something much broader. It is a craving for adventure and discovery, the desire to experience something different. But more than that, it describes a kind of longing for movement that runs as deep in the human psyche as love or fear. It's the desire, as old as human life itself, to see what lies beyond the next mountain, or outside the boundaries of the village — and may leave us with the gnawing feeling that life only makes sense if we are traveling in some direction or another.

When Tissié first met Dadas in the 1880s, the idea that humans might have a natural desire to roam was a popular one. Evolutionary theory had suggested that the human body could play host to ancient impulses, not all of which remained relevant to contemporary life. Tissié believed his patient's urge to wander was an eruption of a long-buried nomadic instinct. He saw it as a kind of irrational outburst (and in many ways, this link between wandering and irrationality is still with us: "doing a geographic," for instance, is Alcoholics Anonymous speak for relocating in the misguided hope that you'll somehow be able to leave your emotional baggage behind). Yet, though Victorians may have feared the eruption of the nomadic instinct, in small doses it was welcomed. Not least because its discovery coincided with the birth of the modern tourist industry. With Cook's Tours, and the publication of the first tourist guides (the Baedeker series), and the popularity of exotic travelers' tales from the likes of Jules Verne and Mark Twain, Europeans had never been more ready to be on the move.

"Pathological tourism" — at least in the way Dadas experienced it — is rarely seen today. Modern psychiatrists would categorize it as a type of fugue state, or state of dissociative amnesia. How might we explain the sudden rise and fall of this strange illness, then, in late-nineteenth-century France? Such transient mental illnesses are sometimes thought to be a kind of *folie à deux*, a half-delusion created by both doctor and patient being willing to see an eccentricity in grandiose terms as symptomatic of an illness. In particular, these syndromes erupt when the cultural climate allows: in the case of dromomania, not only the growth of tourism but also a widespread fear of homeless people created the perfect conditions for anxiety about excessive wandering to fester. Once the symptoms of a new disease enter the psychiatric literature, an epidemic spreads through repeated diagnosis and self-identification (*see also:* SADNESS; NOSTALGIA). Against this backdrop, even a healthy urge to travel could infect those formerly content to stay at home. "Wanderlust arises as an emotional epidemic," wrote one psychologist in 1902. Over a hundred years later, we may still be enjoying its effects.

See also: HOMESICKNESS.

WARM GLOW

Poor Larry David. Even a simple act of charity is fraught for the semifictionalized star of the HBO sitcom *Curb Your Enthusiasm*. Larry is alight with pride when he arrives at the opening of a new museum wing and sees his name immortalized on the wall as a donor. "Pret-ty good," he preens to his wife, Cheryl, ready to soak up the admiration of the VIP guests. But then he notices the donor inscribed on the other new wing. Anonymous. His mood darkens: "Now it looks like I just did mine for the credit." Sure enough, when Cheryl whispers that Larry's friend Ted Danson is the mystery donor, Larry is outraged at Ted's chutzpah. "Nobody told me that I could be anonymous — and tell people!" he fumes. "I would have taken that option!"

We're quick to be suspicious about other people's motives for helping — and sometimes even our own. To Larry David, a gift to charity is motivated by thoughts of one-upmanship and desire for prestige. Others might assume we want something in return (*see:* OIME), or that we just enjoy polishing that little halo (*see:* SMUGNESS).

But truth is, most of us walk off feeling a little bouncier after helping carry a stranger's stroller up the stairs, or bringing in a neighbor's shopping. Random acts of kindness give a HUMBLE feeling of solidarity of the "we're all in this together" variety, even a swell of PRIDE for having been capable enough to do anything useful at all. Yet, though we say "it's my pleasure" after someone thanks us, the English language has not yet dignified this pleasure with a name. Some have suggested "Altru-hedonism." Slightly less ugly is the phrase suggested by the Victorian philosopher Herbert Spencer (not known for being pithy): "altruistic pleasure." With this sort of competition, it might be that "a warm glow," even if it does remind us of halos and the smiles of self-SATISFACTION, is still the best we have.

Perhaps this blind spot in the English language can be traced to a distaste for the concept that kindness should be enjoyable at all. The idea that humans are naturally selfish is well established in Western culture. In his sermons, the sixteenth-century Protestant reformer John Calvin imagined humans to be devious and depraved, and that genuinely acting in another's best interests is hard for us to do. He taught the devout to strive to overcome their worse natures and carry out their "Christian duty." Generosity and kindness weren't instinctual, but required a concerted effort. Kindness should cost us; perhaps even hurt.

Today's neuroscientists argue differently. Over the past ten years, research into altruism has suggested that one of the key pleasure pathways of the brain, the mesolimbic system that carries dopamine to the areas associated with reward, is engaged when we donate to charity in the same way as it is when we receive money ourselves. The fMRI images that accompany these studies depict our brains glowing, quite literally, with the pleasure of giving. There are, of course, many other self-interested reasons to be altruistic: helping others binds our societies together and creates reciprocal networks. But the insight that the pleasure we feel is a biological inevitability, "nature's reward" for behavior that will help our species survive, seems oddly a relief to hear. Perhaps in time this knowledge will shift our way of thinking, until we forget that kindness was ever supposed to be a duty, and relish it only as a pleasure. And perhaps, then, more words for the "warm glow" we feel will not be far behind.

For other reasons we might be reluctant to help, *see*: COMPASSION; PITY.

WONDER

Hidden in the warrenlike shopping arcade deep beneath London's Charing Cross Station, Davenports Magic shop is a mecca for children. They stand slack-jawed and eyes gleaming as shop assistants make playing cards float and squidgy balls disappear from under cups. Their parents loiter near the door, knowing smiles on their faces. Occasionally even one of the adults will suddenly gawp, as momentarily their world unravels, and everything becomes as strange and enchanting as it was when they were small.

Perhaps many of us today associate being stunned or gobsmacked, dazed and astonished with childishness and naivety. Between the twelfth and seventeenth centuries, however, wonder was thought an important response to life's mysteries. At this time, philosophers and scientists believed they lived in a world strewn with rare and miraculous objects. This was a world of fantastical animals, where the wealthy bought alligators' teeth believing they were from dragons, or bezoar stones* thinking they were an antidote to poison, and displayed them in their *Wunderkammer* (often translated as a cabinet of curiosities: "room of wonders" would be correct). It was a world where "monstrous births" — infants born with accessory limbs who lived for only a few hours — were thought divine warnings of catastrophes to come.

With its BEWILDERMENT and dazed submission, awe and FEAR, wonder was thought so powerful it could even harm you: Laertes' lamentations over Ophelia's grave might, according to Hamlet, make the stars "like wonder-wounded hearers" stand still. It was considered such a central human experience that when René Descartes made his inventory of the six "primitive passions" in 1649, he introduced wonder first (following up with love, hatred, desire, joy and sadness). He defined it as a "sudden surprise of the soul, which causes it to apply

---

* Bezoar stones may be familiar from Harry Potter's potions classes, but they were really used by medieval doctors. They are a smooth, and surprisingly light, ball made from the compacted indigestible stuff that makes its way into the stomachs of goats and other ruminants — fruit and vegetable fibers, twigs, and especially hair. Some medieval doctors advised grinding up the valuable and sought-after stones and dissolving them in remedies; others kept the stones on display in ornately decorated stands. In 1575 the French surgeon Ambroise Paré described conducting an experiment to test the effectiveness of bezoar against poison, on a cook who was condemned to be hanged for stealing two silver dishes. The prisoner agreed instead to take poison — and the bezoar antidote — to see if he survived. Unfortunately, he did not.

itself to consider with attention the objects which seem to it rare and extraordinary" (*see also:* SURPRISE).

It is a testament to wonder's importance in this period that it was the subject of fierce debate. To many theologians, wonder, with its submission and HUMILIATION, was the only appropriate response to God's creation. Saint Augustine warned against trying to number the stars or count grains of sand, since this was evidence of vain curiosity, and the pride that barred the way to humble devotion. Others thought that wonder's paralysis could only ever be temporary, quickly transforming itself into purposeful curiosity. "All men by nature desire to know," Aristotle had written, and begin "by wondering that things are." Today we still speak of wondering *how* as well as wondering *that*. As one thirteenth-century text attributed to philosopher and theologian Albertus Magnus put it, the aim of the wise was "to make wonders cease."

Wonders did indeed begin to cease, sometime in the second part of the seventeenth century. In the new cultural atmosphere of the Enlightenment, natural philosophers started to emphasize order over oddity, and tried to uncover timeless laws through their experiments rather than being astonished and awestruck by miracles and other aberrations. This was not only a change in philosophical attitudes. Around the early eighteenth century, the preceding century's vogue for homes that were cluttered with stuffed crocodiles and ostrich eggs gave way to a new desire for space, light and order — and so the old lucrative trade in marvels faded away.

In the centuries that followed, many tried to reinvest wonder with the cultural authority it once had. Both the Romantic poets in the late eighteenth century and the hippies in the twentieth lamented the unweaving of rainbows that had taken place, seeking out — by chemical means if necessary — the feelings of awe and astonishment earlier generations had experienced so readily (*see also:* LONELINESS).

They were not to be successful. Today, curiosity has almost entirely eclipsed wonder as the appropriate emotional attitude of the educated elite.

See also: CURIOSITY; TERROR.

WORRY

Those squiggles of consternation hovering above Charlie Brown's head, give him a permanently frazzled look. He spends his life worrying — about his baseball team, his school grades, his loneliness, his unconventional dog, Snoopy. He's undoubtedly the most conscientious eight-year-old in the history of cartoons. But if being agitated and careworn is not generally for children, it is, however, a very common side effect of adult life.

From the Old English *wyrgan* (to kill or throttle), the oldest meanings of being worried involved strangulation by serpents or asphyxiation by bad smells. Animals worried their prey with biting and shaking ("Said e.g., of dogs or wolves attacking sheep"), but so, in the seventeenth century at least, could lovers worry theirs with kisses and violent hugs. The *Oxford English Dictionary* first identifies worry as a "troubled state of mind arising from the frets and cares of life" in the early nineteenth century. Worrying — or worriting — became a habit of literary characters soon after, evidence of an intense concern for others at the expense of oneself. It could be noisy: when Eliza, the runaway slave in Harriet Beecher Stowe's *Uncle Tom's Cabin*, appears at the house with her child, she is "in great worry, crying and taking on." Or silent, hidden beneath an optimistic smile. But it could still be deadly, exhausting and depleting worriers who, like Little Nell, were eventually killed by their concern.

* * *

In the 1870s the author Samuel Smiles, self-help guru for the Victorian middle classes, emphasized the dangers of worrying. "Cheerfulness," he wrote, "enables nature to recruit its strength; whereas worry and discontent debilitate it." The kind of worry that Smiles was particularly concerned about was that felt in response to vapid problems: the ups and downs of one's social status, breaches of etiquette, the latest romantic intrigue. The fact that worry debilitated was worrying in itself. In a world where being productive and energetically improving oneself were important values, succumbing to worry was emerging as rather irresponsible (*see also:* BOREDOM). It was against this backdrop that, in the 1890s, some of the apprehensiveness associated with worrying was carved off into an important new medical condition: ANXIETY. Initially thought to be caused by unspent sexual arousal, it is now the most regularly diagnosed affective disorder in the United States.

Perhaps the invention of anxiety has left workaday worry with a happier ending. Almost 150 years after Samuel Smiles, modern self-help books still relish the possibility of a worry-free life: *How to Stop Worrying and Start Living; Women Who Worry Too Much — how to stop worry & anxiety from ruining relationships, work and fun*. But more recent psychological research has cautioned against always assuming worry is a problem.

Catastrophizing (always visualizing the worst possible outcome) may be counterproductive, but sometimes worrying at our problems can be an imaginative process. Rattling them apart like a dog shakes its prey and examining them from every angle allows new ideas to come into focus and existing ones to rearrange themselves. And, though it might seem obvious, a longitudinal study reported in the journal *Psychological Medicine* in 2006 has confirmed that worriers have fewer accidents. Some researchers have even suggested that there may be a "worry gene," handed down through the generations, since while stress and anxiety may shorten lives, those who experience the lower-level, more optimal emotion of worry seem to live longer and reproduce more. So perhaps we should welcome at least some of our worries.

After all, not all worries are created equal. Some things are worth getting into a fluster about, as F. Scott Fitzgerald advised his eleven-year-old daughter, Scottie, in 1933:

> *Don't worry about dolls, boys, insects, parents, disappointments, satisfactions or the future.*
> *Things to worry about:*
> *Worry about courage*
> *Worry about cleanliness*
> *Worry about efficiency*
> *Worry about horsemanship…*

See also: DREAD.

Ż

ŻAL

The life of composer and virtuoso pianist Frédéric Chopin was lived in the sharp twists and bitter resentments that come when we lose everything. His exile from Poland, his turbulent relationship with the novelist George Sand, his frail health, which forced him to withdraw from the society of others, the strange episodes of delirium foreshadowing the consumption that killed him at thirty-nine. For Chopin, it was the untranslatable Polish emotion *Żal* that produced the morbid intensity we can still hear in his work, arguably the most haunting piano music ever created. It was, according to Chopin's friend and biographer Franz Liszt, the "soil of his heart."

Żal (pronounced jahl) is melancholy felt at an irretrievable loss. This is not a straightforward dejection. *Żal* is fickle, and shifts its shape, at one moment resigned, the next rebellious. It combines the DISAPPOINT-MENT, REGRET and even violent fury that comes when some part of our lives has been taken away for good. According to Liszt, Chopin's *Żal* was most of all a kind of anger, "full of reproach [and] premeditated vio-lence...feeling itself with a bitter, if sterile, hatred." Chopin's *Żal*, wrote Liszt, found its greatest expression in the composer's later works — the Etudes and Scherzos, which speak of a despair, "sometimes ironic, sometimes disdainfully proud," of recognizing the end of things.

See also: RESENTMENT; VENGEFULNESS.

ACKNOWLEDGMENTS

This book began as an inspired idea by Kirty Topiwala at the Wellcome Collection, and Fay Bound Alberti suggested I might be the one to take it on. Thank you both. Kirty and Cecily Gayford have stewarded the project with great sensitivity and I couldn't have asked for better editors. I am grateful to Elsa Richardson for her diligence as a research assistant in the final stages. Thanks too to Andrew Franklin for his enthusiasm and excellent jokes, to Trevor Horwood for assiduous copyediting, to my agent Jon Elek for his support and expertise, and to Penny Daniel, Drew Jerrison and the teams at both Profile Books and Wellcome Collection for steering this project through to publication and beyond.

Academic research isn't as solitary as it might appear, and I count myself very lucky to have such generous-spirited colleagues. My deepest thanks and respect go to Thomas Dixon, Jen Harvie, Katherine Angel, Elena Carrera and Rhodri Hayward. To all those who have given papers at the Queen Mary Center for the History of Emotions, written for our blog or swapped ideas in the pub, thank you: this project is indebted to your work. I'd also like to thank all in Queen Mary's School of English and Drama, as well as the Wellcome Trust for supporting the Center's activities, and the British Academy for supporting my own research.

While I was doing the research for this book, many people took time to answer my questions, spoke about their emotions and shared unpublished research. My sincere thanks to Carolyn Burdett, Susie Orbach, Dan Susman, Jade Shepherd, Richard Firth-Godbehere, Erin Sullivan, Barbara Taylor, Nathan Abrams, Nadia Davids, Joanna

Cohen, Colin Jones, Adrian Howe, Alice Haddon, Mandy Reichwald, Enda Hughes and Tom and Cat Watt-Smith. And for their help with unfamiliar concepts and foreign words, thanks to Preti Taneja, Yukiko Kinoshita, James and Kyoko Bowskill, Tiziana Morosetti, Margherita Laera, Llyr Gwyn, Gregory Tate, Marta Magalhães, Yaron Shavit, Julia Boffey, and my fellow ambiguphobes, Kieron Humphrey and Stephen Burn. Any inaccuracies are entirely my responsibility.

Thank you to H. Plewis for providing a quiet and inspiring place to work at a crucial moment, and to the many friends who listened patiently as this project took shape. I am, as ever, very grateful to my supportive parents, Ursula and Ian, especially for helping make it possible to juggle having a young child with writing.

And most of all, thank you, Michael. For everything you've done to inspire, encourage, and create the space for me to finish this, my eternal love and deepest admiration. And to Alice, who arrived in the middle of my writing this, thank you, too. You're too young to know it, but you bring the world to life.

NOTES AND
FURTHER READING

Epigraph

"And how delightful…" Oscar Wilde, *The Picture of Dorian Gray* (1891) (Penguin, 2012), p. 12.

Introduction

"key note…" John Constable to Rev. John Fisher, October 23, 1821, quoted in John E. Thornes, *John Constable's Skies: A Fusion of Art and Science* (University of Birmingham Press, 1999), p. 199.

"rather like saying…" Siri Hustvedt, *Living, Thinking, Looking* (Picador, 2012), p. 31.

In a drafty Edinburgh lecture hall… The history of the word "emotion" can be found in Thomas Dixon, "Emotion: The History of a Keyword in Crisis," *Emotion Review* 4(4) (October 2012), 338–44.

"At his 8th day he frowned much…" Darwin's observations of his son are held in the Darwin Archive at Cambridge University Library (DAR 210.11.1). With thanks to the Darwin Correspondence Project.

[fn.] *There is some evidence…* Letter from Emma Wedgwood, January 23, 1839, repr. in Frederick Burkhardt and Sydney Smith (eds.), *The Correspondence of Charles Darwin*, vol. 2: *1837–1843* (Cambridge University Press, 1987).

"common sense says…we meet a bear…" William James, "What Is an Emotion?," *Mind* 9 (1884), 188–205, pp. 190, 195.

"It is not easy to treat feelings scientifically…" Sigmund Freud, *Civilization and Its Discontents* (1930), trans. David McLintock (Penguin, 2002), p. 4.

"Some people would never fall in love…" François de La Rochefoucauld, *Collected Maxims and Other Reflections*, trans. E. H. and A. M. Blackmore and Francine Giguère (Oxford University Press, 2007), V: 136, p. 39.

no word that precisely captures the meaning of "worry"… cited in J. A. Russell, "Culture and the Categorization of Emotions," *Psychological Bulletin* 110(3) (1991), 426–50.

Historians had long suspected… For the history of the history of emotions, and an overview of the field, see Jan Plamper, *The History of Emotions: An Introduction*, trans. Keith Tribe (Oxford University Press, 2015).

The Li Chi... "The Sacred Books of China," *The Sacred Books of the East,* vols. 27 and 28, trans. James Legge (Oxford University Press, 1885).

Descartes thought there were six... René Descartes, "The Passions of the Soul," trans. Elizabeth S. Haldane and G. R. T. Ross, repr. in *What Is an Emotion?: Classic and Contemporary Readings,* ed. Robert C. Solomon (Oxford University Press, 2003).

[fn.] *Emotionologists...argue...* Paul Ekman, E. Richard Sorenson and Wallace V. Friesen, "Pan-Cultural Elements in Facial Displays of Emotion," *Science,* n.s. 164(3875) (April 4, 1969), 86–88. Among the psychologists who have called FACS into question are Rachael Jack and her colleagues: R. Jack et al., "Cultural Confusions Show that Facial Expressions Are Not Universal," *Current Biology,* 19 (2009), 1543–48.

Geertz asked an elegant question... Clifford Geertz, *The Interpretation of Cultures* (New York: Basic Books, 1973), p. 6.

Today's enthusiasm... The idea of EQ was popularized in Daniel Goleman, *Emotional Intelligence: Why It Can Matter More Than IQ* (Bantam Books, 1995), though it is based on earlier research, the most well known of which is P. Salovey and J. D. Mayer, "Emotional Intelligence," *Imagination, Cognition, and Personality* 9 (1990), 185–211.

Abhiman

Rabindranath Tagore's "Punishment" appears in *Selected Short Stories,* ed. William Radice (Penguin, 2005).

translators have offered... Swati Datta, "Locating and Collating Translated Stories of Rabindranath Tagore," *Translation Today* 2(1) (March 2005), 203–4.

Acedia

a "foul darkness" John Cassian, *The Institutes,* trans. Edgar C. S. Gibson (1894), p. 337.

"weighed down"... Amma Theodora's sayings are collected in the *Apophthegmata partum* (Sayings of the Desert Fathers) repr. and trans. in *Women in Early Christianity: Translations from the Greek Texts,* ed. Patricia Cox Miller (Catholic University of America Press, 2005), p. 247.

Amae

"person's love for granted"... Takeo Doi, *The Anatomy of Dependence: The Key Analysis of Japanese Behavior* (1973), trans. John Bester (Kodansha International, 1981), p. 168.

Ambiguphobia

"His ambiguphobic recipe..." Jack Hitt, *In a Word* (Dell, 1992), p. 14.

Anger

The introduction to this section incorporates material from Seneca's "On Anger," Robert A. Kaster, in *Anger, Mercy, Revenge* (Complete Works of Lucius Annaeus Seneca), trans. Robert A. Kaster and Martha C. Nussbaum (University of Chicago Press, 2010).

You might think the idea... For a discussion about the therapeutic uses of anger, and references to the physicians discussed here, see: Elena Carrera, "Anger and the Mind-Body Connection in Medieval and Early Modern Medicine," in her *Emotions and Health, 1200–1700* (Brill, 2013), pp. 95–146.

One example of this approach was the "ventilation therapy"... Eva S. Moskowitz, *In Therapy We Trust: America's Obsession with Self Fulfillment* (Johns Hopkins University Press, 2001), pp. 234–35.

Today's psychotherapists... Leslie S. Greenberg and Sandra C. Paivio, *Working with Emotions in Psychotherapy* (Guilford Press, 2003).

Anticipation

"You just wait and see..." Angela Carter, *Wise Children* (1991) (Vintage, 2006), p. 54.

Anxiety

"Anxiety is the dizziness..." Søren Kierkegaard, *The Concept of Anxiety* (1844), trans. Reidar Thomte (Princeton University Press, 1980), p. 61. All further quotes are to this edition.

Among Angstneurose's *symptoms were*... Sigmund Freud, "On the Grounds for Detaching a Particular Syndrome from Neurasthenia Under the Description 'Anxiety Neurosis' (1895)," in *The Standard Edition of the Complete Psychological Works of Sigmund Freud*, vol. 3 (Vintage, 2001), pp. 87–116.

psychological wreckage caused by the war... Rhodri Hayward, "The Pursuit of Serenity: Psychological Knowledge and the Making of the British Welfare State," in Sally Alexander and Barbara Taylor (eds.), *History and Psyche: Culture, Psychoanalysis and the Past* (Palgrave Macmillan, 2012), pp. 283–304.

"Age of Anxiety." W. H. Auden, *The Age of Anxiety: A Baroque Eclogue* (1947), ed. Alan Jacobs (Princeton University Press, 2011).

"He whose eye happens to look down..." Kierkegaard, *The Concept of Anxiety*, p. 91.

Apathy

"full of love and yet free from passion." Marcus Aurelius, *The Meditations* (Penguin, 2006).

"bystander apathy"... Bibb Latané and John Darley, "Group Inhibition of Bystander Intervention in Emergencies," *Journal of Personality and Social Psychology* 10(3) (1968), 215–21.

In fact, those first reports of the Genovese case...Kevin Cook, *Kitty Genovese: The Murder, the Bystanders, the Crime that Changed America* (W. W. Norton, 2014).

L'Appel du Vide

as Jean-Paul Sartre recognized...Jean-Paul Sartre, *Being and Nothingness: An Essay on Phenomenological Ontology*, trans. Hazel Barnes (Washington Square Press, 1966), p. 345.

Awumbuk

The indigenous Baining people...Jane Fajans, "Shame, Social Action and the Person Among the Baining," *Ethos* 11(3) (1983), 166–80.

[fn.] Peter Goldie, *The Emotions: A Philosophical Exploration* (Clarendon Press, 2002), p. 91.

Basorexia

Discovered in Charles Harrington Elster, *There's a Word for It* (Simon & Schuster), p. 68.

Bewilderment

Mess brings people into analysis...Adam Phillips, "Clutter," repr. in *One Way and Another* (Hamish Hamilton, 2013), pp. 117–28.

"Who is it that can tell me who I am?" William Shakespeare, *King Lear* I.iv.223.

Boredom

When the new emotional category...Patricia Meyer Spacks, *Boredom: The Literary History of a State of Mind* (Chicago University Press, 1995).

many an "overtoiled" Roman citizen...Quoted in Peter Toohey, *Boredom: A Lively History* (Yale University Press, 2012).

"bored to death." Charles Dickens, *Bleak House* (1853) (Oxford University Press, 1948), p. 9.

"look as pretty...and be dull without complaining..." George Eliot, *Daniel Deronda* (1876) (Wordsworth Editions, 2003), p. 110.

There is no coincidence that many creative people...Based on interviews with artists conducted by Dr. Teresa Belton: Teresa Belton, "A Fresh Look at Boredom," *Primary Leadership Today* 13 (2008).

"the root of man's "cultural advance""...Ralph Linton, *The Study of Man* (Appleton-Century, 1936), p. 90.

Brabant

"very much inclined..." Douglas Adams and John Lloyd, *The Deeper Meaning of Liff* (Pan Books, 1990), p. 14.

Broodiness

"the womb is an animal..." Plato, *Timaeus*, ed. and trans. R. G. Bury (Heinemann, 1952), p. 91.

Sociologists studying the desire... R. A. Hadley, The experiences of involuntarily childless men as they age, British Sociological Association Poster (2013).

Calm

He dreamt of a "psychocivilized society"... The discussion of Delgado's experiment and subsequent controversy is based on John Horgan, "The Forgotten Era of the Brain," *Scientific American* 203 (2005), 66–73.

the journalists reporting on Delgado's experiment... Peter J. Snyder et al., *Science and the Media: Delgado's Brave Bulls and the Ethics of Scientific Discourse* (Academic Press, 2009), pp. 32–34.

Carefree

"Slush! slush! sound the scythe-strokes." D. H. Lawrence, "On Insouciance," *D. H. Lawrence: Late Essays and Articles*, vol. 2, ed. James T. Boulton (Cambridge University Press, 2004), pp. 94–97.

Cheerfulness

Disney employees... Anne Reyers and Jonathan Matusitz, "Emotional Regulation at Walt Disney World: An Impression Management View," *Journal of Workplace Behavioral Health* 27(3) (2012), 139–59.

The emergence of cheerfulness... Carol Z. Stearns, "'Lord Help Me Walk Humbly': Anger and Sadness in England and America, 1700–1750," in Carol Z. Stearns and Peter N. Stearns (eds.), *Emotion and Social Change: Toward a New Psychohistory* (Holmes and Meier, 1988); also: Christina Kotchemidova, "From Good Cheer to 'Drive by Smiling': A Social History of Cheerfulness," *Journal of Social History* 39 (2005), 5–37.

"a general air of cheerfulness"... Harriet Martineau, *Retrospect of Western Travel* (1838) (M. E. Sharpe, 2000), vol. 3, pp. 120–21.

the Beecher Sisters' 1869 manual... Catherine Beecher and Harriet Beecher Stowe, *American Women's Home: Or, Principles of Domestic Science* (J. B. Ford and Co., 1869), p. 215.

"Think and act cheerful..." Dale Carnegie, *How to Stop Worrying and Start Living* (World's Work, 1948), p. 112.

In her seminal study... Arlie Russell Hochschild, *The Managed Heart: The Commercialization of Human Feeling* (University of California Press, 1983).

[fn.] The research conducted at the Max Planck Institute is reported in Andreas Hennenlotter, Christian Dresel, Florian Castrop et al., "The Link Between Facial Feedback and Neural Activity with Central Circuitries of

Emotion — New Insights from Botulinum Toxin-Induced Denervation of Frown Muscles," *Cerebral Cortex* 19(3) (2009), 537–42.

Claustrophobia

"They will have to undergo slow suffocation…" William Tebb, *Premature Burial and How It May Be Prevented* (1895) (Swan Sonnenschein & Co., 1905), p. 215.

Collywobbles, The

It's the stomach as well as the heart… For more on the links between stomach, emotions and mind, see Ian Miller, *A Modern History of the Stomach: Gastric Illness, Medicine and British Society 1800–1950* (Pickering and Chatto, 2011).

"It causeth troublesome dreames." Robert Burton, *The Anatomy of Melancholy* (1621) (J. W. Moore, 1867), p. 139.

Comfort

Winnicott suggested that these objects were more than a reliable presence… Donald Winnicott, "Transitional Objects and Transitional Phenomena," *International Journal of Psychoanalysis* 34 (1953), 89–97.

Before the outbreak of the Second World War… M. Vicedo, *The Nature and Nurture of Love: From Imprinting to Attachment in Cold War America* (University of Chicago Press, 2013).

He fashioned two wire structures, or "mothers"… Harry Harlow, "The Nature of Love," *American Psychologist* 13 (1958), 573–685.

Compassion

Compassion is never included in lists of "universal emotions"… Martha Nussbaum, "Compassion: The Basic Social Emotion," *Social Philosophy and Policy* 13(1) (Winter 1996), 27–58.

"When we want to stop an afflicted person…" Gregory I, *Moralia* in Job, quoted in Barbara H. Rosenwein, *Emotional Communities in the Middle Ages* (Cornell University Press, 2006).

Researchers at the Center for Compassion and Altruism… http://ccare .stanford.edu/. Similar results have been found by Helen Weng et al., "Compassion Training Alters Altruism and Neural Responses to Suffering," *Psychological Sciences* 24(7) (2013), 1171–80.

Compersion

[fn.] Steven Alexander, "Free Love Gets a Fit of the Wibbles," *Guardian*, April 4, 2005.

Confidence

"Of all the grifters, the confidence man…" David Maurer, *The Big Con: The Story of the Confidence Man* (1940) (Anchor, 1999), p. 1.

"Let go your conscious self"... *Star Wars Episode IV: A New Hope* (1977).

More recently psychologists have come to think... Tomas Chamorro-Premuzic, *Confidence: The Surprising Truth About How Much You Need and How to Get It* (Profile, 2013).

Contempt

"It was not a simple yawn"... "Clifton Williams, Illinois Man Jailed for Yawning, Freed After 3 Weeks," *Huffington Post*, September 9, 2009.

people "never lose all predisposition to the good." Immanuel Kant, "Religion Within the Boundaries of Mere Reason," *Religion and Rational Theology* (1793), trans. George di Giovanni (Cambridge University Press, 1996), p. 91.

In 1955 the British philosopher J. L. Austin argued...J. L. Austin, "Lecture I: Performatives and Constatives," repr. in *How to Do Things with Words: The William James Lectures Delivered at Harvard University in 1955*, ed. J. O. Urmson and Marina Sbisa (Clarendon Press, 1962), pp. 1–11.

In sixteenth- and seventeenth-century Britain...Sandy Bardsley, *Venomous Tongues: Speech and Gender in Late Medieval England* (University of Pennsylvania Press, 2006).

More recently hundreds of women joined an online campaign... The movement was sparked off by an article by Rebecca Solnit, repr. in her *Men Explain Things to Me and Other Essays* (Haymarket, 2014).

Courage

She quickly became immortalized by the Victorians...John Price, *Everyday Heroism: Victorian Constructions of the Heroic Civilian* (Bloomsbury, 2014), pp. 22–24.

"lots of abundant hair...that is thick and curly"...Quoted in Heather Webb, *The Medieval Heart* (Yale University Press, 2010), p. 112.

"stand immovable in the midst of dangers"...Thomas Aquinas, "The Virtues," *Summa Theologiæ* (1271–72), 1–2, 55–57, in *Selected Writings* (Penguin, 1998), pp. 653–81.

"We esteem the man who supports pain..." Adam Smith, *The Theory of Moral Sentiments*, VI.iii.17 (1759) (Wells and Lilly, 1817), p. 75.

Curiosity

Yet, even in the age historians have dubbed the "Age of Curiosity"...For the history of curiosity see Barbara M. Benedict, *Curiosity: A Cultural History of Early Modern Inquiry* (University of Chicago Press, 2001).

"the speculative part of swimming..." Thomas Shadwell, *The Virtuoso* (1676), ed. Marjorie Hope Nicolson and David Stuart Rodes (University of Nebraska Press, 1966), II.ii.84, p. 47.

Evolutionary psychologists have suggested...Robin Dunbar, *Grooming, Gossip and the Evolution of Language* (Faber and Faber, 2010).

a "listen-thief." For more on listen-thiefs, see John L. Locke, *Eavesdropping: An Intimate History* (Oxford University Press, 2010).

Delight

For the eighteenth-century English philosopher John Locke...John Locke, *An Essay Concerning Humane Understanding* (1689), ed. Peter N. Nidditch (Clarendon Press, 1975), book II, chapter XX, pp. 229–32.

Dépaysement

Each day, under cover of cleaning the guests' rooms...Excerpts from *L'Hôtel* are reproduced in Sophie Calle, *M'as-tu vue* (Prestel, 2003), pp. 159–65.

Desire

"It was a long time..." Samuel Beckett, "The End" (1946), in *Stories and Texts for Nothing* (Grove Press, 1968), pp. 47–74, p. 52.

"his departed idol"...Emily Brontë, *Wuthering Heights* (1847) (Harper & Brothers, 1858), p. 227.

In the twentieth century, the philosopher Georges Bataille suggested...This section incorporates material from Georges Bataille, *Death and Sensuality: A Study of Eroticism and the Taboo* (Walker & Co., 1962), p. 237.

Twentieth-century sexologists...William H. Masters and Virginia E. Johnson, *Human Sexual Response* (Little, Brown, 1966).

Despair

"the greatest hazard of all, losing one's self..." Søren Kierkegaard, *The Sickness Unto Death: A Christian Psychological Exposition for Upbuilding and Awakening* (1849) (Princeton University Press, 1941), p. 32.

"eternall rest / And happie ease..." Edmund Spenser, *The Fairie Queene* (1590), IX: 40 (Wordsworth Editions, 1999), p. 97.

"I see that man going back down..." Albert Camus, *The Myth of Sisyphus and Other Essays* (1942), trans. Justin O'Brien (Hamish Hamilton, 1955), pp. 76–77.

Disappear, The Desire to

"a chance...to totally erase the past"...Neil LaBute, *The Mercy Seat* (Faber and Faber, 2013), p. 32.

Disappointment

"his pleasure by trotting gravely..." Charles Darwin, *The Expression of the Emotions in Man and Animals* (John Murray, 1872), p. 57.

Her defense was "double insanity"... Official Report of the Trial of Mary Harris, Supreme Court of the District of Columbia, Monday, July 3, 1865 (W. H. & O. H. Morrison, 1865), p. 51.

He coined the phrase "the family romance"... Sigmund Freud, "Family Romances" (1909), in *The Standard Edition of the Complete Psychological Works of Sigmund Freud*, vol. 9, ed. and trans. James Strachey and Anna Freud (Hogarth Press, 1959), pp. 235–42.

"no really ideal part of the self exists." Melanie Klein, "On the Sense of Loneliness," in *Envy and Gratitude and Other Works 1946–63* (Hogarth, 1975), p. 305.

"a sense of treachery..." William Wordsworth, *The Prelude; or, Growth of a Poet's Mind* (1799), ed. Jonathan Wordsworth, M. H. Abrams and Stephen Gill (W. W. Norton, 1979), 10.378–80.

Disgruntlement

"If not actually disgruntled..." P. G. Wodehouse, *The Code of the Woosters* (1938) (Arrow Books, 2008), p. 9.

Raoul Silva, villain of the Bond film Skyfall...Sam Mendes (2012).

"Right here and now we thankfully..." "Ever Onward: IBM Rally Song," *IBM Songbook* (IBM Corporation, 1958).

"flexibility, adaptability and a readiness to reconfigure oneself." Paolo Virno is quoted in Sainne Ngai, *Ugly Feelings* (Harvard University Press, 2005), pp. 4–5.

Corporations have begun to use cybersecurity consultants... This paragraph incorporates language from Eric Shaw and Harley Stock, *Behavioral Risk Indicators of Malicious Insider Theft of Intellectual Property: Misreading the Writing on the Wall* (NASDAQ: SYMC, 2011).

"despondence and grumpiness..." Quoted in Olivia Lang, "Can Governments Spot Whistle-Blowers?" BBC News, January 7, 2011, www.bbc.co.uk/news/world-us-canada-12120850.

Disgust

When evolutionary psychologists talk of "universal basic emotions"... Paul Ekman, "Biological and Cultural Contributions to Body and Facial Movement," in John Blacking (ed.), *The Anthropology of the Body* (Academic Press, 1977).

To start with, there are at least three types... Colin McGinn, *The Meaning of Disgust* (Oxford University Press, 2011); William Ian Miller, *The Anatomy of Disgust* (Harvard University Press, 1997).

"Dirt is matter out of place"... Mary Douglas, *Purity and Danger: An Analysis of Concepts of Pollution and Taboo* (1966) (Routledge, 2003), p. 41.

Early moderns didn't talk of disgust... This history of disgust is based on research by Richard Firth-Godbehere, a PhD student at Queen Mary Center for the History of the Emotions. I am grateful to him for sharing his unpublished research with me.

In the late 1980s psychologists... Paul Rozin, Linda Milman and Carol Nemeroff, "Operation of the Laws of Sympathetic Magic in Disgust and Other Domains," *Journal of Personality and Social Psychology*, 50(4) (April 1986), 703–12.

Dismay

In Dickens's novels... Mr. Pickwick "almost fainted with horror and dismay" in *The Pickwick Papers* (1836) (Amalgamated Press, 1905), p. 294.

"What myghte he seyn? He felte he nas but deed"... Geoffrey Chaucer, *Troilus and Criseyde*, book 3, lines 1058–1141, repr. in *The Riverside Chaucer* (Oxford University Press, 1987), p. 528.

Those who suffer from Stendhal... I. Bamforth, "Stendhal's Syndrome," *British Journal of General Practice* 60(581) (2010), 945–46.

Dread

a "rootless phantom." Jeuan Gethin (1349). Quoted in Philip Ziegler, *The Black Death* (Sutton, 2003), p. 162.

Some chroniclers reported... There is disagreement only about the number of people who died. R. S. Bray, *Armies of Pestilence: The Impact of Disease on History* (James Clark, 1996), gives an account of the different estimates.

In his account of the outbreaks of the plague... Giovanni Boccaccio, *The Decameron of Giovanni Boccaccio*, vol. 1 (1353), trans. Richard Aldington (Covici, 1930), p. 3.

Ecstasy

"The pain was so great that I screamed aloud"... *The Collected Works of St. Teresa of Avila*, vol. 1: *The Book of Her Life*, trans. K. Kavanaugh and O. Rodriguez (Institute of Carmelite Studies, 1976), pp. 193–94.

"When you've the air of dervishood inside..." Rumi, *The Masnavi: Book One*, trans. Jawi Mojaddedi (Oxford University Press, 2004), p. 63.

One is entitled "Extase 1878." D. M. Bourneville and P. Regnard, "Attitudes Passionnelles — Extase (1878)," Plate 23, *Iconographie Photographique de la Salpêtrière*, vol. 2 (Aux Bureaus du Progrès Médical, 1876–80).

"What does it matter if it is a disease?"... Fyodor Dostoevsky, *The Idiot* (1869) (Wordsworth Editions, 1996), p. 210.

Embarrassment

According to the sociologist Erving Goffman... Erving Goffman, "Embarrassment and Social Organization," *American Journal of Sociology* 62(3) (1956), 264–71.

In the film Four Weddings and a Funeral... Mike Newell (1994).

"instrument of conformity." Rom Harré, "Embarrassment: A Conceptual Analysis," in Roy Crozier (ed.), *Perspectives from Social Psychology* (Cambridge University Press, 1990), pp. 181–204, p. 181.

"sign of indignation"...See "The Guillotine: Some of Its Victims," *The Courier*, June 14, 1844.

The true blush...Thomas Henry Burgess, *The Physiology or Mechanism of Blushing* (John Churchill, 1839), pp. 48–61.

One particular "servant Negress"...Charles Darwin, *The Expression of the Emotions in Man and Animals*, 2nd ed. (John Murray, 1890), p. 381.

He argued that blood rushes to the surface of the skin...Ibid., pp. 310–47.

Empathy

In the 1890s the novelist Vernon Lee...Vernon Lee and C. Anstruther-Thomson, "Beauty and Ugliness" (1897), repr. in *Beauty and Ugliness and Other Studies in Psychological Aesthetics* (London: John Lane, 1912), pp. 45–76.

a "universal solvent"...Simon Baron-Cohen, *Zero Degrees of Empathy: A New Theory of Human Cruelty* (Penguin, 2012), p. 127.

"mirror neurons will do for psychology..." Vilayanur Ramachandran, "Mirror Neurons and Imitation Learning as the Driving Force Behind the 'Great Leap Forward' in Human Evolution," *The Edge*, May 29, 2000.

"When we see a stroke aimed..." Adam Smith, *The Theory of Moral Sentiments* (1759) (Millar, 1761), p. 4.

"Nature" makes men "apt to invade, and destroy one another." Thomas Hobbes, *Leviathan* (Andrew Crooke, 1651), p. 61.

The eighteenth-century interest in sympathy...Barbara Taylor and Adam Phillips, *On Kindness* (Penguin, 2009).

"Weeping for the affliction of others..." "Moral Weeping," in *Man: A Paper for Ennobling the Species* (1755) (written by the King's physician, Peter Shaw, though published anonymously).

Envy

"it was as if she hadn't a single penny." *The Tain. A New Translation of "The Táin bó Cúailnge,"* trans. Ciaran Carson (Penguin, 2007), p. 5.

"the one emotion in all human life..." Nancy Friday, *Jealousy* (1985) (M. Evans, 1997), p. 9.

the impulse to "take it away or to spoil it." Melanie Klein, "Envy and Gratitude" (1957), repr. in *Envy and Gratitude and Other Works, 1946–1963* (Hogarth Press, 1975), pp. 176–235.

Fredric Jameson has argued...Fredric Jameson, *The Political Unconscious: Narrative as a Socially Symbolic Act* (1981) (Routledge, 2002).

Euphoria

*As the Tunisian activist and blogger…*Lina Ben Mhenni, "A Tunisian Girl," http://atunisiangirl.blogspot.co.uk/.

[fn.] John Jones, *The Mysteries of Opium Revealed* (Richard Smith, 1701).

or what they called "silly cheerfulness." Théodore Ribot, *The Psychology of the Emotions* (1896) (Scott, 1897).

*In 1926 two physicians…*S. S. Cottrell and S. A. K. Wilson, "The Affective Symptomatology of Disseminated Sclerosis," *Journal of Neurology and Psychopathology* 7 (1926), 1–30.

*Today, only 13 percent…*C. Diaz-Olavarrieta et al., "Neuropsychiatric Manifestations of Multiple Sclerosis," *Journal of Neuropsychiatry and Clinical Neuroscience* 11 (1999), 51–57.

Dr. Feelgood guitarist Wilko Johnson…"Terminal Cancer Has Made Me Feel Alive," BBC News, January 25, 2013, www.bbc.co.uk/news/entertainment-arts-21187740.

Excitement

"laughing, talking and kissing." Charles Darwin, *The Expression of the Emotions in Man and Animals* (John Murray, 1872), p. 212.

excitement was an "emotion of action"…Alexander Bain, *The Emotions and the Will*, 2nd ed. (Longmans, Green & Co., 1865), pp. 148–62.

In adrenaline, they had found the secret of excitement…Otniel Dror, "What Is an Excitement?," in Frank Biess and Daniel M. Gross (eds.), *Science and Emotions After 1945: A Transatlantic Perspective* (University of Chicago Press, 2014), pp. 121–38.

"Men and women must have their adrenals stimulated…" Aldous Huxley, *Brave New World* (1932) (Vintage, 2007), p. 211.

Fago

"The implicit poetry in Ifaluk…" Catherine Lutz, *Unnatural Emotions: Everyday Sentiments on a Micronesian Atoll and Their Challenge to Western Theory* (University of Chicago Press, 1988), p. 119.

Fear

"fear was expressed from an extremely remote period…" Charles Darwin, *The Expression of the Emotions in Man and Animals* (John Murray, 1872), p. 362.

*Fear is that simple. And yet…*For more on fear and its history, see Joanna Bourke, *Fear: A Cultural History* (Virago, 2005).

"The only thing we have to fear is fear itself"…Franklin D. Roosevelt, *Inaugural Address*, March 4, 1933.

"The thing I fear most is fear." Michel de Montaigne, "Of Fear," in *The Essays of Michel de Montaigne*, vol. 1 (C. Baldwin, 1811), pp. 63–66, p. 64.

According to the seventh-century medical manual... *The Eight Books on Medicine of Aurelius Cornelius Celsys: Adapted for Students of Medicine*, vol. 2, ed. John William Underwood (Underwood, 1830), p. 108.

"frighted" to death. Bill of Mortality, September 1665, Museum of London.

The situation is exacerbated...Frank Furedi, *Culture of Fear: Risk Taking and the Morality of Low Expectation* (Cassell, 1997).

"It did what all ads are supposed to do..." David Foster Wallace, *Infinite Jest* (Little, Brown, 1996), p. 414.

Feeling Good (About Yourself)

"lightness about the heart"...William James, "The Will to Believe," in *The Will to Believe and Other Essays in Popular Philosophy* (1897) (Dover, 1956), p. 19.

But as a result of the interest in positive psychology...For more on the history of the self-esteem movement see Peter N. Stearns, *Anxious Parents: A History of Modern Child-rearing in America* (New York University Press, 2003).

In the last ten years, the self-esteem movement...Jean M. Twenge, *Generation Me* (Free Press, 2006).

Formal Feeling, A

Emily Dickinson, "After Great Pain, A Formal Feeling Comes," in *The Poems of Emily Dickinson*, ed. Thomas H. Johnson (Harvard University Press, 1996), p. 272.

Fraud, Feeling Like a

"like a bank clerk who had committed a fraud." Franz Kafka, "Letter to his father," trans. Ernst Kaiser and Eithne Wilkins, repr. in *The Metamorphosis and Other Writings* (Continuum, 2002), p. 207.

In the 1970s two psychologists...P. R. Clance and S. A. Imes. "The Imposter Phenomenon in High Achieving Women: Dynamics and Therapeutic Intervention," *Psychotherapy: Theory, Research and Practice*, 15, (1978), 241–47.

The suspicion that she's a phony...Maria Klawe was interviewed on imposterism here: www.nytimes.com/2012/04/03/science/giving-women-the-access -code.html?_r=0.

Glee

After a series of security leaks in 2013... "NSA Leaks: UK's Enemies Are 'rubbing their hands with glee,' Says MI6 Chief," *Guardian*, November 8, 2013.

The answer can be found in...John Bulwer, *Chirologia or The Naturall Language of the Hand* (1644) (Southern Illinois Press, 1974), p. 40.

Gratitude

It might seem "hokey"...Sonja Lyubomirsky, *The How of Happiness: A Practical Guide to Getting the Life You Want* (Piatkus, 2010), p. 95.

to make "the lives of relatively untroubled people happier." Martin Seligman, *Authentic Happiness: Using the New Positive Psychology to Realize Your Potential for Lasting Fulfillment* (Simon & Schuster, 2002), p. 19.

the "invisible hand" of the free market. Adam Smith, *An Enquiry into the Nature and Causes of the Wealth of Nations* (1776).

"to recompense, to remunerate, to return good for good received"... Adam Smith, *The Theory of Moral Sentiments* (1759) (Oxford University Press, 1976), II.i.1.2, 68.

McDougall thought gratitude produced "negative self-feeling"... William McDougall, *Outline of Abnormal Psychology* (Scribners, 1929), p. 334.

Lyubomirsky and her colleagues define gratitude... Kennon M. Sheldon and Sonja Lyubomirsky, "How to Increase and Sustain Positive Emotion: The Effects of Expressing Gratitude and Visualizing Best Possible Selves," *Journal of Positive Psychology*, 1(2) (April 2006), 73–82.

Grief

The stone sculpture... "A Heavily Pregnant Woman," Kunstkamera, St. Petersburg, repr. in Jill Cook, *Ice Age Art: Arrival of the Modern Mind* (British Museum Press, 2013), p. 81.

"It's useless for me to describe..." Lemony Snicket, *A Series of Unfortunate Events: The Bad Beginning* (1999) (HarperCollins, 2007), p. 11.

"For a week, almost without speaking..." Gabriel García Márquez, *One Hundred Years of Solitude* (1967) (New York Classics, 1981), p. 12.

Among the Koma of northern Ghana... Franz Kröger and Ben Baluri Saibu, *First Notes on Koma Culture: Life in a Remote Area of Northern Ghana* (Lit Verlag, 2010), pp. 405–6.

"permanently provisional feeling"... C. S. Lewis, *A Grief Observed* (Faber and Faber, 1961), p. 29.

"the deceased is tortured in his grave..." Sahih Bukhari, Book 23, Book of Funerals (Al-Janaaiz), Hadith Number 379, narrated Ibn Umar.

"grief not only had to be done but had to be seen to be done." Jacqueline Rose, "The Cult of Celebrity," *London Review of Books*, August 20, 1998.

This "five stages of grief" model... Elisabeth Kübler-Ross, *On Death and Dying* (Routledge, 1969).

"You don't come out of it like a train..." Julian Barnes, *Flaubert's Parrot* (1984) (Picador, 2004), p. 191.

Guilt

"Remember what happens to me is your responsibility..." *The Odd Couple*, Gene Sacks (1968).

It begins with a dream Freud had in 1895. Sigmund Freud, *The Interpretation of Dreams* (1899) (Dover, 2015), pp. 80–108.

Freud called this inner monologue the "voice of the Father." Sigmund Freud, "The Ego and the Id" (1923), in *The Standard Edition of the Complete Psychological Works of Sigmund Freud*, vol. 19, ed. and trans. James Strachey in collaboration with Anna Freud (Hogarth Press, 1961), pp. 3–66.

a "combination of self-accusation and repentance"...Alfred Adler, "More on Individual Psychological Dream Theory" (1927), in *The Collected Clinical Works of Alfred Adler: Journal Articles: 1927–1931*, ed. Henry T. Stein (Adlerian Translation Project, 2004), p. 22.

Han

"If we lived in paradise..." Park Kyung-ni, "The Feelings and Thoughts of the Korean People in Literature," speech delivered at the University of Paris, November 1994.

Happiness

"Even if the feeling of happiness this gives me..." Karl Ove Knausgaard, *A Death in the Family* (2009), trans. Don Bartlett (Vintage, 2013), p. 31.

"Ask yourself if you are happy, and you cease to be so." John Stuart Mill, *Collected Works of John Stuart Mill: Autobiography and Literary Essays*, vol. 1, ed. John M. Robertson and Jack Stillinger (Routledge, 1996), p. 249.

"O Happiness! Our Being's End and Aim!"...Alexander Pope, "An Essay on Man: Epistle IV," repr. in *The Works of Alexander Pope* (10 vols.), vol. 3 (Cadell and Davies, 1807), p. 145.

"catalogue of pleasures." Jeremy Bentham, "Value of a Lot of Pleasure or Pain, How to be Measured," in *Introduction to the Principles of Morals and Legislation* (1789) (Clarendon Press, 1907), XVI.14.

"Let your self-consciousness, your scrutiny..." John Stuart Mill, *Collected Works of John Stuart Mill: Autobiography and Literary Essays*, vol. 1, ed. John M. Robertson and Jack Stillinger (Routledge, 1996), p. 146.

It may not even always be desirable... M. Joshanloo and D. Weijers, "Aversion to Happiness Across Cultures: A Review of Where and Why People Are Averse to Happiness," *Journal of Happiness Studies* 15(3) (2013), 717–35.

"perfect bridge over the crocodiles." Stephen Dunn, "Happiness," in *Between Angels* (W. W. Norton, 1989), p. 92.

Hatred

Abdel, a local youth from the banlieues...*La Haine*, Mathieu Kassovitz (1995).

"For if we believe that someone is a certain kind of person"...Aristotle, *Rhetoric* 2.4, 1382a, l. 14.

Many legal scholars... Paul Iganski, *Hate Crime and the City* (Policy Press, 2008).

"We grow tired of everything…" William Hazlitt, "On the Pleasure of Hating" (1823), repr. in *The Oxford Book of Essays*, ed. John Gross (Oxford University Press, 1991), pp. 112–22.

Hoard, The Urge to

"For it is invariably oneself that one collects"…Jean Baudrillard, "The System of Collecting," in John Elsner and Roger Cardinal (eds.), *The Cultures of Collecting* (Reaktion Books, 1968), p. 24.

As the psychoanalyst Stephen Grosz has suggested…Stephen Grosz, *The Examined Life: How We Lose and Find Ourselves* (W. W. Norton, 2014), p. 113.

Oscar the Grouch knew this. Jeff Moss, "I Love Trash" (sung by Oscar the Grouch).

Homefulness

"I felt myself in home's way." John Clare, "Journey Out of Essex" (1841) in *John Clare by Himself,* ed. David Powell and Eric Robinson (Routledge, 2002), pp. 257–65, p. 264.

The writer Iain Sinclair…Radio 3 Free Thinking documentary, May 20, 2014.

Homesickness

By the American Civil War…Susan Matt, *Homesickness: An American History* (Oxford University Press, 2011).

Families and friends are also urged to write…"Social Media Guide for Military Families," www.jber.af.mil/shared/media/document/AFD-120302-082.pdf.

Some psychologists have even called it a taboo…Roger Brown, *Social Psychology* (Free Press, 2003), p. 536.

"unhealable rift…" Edward Said, "Reflections on Exile," in *Reflections on Exile: And Other Literary and Cultural Essays* (Granta, 2001), pp. 173–86, p. 173.

Hopefulness

When the sociologist Barbara Ehrenreich was diagnosed…Barbara Ehrenreich, *Smile or Die: How Positive Thinking Fooled America and the World* (Granta, 2009), pp. 32–33.

Ehrenreich also cites a 2004 study…Patricia L. Tomich and Vicki S. Helgeson, "Is Finding Something Good in the Bad Always Good? Benefit Finding Among Women with Breast Cancer," *Health Psychology* 23(1) (January 2004), 16–23.

Huff, In a

The ancients took for granted…Shiegehisa Kuriyama, *The Expressiveness of the Body and the Divergence of Greek and Chinese Medicine* (Zone, 1999), p. 237.

"*bitter-blowing winds…*" Sophocles, *Antigone*, trans. by and quoted in Ruth Padel, *In and Out of the Mind: Greek Images of the Tragic Self* (Princeton University Press, 1992), p. 91.

Humiliation

"*a day of national humiliation.*" Abraham Lincoln, "Proclamation 97: Appointing a Day of National Humiliation, Fasting and Prayer," March 30, 1863.

"*all the cruel and brutal things…*" "Guest Biography: Kofi Annan," Maya Angelou's Black History Month Special (2013); http://mayaangelouonpublicradio.com/guest-bios/kofi-annan/.

"*nuclear bomb of the emotions*"…Evelin Linder, *Making Enemies: Humiliation and International Conflict* (Greenwood Press, 2006), p. xii.

"*many of those who are humiliated are not humble…*" Bernard of Clairvaux, *Sermons on the Song of Songs* (1136–1153), Sermon 34, repr. in *The Works of Bernard of Clairvaux*, vol. 2, trans. Kilian Walsh and Irene M. Edmonds (Cistercian Publications, 1976).

"*check your privilege*"…For more on this see Roxanne Gay, *Bad Feminist: Essays* (Corsair, 2014).

Hunger

But our emotions also lead us to overeat. For more on this idea see: Susie Orbach, *Fat Is a Feminist Issue* (Paddington Books, 1978).

"*The ambiowa cries for me…*" In Jane Fajans, *They Make Themselves: Work and Play Among the Baining of Papua New Guinea* (University of Chicago Press, 1997), p. 119.

Ijirashii

"*I think I can I think I can I think I can*"…Watty Piper, *The Little Engine That Could* (Platt & Munk, 1930).

as did Churchill… Thomas Dixon, *Weeping Britannia: Portrait of a Nation in Tears* (Oxford University Press, 2015).

Ilinx

"*strange excitement*"…Roger Caillois, *Man, Play and Games* (1958), trans. Meyer Barash (Free Press, 2001), p. 24.

Impatience

It was these waiting-room chairs… Meyer Friedman and Ray H. Rosenman, *Treating Type A Behavior — And Your Heart* (Fawcett, 1985).

"*the greatest poets did not disdain…*" Friedrich Nietzsche, *Human, All Too Human* (1878), trans. Gary Handwerk (Stanford University Press, 1995), p. 60.

"Time goes on crutches till love have all his rites"...William Shakespeare, *Much Ado About Nothing*, II.i.357–58.

Indignation

"majestic in his wrath..." Theodore Stanton and Harriet Stanton Blanche (eds.), *Elizabeth Cady Stanton, As Revealed in Letters, Diary and Reminiscences* (Harper & Brothers, 1922), pp. 311–12.

Aristotle thought indignation... David Konstan, *The Emotions of the Ancient Greeks: Studies in Aristotle and Classical Literature* (University of Toronto Press, 2007), pp. 114–15.

"anger for great Hurt..." Thomas Hobbes, *Leviathan* (Andrew Crooke, 1651), pp. 26, 182–83.

Think of the pyrotechnics of the speech... Transcript of Julia Gillard speech, *Sydney Morning Herald*, October 10, 2012.

"scathing denunciations of slaveholders..." Frederick Douglass, *Narrative of the Life of Frederick Douglass: An American Slave. Written by Himself* (1845), intro. Robert B. Stepto (Harvard University Press, 2009), p. 114.

Inhabitiveness

"love of continuity..." Sidney Smith, *The Principles of Phrenology* (William Tait, 1838), p. 98.

Irritation

"On the pleasures of being booed"...Filippo Tommaso Marinetti, *Manifesto of the Futurist Dramatists* (1911), in *Marinetti, Selected Writings*, ed. R.W. Flint (Farrar, Straus and Giroux, 1972), pp. 113–15.

"irritable muscles"...Edwin Clarke and L. S. Jacyna, *Nineteenth-Century Origins of Neuroscientific Concepts* (University of California Press, 1987), p. 105.

"irritable heart." Charles F. Wooley, *The Irritable Heart of Soldiers and the Origins of Anglo-American Cardiology: The US Civil War to World War I* (Ashgate, 2002).

Jealousy

"He who is not jealous can not love"...Andreas Capellanus, *The Art of Courtly Love* (1180) in *The Broadview Anthology of British Literature*, vol. 1, ed. Joseph Black et al. (Broadview Press, 2009), pp. 366–68.

"green-eyed monster." William Shakespeare, *Othello*, III:iii:169.

"directed the executioner to burn him gently..." Collected in Sir Thomas Raymond, *Reports of Divers Special Cases, Adjudged in the Courts of King's Bench, Common Pleas and Exchequer in the Reign of King Charles II* (James Moore, 1793), p. 212.

"*the rage of a man...*" *R v. Mawgridge* (1707) 84 Eng. Rep. 1107. Lord Chief Justice Holt's argument that "jealousy is the rage of a man" was a quotation from the King James Bible, Proverbs 6:34.

The jealous man suffers "four times over"...Roland Barthes, *A Lover's Discourse* (Vintage, 2002), pp. 145–46.

research has shown that judges still show sympathy...Jeremy Horder, interviewed on *Woman's Hour*, BBC Radio 4, October 15, 2014, www.bbc.co.uk/news/magazine-29612916.

Joy

"*Although Bertha Young was thirty...*" Katherine Mansfield, "Bliss" (1920), in *The Collected Works of Katherine Mansfield* (Penguin, 2007), pp. 32–41.

"*Joy is pleasure...*" Baruch Spinoza, *Ethics III: On the Origin and Nature of Emotions* (1677), XVI, trans. R. H. M. Elwes, repr. in *What Is an Emotion?: Classic and Contemporary Readings*, ed. Robert C. Solomon (Oxford University Press, 2003), pp. 32–43, p. 38.

"*the clammy joys.*" James Wilmot, Earl of Rochester, "The Imperfect Enjoyment," in *Selected Poems*, ed. Paul Davis (Oxford University Press, 2013), pp. 39–40.

"*She hovered like a hawk suspended...*" Virginia Woolf, *To the Lighthouse* (1927) (Broadview Press, 2000), pp. 158–59.

Liget

"*If it were not for liget...*" Michelle Z. Rosaldo, *Knowledge and Passion: Ilongot Notions of Self and Social Life* (1980) (Cambridge University Press, 1993), p. 44.

the rage of grief...Renato Rosaldo, *Culture and Truth: The Remaking of Social Analysis* (Beacon Press, 1989).

Litost

"*a state of torment...*" Milan Kundera, *Book of Laughter and Forgetting* (1979), trans. Michael H. Heim (Alfred A. Knopf, 1980), p. 122.

Loneliness

The passengers climb in... *Taxi Driver*, Martin Scorsese (1976).

"*Solitude produces ignorance...*" John Evelyn, *Public Employment and an Active Life Prefer'd to Solitude* (1667), in *The Miscellaneous Writings of John Evelyn*, ed. William Upcott (Henry Colburn, 1825), p. 552.

"*utter lonesomeness*"...Georg Simmel, "The Metropolis and Mental Life" (1903), repr. in Charles Harrison and Paul Wood (eds.), *Art in Theory, 1900–1990: An Anthology of Changing Ideas* (Blackwell, 1993), pp. 130–34, p. 132.

And the stakes are high...This claim is based on research described in John T. Cacioppo, *Loneliness and the Need for Social Connection* (W. W. Norton, 2009).

In Japan, hikikomori...Tamaki Saito, *Hikikomori: Adolescence Without End,* trans. Jeffrey Angles (University of Minnesota Press, 2013).

Love

Oh that you were, my Susie...Emily Dickinson to Susan Gilbert, June 11, 1852, in *The Collected Letters of Emily Dickenson,* ed. Thomas H. Johnson and Theodora Ward (Harvard University Press, 1986), pp. 211–12.

"My lost voice stutters..." Sappho, *Stung with Love: Poems and Fragments,* trans. Aaron Poochigian (Penguin, 2009), p. 23.

"We ought to move on..." Stendhal, *On Love* (1822), trans. Gilbert and Suzanne Sale (Penguin Classics, 1975), p. 73.

Ibn-Sīna...For a discussion of these terms and the medical history of love-sickness, see Marion A. Wells, *The Secret Wound: Love-Melancholy and Early Modern Romance* (Stanford University Press, 2007), pp. 19–95.

Day-long I stretch, all times, like a bird preening...Arnaut Daniel, "Sweet Cries and Cracks," repr. and trans. in *Lark in the Morning: The Verses of the Troubadours,* ed. Robert Kehew, trans. Ezra Pound, W. D. Snodgrass and Robert Kehew (University of Chicago Press, 2005), p. 205.

"I love you," says Alec...*Brief Encounter,* David Lean (1945).

Mehameha

A Tahitian named Tano...Robert Levy, *Tahitians: Mind and Experience in the Society Islands* (University of Chicago Press, 1973), p. 151.

Melancholy

a "sugarcoated misery." In the song "Sentimental and Melancholy" by Johnny Mercer and Richard Whiting.

"at every trifle...inflamed"...Thomas Wright, *The Passions of the Minde in General* (London, 1604).

"terrible monstrous fictions..." Robert Burton, *The Anatomy of Melancholy* (1621) (J. W. More, 1857), p. 254.

In the mid-fifteenth century...Marsilio Ficino, *Three Books on Life* (1489) ed. Carol V. Kaske and John R. Clarke (Arizona State University Press, 1989).

"but the trappings and the suits of woe." William Shakespeare, *Hamlet,* I.ii.85–86.

Mono no Aware

"The autumn flowers were gone..." Murasaki Shikibu, "The Sacred Tree," from *The Tale of Genji,* repr. in *Traditional Japanese Literature: An Anthology, Beginnings to 1600,* ed. Haruo Shirane (Columbia University Press, 2007), pp. 343–45.

Morbid Curiosity

In The Republic...Plato, *The Republic,* trans. Desmond Lee (Penguin, 1988), IV, 439e–440a, pp. 215–16.

"*as to a theater play*"...Immanuel Kant, *Anthropology from a Pragmatic Point of View* (1798), trans. Robert B. Louden (Cambridge University Press, 2006), p. 135.

"*shadow aspect*"...The idea of a shadow and its integration is discussed in chapter 2 of Carl Jung, *Aion: Researches into the Phenomenology of the Self* (1951), repr. in *The Collected Works of C. G. Jung*, trans. R.F. C. Hull, vol. 9, part 2 (Princeton University Press, 1959).

"*The rest of us are voyeurs...*" Susan Sontag, *Regarding the Pain of Others* (Hamish Hamilton, 2003), p. 37.

Mudita

"*it is not enough to succeed. Others must fail.*" Gore Vidal, attributed to a quote by Gerard Irvine, "Antipanegyric for Tom Driberg," [memorial service for Driberg], December 8, 1976.

Nakhes

"*I didn't know they made Ninth Place ribbons*"...*Meet the Fockers*, Jay Roach (2004).

Nginyiwarrarringu

For the Pintupi...J. A. Russell, "Culture and the Categorization of Emotions," *Psychological Bulletin* 110(3) (1991), 426–50.

Nostalgia

"*frequent sighs*" *and* "*disturbed sleep.*" Johannes Hofer, "Medical Dissertation on Nostalgia (1688)," trans. Carolyn Kiser Anspach, *Bulletin of the History of Medicine* 2(6) (August 1934), 376–91.

In the early twentieth century...For the history of nostalgia see: Jean Starobinski, "The Idea of Nostalgia," trans. William S. Kemp, *Diogenes* 14 (Summer 1966), 81.

a "coherence in things, a stability"...Virginia Woolf, *To the Lighthouse* (1927) (Broadview Press, 2000), p. 158.

[fn.] "*US Dept. of Retro Warns...*" *The Onion*, November 4, 1997, www.theonion .com/articles/us-dept-of-retro-warns-we-may-be-running-out-of-pa-873/.

A surprising number...One early and influential study is Clay Routledge et al., "The Past Makes the Present Meaningful: Nostalgia as an Existential Resource," *Journal of Personality and Social Psychology* 101(3) (2001), 638–52.

"*nostalgia workouts*"...Clay Routledge, "Nostalgia Is Good Medicine," *Psychology Today*, August 11, 2009, https://www.psychologytoday.com/blog/more -mortal/200908/nostalgia-is-good-medicine.

A team of researchers in southern China...Xinyue Zhon et al., "Heartwarming Memories: Nostalgia Maintains Physiological Comfort," *Emotion* 12(4) (August 2012), 678–84.

Overwhelmed, Feeling

she "excelled" in poetry... Ibn Bashkuwal, *Kitab al-Silla*, vol. 2 (Cairo, 2008), p. 324.

"Is there anywhere on earth exempt..." Desiderius Erasmus, *The Adages of Erasmus*, ed. William Barker (University of Toronto Press, 2001) II.i.1, p. 145.

One more practical response... Ann M. Blair, *Too Much to Know: Managing Scholarly Information Before the Modern Age* (Yale University Press, 2010).

"hard study..." Samuel Johnson, *The Adventurer* 115 (December 11, 1753), in W. J. Bate, John M. Bullitt and L. F. Powell (eds.), *The Idler and The Adventurer* (Yale University Press, 1963), pp. 456–61.

Panic

"we've got a panic on our hands." Jaws, Steven Spielberg (1975).

They believed that when individuals became part of a crowd... Gustave Le Bon, *The Crowd: A Study of the Popular Mind* (T. Fisher Unwin, 1896).

Paranoia

Inspired in part by the memoirs of a German judge... Daniel Paul Schreber, *Memoirs of my Nervous Illness* (1903), trans. and ed. Ida Macalpine and Richard A. Hunter (W. Dawson, 1955).

"There is nothing... more banal and bourgeois..." Vladimir Nabokov, *Pnin* (1957) (Penguin, 2010), p. 82.

Daniel Freeman, who has studied... Daniel Freeman and Jason Freeman, *Paranoia: The 21st-Century Fear* (Oxford University Press, 2008).

Penny Garner, who became interested in dementia... Oliver James, *Contented Dementia: 24-Hour Wraparound Care for Lifelong Well-being* (Ebury Press, 2008).

Perversity

"The more reason deters us from the brink..." Edgar Allan Poe, "The Imp of the Perverse," *Graham's Magazine* (July 1845), repr. in *The Complete Tales and Poems of Edgar Allan Poe* (Penguin, 2011), pp. 280–85, p. 282.

Peur des Espaces

Madame B cluttered up her apartment with furniture. Henri Legrand du Saulle, "Etude Clinique sur la Peur des Espaces (Agoraphobie des Allemands)," *Annales Médico-Psychologiques* 34 (1878), 405–33.

Carl Otto Westphal came up with the name... Carl Friedrich Otto Westphal, "Die Agoraphobie, ein neuropathische Erscheinung," *Archiv für Psychiatrie und Nervenkrankheiten* 3 (1871), 138–61.

Researchers at University College London and Southampton University... L. Yardley et al., "Relationship Between Balance System Function and Agoraphobic Avoidance," *Behavior Research and Therapy* 33(4) (June 1995), 435–39.

Feminist critics... Joyce Davidson, "'...the world was getting smaller': Women, Agoraphobia and Bodily Boundaries," *Area* 32(1) (2000), 31–40.

Philoprogenitiveness

"the glowing impulse..." Johann Gaspar Spurzheim, *Outlines of Phrenology* (Treuttel, Wurtz and Richer, 1827), p. 26.

"a slave to maternal duties." Samuel Robert Wells, *New Physiognomy* (Samuel R. Wells, 1875), p. 133.

Pity

"Nothing...dries more quickly..." Cicero attributes this to Apollonius the rhetorician, in Marcus Tullius Cicero, *Treatise on Rhetorical Invention*, vol. 1, trans. C. D. Yonge (Digireads, 2009), p. 45.

In medieval Christian Europe... For more on this era's emotional culture of pity see Sarah McNamer, *Affective Meditation and the Invention of Medieval Compassion* (University of Pennsylvania Press, 2011).

"How well you're looking today, and how splendidly you're walking..." Stefan Zweig, *Beware of Pity* (1939), trans. Anthea Bell (Puskin Press, 2012), p. 110.

"since the world began..." Theodore Zeldin, *An Intimate History of Humanity* (Vintage, 1998), p. 243.

Postal, Going

Among the Gurumba tribe of New Guinea... Philip Newman, "Wild Man Behavior in a New Guinea Highlands Community," *American Anthropologist* 66(1) (1964), 1–19.

Compare this to amok... J. E. Carr and E. K. Tan, "In Search of the True Amok: Amok as Viewed with the Malay Culture," *American Journal of Psychiatry* 133(11) (1976), 1295–99.

Pride

"She was right. But how could I explain..." Alice Munro, "Pride," in *Dear Life* (Chatto & Windus, 2012), pp. 133–53, p. 151.

In 2010 the director of the British Museum... "In Conversation with Wole Soyinka," www.britishmuseum.org/channel/events/2010/audio_wole_soyinka.aspx.

Rage

"grossly out of proportion"... "Intermittent Explosive Disorder," *Diagnostic and Statistical Manual of Mental Disorders: DSM-V* (American Psychiatric Publishing, 2013).

"only where there is reason..." Hannah Arendt, *Crises of the Republic* (Harcourt, 1972), p. 160.

Regret

"For this deed thou shalt…" Francis Rous, *Thule, or Vertues Historie,* II (1598) (The Spencer Society, 1878).

Researchers from Stanford University's School of Business… Rebecca L. Schaumberg and Francis J. Flyn, "Uneasy Lies the Head that Wears the Crown: The Link Between Guilt-Proneness and Leadership," *Journal of Personality and Social Psychology* 103(2) (August 2012), pp. 327–42.

Relief

"Would you mind if I cry a little?"…Fanny and Alexander, Ingmar Bergman (1982).
"If tears reduce stress…" Robert R. Provine, *Curious Behavior: Yawning, Laughing, Hiccupping, and Beyond* (Harvard University Press, 2012), p. 80.

Reluctance

"You must know again…" Amelia Earhart to George Putnam, February 7, 1931, repr. in *Letters of Note,* ed. Shaun Usher (Canongate, 2013), no. 45.

Remorse

In the painting by… Antonio Vivarini, *Saint Peter Martyr Healing the Leg of a Young Man.*

It is in childhood… Melanie Klein, "Love, Guilt and Reparation" (1937), in *The Writings of Melanie Klein,* vol. 1 (Hogarth Press, 1975).

An apology, to use the philosopher J. L. Austin's theory… J. L. Austin, "Lecture I: Performatives and Constatives," repr. in *How to Do Things with Words: The William James Lectures Delivered at Harvard University in 1955,* ed. J. O. Urmson and Marina Sbisa (Clarendon Press, 1962), pp. 1–11.

On November 7, 1497… Durham Cathedral Archives and Library: Court Book of Prior's Official, 1487–1498, repr. and trans. Philippa Maddern. http://emotions.arts.uwa.edu.au/wiki/items/show/12.

Resentment

In Cesare Ripa's Iconologia… Cesare Ripa, *Iconologia, or, Moral Emblems* (1593) (Benji Mott, 1709), p. 255.

terrorism is motivated by the "perversion" of resentment. Slavoj Žižek, *Violence* (Picador, 2008), p. 74.

"the human soul became deep." Friedrich Nietzsche, *On the Genealogy of Morality* (1887), ed. Keith Ansell-Pearson (Cambridge University Press, 2003), p. 18.

Ringxiety

According to the psychologist David Laramie… Laramie's research was reported in "Do You Suffer from Ringxiety," *Guardian,* June 1, 2006, www.theguardian.com/technology/2006/jun/01/mobilephones.guardianweeklytechnologysection.

Rivalry

"warre of every one against every one." Thomas Hobbes, *Leviathan* (Andrew Crooke, 1651), p. 82.

"It is best they should die"...Herbert Spencer, *Social Statics: or the Conditions Essential to Human Happiness Specified*...(London, 1851), pp. 379–80.

In the first decades of the twentieth century...Peter Stearns, "The Rise of Sibling Jealousy in the Twentieth Century," *Symbolic Interaction* 13(1) (Spring 1990), 83–101.

"The competition is maddening!" Arthur Miller, *Death of a Salesman* (1949) I. i (Heinemann, 1994), p. 7.

children display ingenuity and creativity...Claire Hughes, *Social Understanding and Social Lives: From Toddlerhood Through to the Transition to School* (Psychology Press, 2011), pp. 105–21.

"ease and slack facility..." Michel de Montaigne, "Of the Disadvantage of Greatness" (1585–88), repr. in his *The Complete Works*, trans. Donald M. Frame (Everyman's Library, 2003), pp. 849–53.

Road Rage

In a now classic study on prosocial behavior...K. J. Haley and D. M. T. Fessler, "Nobody's Watching? Subtle Cues Affect Generosity in an Anonymous Economic Game," *Evolutionary Human Behavior* 26 (2005), 245–56.

Sadness

From its earliest incarnations...This idea is suggested by Erin Sullivan in *Beyond Melancholy: Sadness and Selfhood in Renaissance England* (Oxford University Press, 2016). I am grateful to Erin for sharing her work with me prior to publication.

"I am a lonely thing"...Paull Franklin Baum, *Anglo-Saxon Riddles of the Exeter Book* (Duke University Press, 1963), 49 [K-D.5].

In his Castell of Helth...Thomas Elyot, *The Castell of Helth* (1595), 100–102.

Among those who fear...A. Horwitz and J. C. Wakefield, *The Loss of Sadness: How Psychiatry Transformed Normal Sorrow into Depressive Disorder* (Oxford University Press, 2007).

"pain can't be borne..." Susie Orbach, "Prozac," in *Toward Emotional Literacy* (Virago, 1999), pp. 237–41, p. 240.

Satisfaction

"You're a fake and a phony...," Grease, Randal Kleiser (1978).

The origins of this "smile revolution"...Colin Jones, *The Smile Revolution in Eighteenth Century Paris* (Oxford University Press, 2014).

a "secret joy"... "Satisfaction," in *Encyclopaedia, or a Systematic Dictionary of the Sciences, Arts and Crafts*, ed. Denis Diderot and Jean le Rond d'Alembert (Briasson, David, Le Breton and Durand, 1751–72).

Schadenfreude

"it is sweet to perceive..." Lucretius, *Lucretius on the Nature of Things*, trans. Cyril Bailey (Clarendon Press, 1910), p. 65.

"a glow of excitement and pleasure..." Iris Murdoch, *A Severed Head* (1961) (Random House, 2008), p. 33.

Self-pity

Marvin the Paranoid Android...Douglas Adams, *The Hitchhiker's Guide to the Galaxy* (Pan, 1979).

"regards himself 'as if he were someone else'"...Max Scheler, "Fellow Feeling, Benevolence, Forms and Kind of Love," *On Feeling, Knowing, and Valuing: Selected Writings*, ed. Harold J. Bershady (University of Chicago Press, 1992), pp. 70–82, p. 72.

Shame

"one of the greatest shaking cracks that our soul can receive." Plutarch, *Moralia* (1603), trans. P. Holland (Dent, 1911), p. 187.

an "internal hemorrhage." Jean-Paul Sartre, *Being and Nothingness: An Essay on Phenomenological Ontology*, trans. Hazel Barnes (Washington Square Press, 1966), p. 345.

"How shall I behold the face..." John Milton, *Paradise Lost* (1674), Book 9, 1080–90, repr. in John Milton, *The Complete Poems*, ed. John Leonard (Penguin, 2005).

In the 1940s...Ruth Benedict, *The Chrysanthemum and the Sword: Patterns of Japanese Culture* (Houghton Mifflin, 1946).

Feeling ashamed..."is not the exclusive property of the East." Salman Rushdie, *Shame* (1983) (Random House, 2011), p. 28.

"to be present at the whipping post..." Quoted in John Demos, "Shame and Guilt in Early New England," in Rom Harré and W. Gerrod Parrott (eds.), *The Emotions: Social, Cultural and Biological Dimensions* (Sage, 2000), pp. 74–88, p. 76.

They have initiated a "gay shame" movement. Helen Love, *Feeling Backwards: Loss and the Politics of Queer History* (Harvard University Press, 2009).

Shock

the strange symptoms were caused...C. S. Myers, "A Contribution to the Study of Shell-Shock," *The Lancet* 1 (February 13, 1915), 316–20.

"shocke of armes." William Shakespeare, *Richard III*, V: iii. 3565.

He had carefully dissected the corpses of hanged criminals... For the results of these labors, see Thomas Willis, *Cerebri Anatome: cui accessit nervorum desciptio et usus* (1664).

"our senses have been opened..." Johann Wolfgang von Goethe, *The Sorrows of Young Werther* (1774), trans. David Constantine (Oxford University Press, 2012), p. 22.

Smugness

"Handsome, clever, and rich"... Jane Austen, *Emma* (1815), in *The Complete Novels of Jane Austen* (Wordsworth, 2007), p. 777.

Song

Those who live on the Pacific island of the Ifaluk... Catherine Lutz, *Unnatural Emotions: Everyday Sentiments on a Micronesian Atoll and Their Challenge to Western Theory* (University of Chicago Press, 1988).

Surprise

"with the firm determination..." Charles Darwin, *The Expression of the Emotions in Man and Animals* (John Murray, 1872), p. 38.

Like the early-twentieth-century theorist of laughter... Henri Bergson, *Laughter: An Essay on the Meaning of the Comic (Le Rire)* (1900), trans. Cloudesley Brereton and Fred Rothwell (London: Macmillan, 1911), p. 9.

a "sudden surprise of the soul." René Descartes, *The Passions of the Soul*, trans. Stephen H. Vass (Hackett, 1989), p. 56.

Technostress

Aristotle observed... Aristotle, *Rhetoric*, bk II, ch. 2 (Dover, 2002), p. 60.

Terror

"It's when the lights go out..." https://www.facebook.com/OfficialStephenKing/posts/355794961226759.

"in terror, even the most intrepid men..." Angelo Mosso, *Fear* (1884), trans. E. Lough and Frederich Kiesow (Longmans, 1896), p. 11.

"The axe, the wheel, sawdust and the bloodstained sheet"... Henry Fuseli, *The Life and Writings of Henry Fuseli*, vol. 3 (Henry Colburn, 1831), p. 91.

"terror and wonder"... Edmund Burke, *A Philosophical Enquiry into the Origin of Our Ideas of the Sublime and the Beautiful* (1757) (J. Dodsley, 1767), p. 98.

"huge and mighty forms..." William Wordsworth, *The Prelude; or, Growth of a Poet's Mind* (D. Appleton, 1850), I.19.

"It is natural to wonder..." "President Bush Addresses the Nation," *Washington Post*, September 20, 2001.

"the only thing we have to fear is fear itself." Franklin D. Roosevelt, *Inaugural Address*, March 4, 1933.

Toska

"a dull ache…a longing with nothing to long for"… Vladimir Nabokov, *Eugene Onegin, a Novel in Verse*, vol. 2 (Princeton University Press, 1991), p. 141.

Triumph

the *"dreadful screech"*…J. M. Barrie, *Peter Pan* (1915) (Sovereign, 2013), p. 25.

Uncertainty

"All things are so very uncertain…" Tove Jansson, *Moominland Midwinter*, trans. Thomas Warburton (Ernest Benn Ltd, 1958), p. 28.

"capable of being in uncertainties…" John Keats to George and Tom Keats, December 27, 1817, *Selected Letters of John Keats*, revised ed., ed. Grant F. Scott (Harvard University Press, 2002), p. 60.

Vengefulness

"Dishonor consists not…" Jeremy Bentham, "Honorary Satisfaction," in *Collected Works*, vol. 2, ed. John Bowring (William Tait, 1838), p. 379.

"wild, cruel, prone to violent outbursts"…Norbert Elias, *The Civilizing Process: The History of Manners* (1939) (Polity Press, 1994), p. 319.

"Revenge is a kind of wild justice…" Francis Bacon, "Of Revenge," in *Bacon's Essays*, ed. Richard Whately (John W. Parker, 1858), pp. 53–100, p. 53.

Hieronimo, *"tears the papers"*…Thomas Kyd, *The Spanish Tragedy* (Bloomsbury, 2013), p. 92.

Vergüenza Ajena

These apparently contradictory impulses…Immaculada Iglesias, "Verguenza ajena," in Rom Harré and W. Gerrod Parrott (eds.), *The Emotions: Social, Cultural and Biological Dimensions* (Sage, 1996), pp. 122–31.

Viraha

"I was shy at our first union…" Quoted and discussed in William M. Reddy, *The Making of Romantic Love: Longing and Sexuality in Europe, South Asia and Japan, 900–1200 CE* (University of Chicago Press, 2012), pp. 256–66.

"Batter my heart…ravish me." John Donne, "Batter my heart, three-personed God," Holy Sonnet 14 (1633), repr. in *John Donne, The Complete English Poems* (Penguin, 1982), pp. 314–15.

Vulnerability

"Tread softly…" W. B. Yeats, "He Wishes for the Cloths of Heaven," repr. in *W. B. Yeats Collected Poems*, ed. Augustine Martin (Vintage, 1992), p. 68.

In the last ten years... Brené Brown, "The Power of Vulnerability," https://www.ted.com/talks/brene_brown_on_vulnerability.

Even precariats working in the creative industries... Guy Standing, *The Precariat: The New Dangerous Class* (Bloomsbury, 2011).

Wanderlust

"pathological tourism"... Philippe Tissié wrote up his account of Dada's case in his PhD thesis: Philippe Auguste Tissié, "Les aliénés voyageurs: essai médico-physiologique thèse de médicine de Bordeaux no. 29" (1887). The case is discussed in detail in Ian Hacking, *Mad Travelers: Reflections on the Reality of Transient Mental Illnesses* (University Press of Virginia, 1998).

Such transient mental illnesses are sometimes thought to be a kind of folie à deux... Ibid., p. 18.

"Wanderlust arises as an emotional epidemic"... Daniel Garrison Brinton and Livingston Farrand, *The Basis of Social Relations: A Study in Ethnic Psychology* (G. P. Putnam & Sons, 1902), p. 113.

Warm Glow

Larry is alight with pride when he arrives... Curb Your Enthusiasm, season 6, episode 2: "The Anonymous Donor."

"altruistic pleasure." Herbert Spencer, *The Data of Ethics* (Williams and Norgate, 1879), pp. 201–18.

The idea that humans are naturally selfish... For the evolution of this idea, see Barbara Taylor, "A Short History of Kindness," in Barbara Taylor and Adam Phillips, *On Kindness* (Penguin, 2009), pp. 15–47 (Calvin is discussed on p. 22).

Over the past ten years... See: J. Moll et al., "Human Fronto-Mesolimbic Networks Guide Decisions About Charitable Donation," *Proceedings of the National Academy of Sciences* 103(42) (October 17, 2006), pp. 15623–28.

Wonder

Between the twelfth and seventeenth centuries... Lorraine Daston and Katharine Park, *Wonders and the Order of Nature, 1150–1750* (Zone, 1998).

[fn] Ambroise Paré, "Concerning Poisons etc.", repr. in *The Workes of That Famous Chirurgion Ambrose Parey* [sic], trans. Thomas Johnson (Richard Cotes, 1649), pp. 529–30.

"like wonder-wounded hearers"... William Shakespeare, *Hamlet*, V.i. 257.

a "sudden surprise of the soul..." René Descartes, *The Passions of the Soul* (1649), trans. Stephen H. Vass (Hackett, 1989), p. 56.

Saint Augustine warned... Saint Augustine, *Confessions* (Book 5.3.4), trans. Henry Chadwick (Oxford University Press, 2008), p. 74.

"All men by nature desire to know"...Aristotle, *Metaphysics* (980), in *The Complete Works of Aristotle*, vol. 1, ed. Jonathan Barnes (Princeton University Press, 1984), p. 1552.

"to make wonders cease." Albertus Magnus, "Metaphysica," 1.2.6, in *Opera Omnia*, 40 vols., vol. 16, ed. Bernhard Geyer (Aschendorff, 1951).

Worry

"in great worry, crying and taking on." Harriet Beecher Stowe, *Uncle Tom's Cabin* (1853) (Oxford University Press, 2002), p. 37.

like Little Nell...Charles Dickens, *The Old Curiosity Shop* (Chapman & Hall, 1841).

"Cheerfulness enables nature to recruit its strength..." Samuel Smiles, *Character* (Harper & Brothers, 1872), p. 225.

a longitudinal study...W. E. Lee, M. E. J. Wadsworth and M. Hotop, "The Protective Role of Trait Anxiety: A Longitudinal Cohort Study," *Psychological Medicine* 36 (2006), 345–51.

Some researchers have even suggested that there may be a "worry gene"...Christian Montag et al., "COMT Genetic Variation Affects Fear Processing: Psychophysiological Evidence," *Behavioral Neuroscience* 122(4) (2008), 901–9.

"Things to worry about..." "F. Scott Fitzgerald to his 11-Year-Old Daughter in Camp," *New York Times Magazine*, June 15, 1933.

Żal

"the soil of his heart." Franz Liszt, *The Life of Chopin*, trans. Martha Walker Cook (Leypoldt and Holt, 1863), p. 77.

ABOUT THE AUTHOR

TIFFANY WATT SMITH is a research fellow at the Center for the History of the Emotions, Queen Mary University of London, and was also a 2014 BBC New Generation Thinker. Before beginning her academic career she worked as a theater director, including as an Associate Director at the Arcola Theatre and International Associate at the Royal Court. She lives in London.